Lecture Notes in Computer Science 10165

Commenced Publication in 1973
Founding and Former Series Editors:
Gerhard Goos, Juris Hartmanis, and Jan van Leeuwen

More information about this series at http://www.springer.com/series/7412

Kamal Nasrollahi · Cosimo Distante
Gang Hua · Andrea Cavallaro
Thomas B. Moeslund · Sebastiano Battiato
Qiang Ji (Eds.)

Video Analytics

Face and Facial Expression Recognition and Audience Measurement

Third International Workshop, VAAM 2016
and Second International Workshop, FFER 2016
Cancun, Mexico, December 4, 2016
Revised Selected Papers

 Springer

Editors
Kamal Nasrollahi
Aalborg University
Aalborg
Denmark

Cosimo Distante
Institute of Applied Sciences
  and Intelligent Systems
Lecce
Italy

Gang Hua
Stevens Institute of Technology
Hoboken, NJ
USA

Andrea Cavallaro
Queen Mary University of London
London
UK

Thomas B. Moeslund
Aalborg University
Aalborg
Denmark

Sebastiano Battiato
Università di Catania
Catania
Italy

Qiang Ji
Rensselaer Polytechnic Institute
Troy, NY
USA

ISSN 0302-9743   ISSN 1611-3349   (electronic)
Lecture Notes in Computer Science
ISBN 978-3-319-56686-3   ISBN 978-3-319-56687-0   (eBook)
DOI 10.1007/978-3-319-56687-0

Library of Congress Control Number: 2017936357

LNCS Sublibrary: SL6 – Image Processing, Computer Vision, Pattern Recognition, and Graphics

Printed on acid-free paper

This Springer imprint is published by Springer Nature
The registered company is Springer International Publishing AG
The registered company address is: Gewerbestrasse 11, 6330 Cham, Switzerland

Preface

This book collects the papers presented at two workshops during the 23rd International Conference on Pattern Recognition (ICPR): the Third Workshop on Video Analytics for Audience Measurement (VAAM) and the Second International Workshop on Face and Facial Expression Recognition (FFER) from Real World Videos. The workshops were run on December 4, 2016, in Cancun in Mexico.

The two workshops together received 13 papers. Each paper was then reviewed by at least two expert reviewers in the field. In all, 11 papers were accepted to be presented at the workshops.

The topics covered in the papers include: re-identification, consumer behavior analysis, utilizing pupillary response for task difficulty measurement, logo detection, saliency prediction, classification of facial expressions, face recognition, face verification, age estimation, super-resolution, pose estimation, and pain recognition.

The organizers of the two workshops would like to express their sincere thanks to the authors of the contributed papers, the reviewers who made sure of the good quality of the papers, and the attendees of the workshops.

February 2017

Kamal Nasrollahi
Cosimo Distante
Gang Hua
Andrea Cavallaro
Thomas B. Moeslund
Sebastiano Battiato
Qiang Ji

Organization

FFER Organizers

Kamal Nasrollahi	Aalborg University, Denmark
Gang Hua	Stevens Institute of Technology, USA
Thomas B. Moeslund	Aalborg University, Denmark
Qiang Ji	Rensselaer Polytechnic Institute, USA

FFER Program Committee

Abdenour Hadid	University of Oulu, Finland
Abhinav Dhall	University of Waterloo, Australia
Gholamreza Anbarjafari	University of Tartu, Estonia
Jordi Gonzalez	Universitat Autònoma de Barcelona, Spain
Jose Alba-Castro	Vigo University, Spain
Karl Ricanek	University of North Carolina Wilmington, USA
Mohammad A. Haque	Aalborg University, Denmark
Paulo Correia	Universidade de Lisboa, Portugal
Sergio Escalera	University of Barcelona, Spain
Shangfei Wang	University of Science and Technology of China, China
Sichuan Du	LENA Research Foundation, USA
Vladimir Pavlovic	Rutgers University, USA
Xiaoming Liu	Michigan State University, USA
Xilin Chen	Chinese of Academy of Sciences, China
Yan Tong	University of South Carolina, USA
Yun Fu	Northeastern University, USA

VAAM Organizers

Sebastiano Battiato	University of Catania, Italy
Andrea Cavallaro	Queen Mary University of London, UK
Cosimo Distante	National Research Council – CNR, Italy

VAAM Program Committee

Abdenour Hadid	University of Oulu, Finland
Dit-Yan Yeung	Hong Kong University of Science and Technology, SAR China
Djamal Merad	CNRS, France
Emanuele Frontoni	Università Politecnica delle Marche, Italy
Gabriella Sanniti di Baja	National Research Council – CNR, Italy
Giovanni M. Farinella	University of Catania, Italy

Contents

Person Re-identification Dataset with RGB-D Camera in a Top-View Configuration

Daniele Liciotti, Marina Paolanti$^{(\boxtimes)}$, Emanuele Frontoni, Adriano Mancini,
and Primo Zingaretti

Dipartimento di Ingegneria dell'Informazione, Università Politecnica delle Marche,
Via Brecce Bianche, 60131 Ancona, Italy
{d.liciotti,m.paolanti}@pm.univpm.it,
{e.frontoni,a.mancini,p.zingaretti}@univpm.it

Abstract. Video analytics, involves a variety of techniques to monitor, analyse, and extract meaningful information from video streams. In this light, person re-identification is an important topic in scene monitoring, human computer interaction, retail, people counting, ambient assisted living and many other computer vision research. The existing datasets are not suitable for activity monitoring and human behaviour analysis. For this reason we build a novel dataset for person re-identification that uses an RGB-D camera in a top-view configuration. This setup choice is primarily due to the reduction of occlusions and it has also the advantage of being privacy preserving, because faces are not recorded by the camera. The use of an RGB-D camera allows to extract anthropometric features for the recognition of people passing under the camera. The paper describes in details the collection and construction modalities of the dataset TVPR. This is composed by 100 people and for each video frame nine depth and colour features are computed and provided together with key descriptive statistics.

Keywords: Person re-identification · Top-view dataset · RGB-D camera · TVPR

1 Introduction

In the last decades, video analytics has been rapidly evolving as autonomous understanding of events occurring in a scene monitored by multiple video cameras. One of the fundamental problems in video surveillance is person re-identification (re-id), which is the process to determine if different instances or images of the same person, recorded in different moments, belong to the same subject. In every day life, this is done by humans without much effort. Our brains are trained to localise and detect people and later to properly re-identify them. In the recent years, this problem has gained a rapid increase in attention in both academic research communities and industrial laboratories.

Person re-id has many important applications in video surveillance, because it saves human efforts on exhaustively searching for a person from large amounts

© Springer International Publishing AG 2017
K. Nasrollahi et al. (Eds.): VAAM 2016/FFER 2016, LNCS 10165, pp. 1–11, 2017.
DOI: 10.1007/978-3-319-56687-0_1

of video sequences. Identification cameras are widely employed in most of public places like malls, office buildings, airports, stations and museums. These cameras generally provide enhanced coverage and overlay large geospatial areas because they have non-overlapping fields-of-views. Huge amounts of video data, monitored in real time by law enforcement officers or used after the event for forensic purposes, are provided by these networks. An automated analysis of these data improves significantly the quality of monitoring, in addition to process the data faster [20].

The behaviour characterization of people in a scene and their long term activity can be possible using video analysis, which is required for high-level surveillance tasks in order to alert the security personnel.

Recent literature about re-id approaches is mostly focused on appearance-based models. Researchers have paid attention on interest points, structural information and colour as principal appearance cues [5]. The introduction of RGB-D cameras provides affordable and additional rough depth information coupled with visual images, offering sufficient accuracy and resolution for indoor applications. Due to this fact, this camera has already been successfully applied in retail field to univocally identify customers and to analyse behaviours and interactions of shoppers [12].

In this paper, we present a new dataset of person re-id that uses an RGB-D camera in a top-view configuration: the TVPR (Top View Person Re-identification) dataset. We chose an Asus Xtion Pro Live RGB-D camera because it allows acquiring colour and depth information in an affordable and fast way. The camera is installed on the ceiling above the area to be analysed.

For re-id evaluation, we collect data of 100 people, acquired across intervals of days and in different times. This choice is due to its greater suitability compared with a front view configuration, usually adopted for gesture recognition or even for video gaming. The top-view configuration reduces the problem of occlusions [13] and has the advantage of being privacy preserving, because the face is not recorded by the camera. Main motivations of our top-view dataset and some related applications/works are described in Table 1.

The process of extraction of a high number of significant features derived from both depth and colour information is presented. Among all possible features, we selected the nine features described in following sections as the most interesting ones. The set of features extracted by the colour and depth images is used to perform in future works the re-id process.

The paper is organized as follow: Sect. 2 is an overview of the approaches in the context of re-id; Sect. 3 gives details on the proposed setup for the collection of data, which is the core of this work; next section (Sect. 4) provides some samples and key statistics of the dataset (Subsects. 4.1 and 4.2), followed by conclusions and our future works (Sect. 5).

2   State of Art

Over the past years, in the field of object recognition a significant amount of research has been performed by comparing video sequences. Colour-based

Table 1. Main motivations and possible applications of TVPR.

Research challenges	Applications	Related works
Reliable and occlusion free people counting	Safety and security in crowded environments; people flow analysis; access control and counting	[4, 11, 21, 24, 25]
Interaction detection between people and environment	Intelligent retail environment shelf: Shopper Analytics; Ambient Assisted Living (AAL)	[6, 12, 16]
Fall detection, Human Behaviours Analysis (HBA)	High reliability fall detection; occlusion free; HBA at home and AAL	[10, 13]

features of video sequences are usually described with the use of a set of key frames that characterize well a video sequence. The HSV colour histogram and the RGB colour histogram are robust against the perspective and the variability of resolution [9]. The clothing colour histograms taken over the head, trousers and shirt regions together with the approximated height of the person have been used as discriminative features.

Recently, the person re-id problem has received a considerable attention, and various reviews and surveys are available, pointing out different aspects of this topic [15]. Research works on person re-id can be divided into two categories: feature and learning [22].

The use of anthropometric measures for re-id was proposed for the first time in [14]. In this case, height was estimated from RGB cameras as a cue for associating tracks of individuals coming from non-overlapping views.

In [7], the authors proposed the use of local motion features to re-identify people across camera views. They obtained correspondence between body parts of different persons through space-time segmentation. On this body parts, color and edge histograms are extracted. In this approach, person re-id is performed by matching the body parts based on the features and correspondence.

Shape and appearance context, which computes the co-occurrence of shape words and visual words for person re-id is proposed in [23]. Human body is partitioned into L parts with the shape context and a learned shape dictionary. Then, these parts is further segmented into M subregions by a spatial kernel. The histogram of visual words is extracted on each subregion. Consequently, for person re-id the $L \times M$ histograms are used as visual features.

In [3] the appearance of a pedestrian is represented by combining three kinds of features (sampled according to the symmetry and asymmetry axes obtained from silhouette segmentation): the weighted color histograms, the maximally stable color regions, and recurrent highly structured patches.

Another method to face the problem of person re-id is learning discriminant models on low-level visual features. Adaboost is used to select an optimal ensemble of localized features for pedestrian recognition in [9]. Partial least squares is used to perform person re-id in [19]. Instead, Prosser et al. [18] have used ranking SVM to learn the ranking model.

In last years, it is well-known the metric learning for person re-id. A probabilistic relative distance comparison model has been proposed [26]. It maximizes the probability that the distance between a pair of true match is smaller than that between an incorrect match pair.

In [17], the authors investigate whether the re-id accuracy of clothing appearance descriptors can be improved by fusing them with anthropometric measures extracted from depth data, using RGB-D sensors, in unconstrained settings. They also propose a dissimilarity-based framework for building and fusing the multimodal descriptors of pedestrian images for re-id tasks, as an alternative to the widely used score-level fusion.

Several datasets used to test re-id models are available: *VIPeR*[1], *iLIDS*,[2] *ETHZ*[3] and the more recent *CAVIAR4REID*[4]. These datasets cover many aspects of the person re-id problem, such as shape deformation, occlusions, illumination changes, very low resolution images, image blurring, etc. [8]. Another re-id dataset is proposed in [2]; this is composed by 79 people and four groups. Data are gathered using RGB-D technology, but are not suitable for our purposes as mentioned above in Table 1.

3 Setup and Acquisition

We have built a dataset, TVPR[5], of 100 individuals recorded from an RGB-D camera installed in a top-view configuration. The 100 people were captured in several days (see more information on TVPR in Sect. 4). The camera is installed on the ceiling of a laboratory at 4 m above the floor and covers an area of $14.66\,\mathrm{m}^2$ ($4.43\,\mathrm{m} \times 3.31\,\mathrm{m}$). The camera is positioned above the surface which as to be analysed (Fig. 1).

The first step is the processing of the data acquired from the RGB-D camera. The camera captures depth and colour images, both with dimensions of 640×480 pixels, at a rate up to approximately 30 fps and illuminates the scene/objects with structured light based on infrared patterns.

Seven out of the nine features selected are the *anthropometric features* extracted from the depth image:

- distance between floor and head, d_1;
- distance between floor and shoulders, d_2;
- area of head surface, d_3;
- head circumference, d_4;
- shoulders circumference, d_5;

---

[1] https://vision.soe.ucsc.edu.

[2] http://www.eecs.qmul.ac.uk.

[3] https://data.vision.ee.ethz.ch/cvl/aess/dataset.

[4] http://www.lorisbazzani.info/datasets.

[5] http://vrai.dii.univpm.it/re-id-dataset.

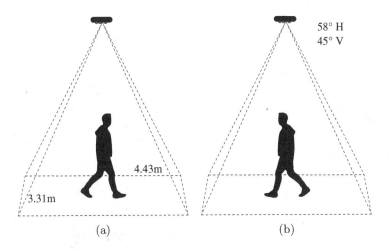

Fig. 1. System architecture.

- shoulders breadth, d_6;
- thoracic anteroposterior depth, d_7.

The remaining two *colour-based features* are acquired by the colour image. We also define *TVH*, *TVD* and *TVDH*.

- *TVH* is the colour descriptor:

$$TVH = \{H_h^p, H_o^p\} \tag{1}$$

- *TVD* is the depth descriptor:

$$TVD = \{d_1^p, d_2^p, d_3^p, d_4^p, d_5^p, d_6^p, d_7^p\} \tag{2}$$

- Finally, *TVDH* is the signature of a person defined as:

$$TVDH = \{d_1^p, d_2^p, d_3^p, d_4^p, d_5^p, d_6^p, d_7^p, H_h^p, H_o^p\} \tag{3}$$

Colour is an important visual attribute for both computer vision and human perception. It is one of the most widely used visual feature in image/video retrieval. To extract this two features we used HSV histograms. Local histograms have proven to be largely adopted and very effective. The signature of a person is also composed by two colour histograms computed for head/hairs and outerwear: H_h^p, H_o^p in (3), such as in [1], with $n = 10$ bin quantization, for both H channel and S channel.

Figure 2 depicts the set features considered: anthropometric and the colour-based ones.

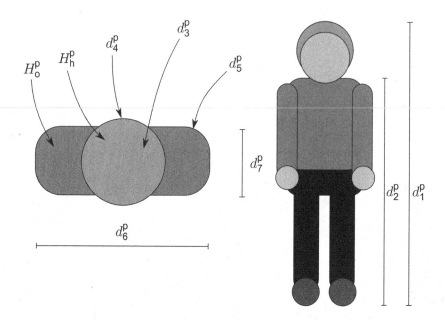

Fig. 2. Anthropometric and colour-based features.

4   Evaluation Results

4.1   Dataset Description

The 100 people of our dataset were acquired in 23 registration session. Each of the 23 folders contains the video of one registration sessions. The recording time [s] for the session and the number of persons of that session are reported in Table 2. Acquisitions have been performed in 8 days and the total recording time is about 2000 s. Registrations are made in an indoor scenario, where people pass under the camera installed on the ceiling. Another big issue is environmental illumination. In each recording session, the illumination condition is not constant, because it varies in function of the different hours of the day and it also depends on natural illumination due to weather conditions. The video acquisitions, in our scenario, are depicted in Fig. 3, which are examples of person registration respectively with sunlight and artificial light. Each person during a registration session walked with an average gait within the recording area in one direction, then it turned back and repeated the same route in the opposite direction. This methodology is used for a better split of TVPR in training set (the first passage of the person under the camera) and testing set (when the person passed again under the camera).

The recruited people are aged between 19–36 years: 43 females and 57 male; 86 with dark hair, 12 with light hair and 2 are hairless. Furthermore, of these people 55 have short hair, 43 have long hair. The subjects were recorded in their everyday clothing like T-shirts/sweatshirts/shirts, loose-fitting trousers, coats, scarves and hats. In particular, 18 subjects wore coats and 7 subjects

Table 2. Time [s] of registration for each session and the number of people of that session.

Session	Time [s]	# people	Session	Time [s]	# people
g001	68.765	4	g013	102.283	6
g002	53.253	3	g014	92.028	5
g003	50.968	2	g015	126.446	6
g004	59.551	3	g016	86.197	4
g005	75.571	4	g017	95.817	5
g006	128.827	7	g018	57.903	3
g007	125.044	6	g019	82.908	5
g008	75.972	3	g020	87.228	4
g009	94.336	4	g021	42.624	2
g010	116.861	6	g022	68.394	3
g011	101.614	5	g023	56.966	3
g012	155.338	7			
			Total	**2004.894**	**100**

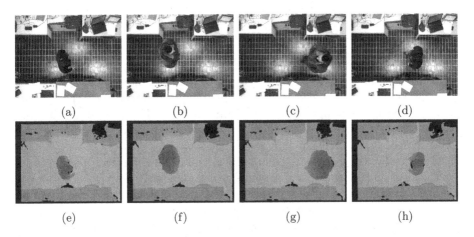

(a)   (b)   (c)   (d)

(e)   (f)   (g)   (h)

Fig. 3. Snapshots of a registration session of the recorded data, in an indoor scenario, with artificial light. People had to pass under the camera installed on the ceiling. The sequence a–e, b–f corresponds to the sequence d–h, c–g respectively training and testing set of the classes 8-9 for the registration session g003.

wore scarves. All videos have fixed dimensions and a frame rate of about 30 fps. Videos are saved in native .oni files, but can be converted in any other format. Colour stream is available in a non compressed format.

Figure 4 reports the histograms of each extracted anthropometric feature. Due to the dissimilarity of the analysed subjects a Gaussian curve is obtained from the data.

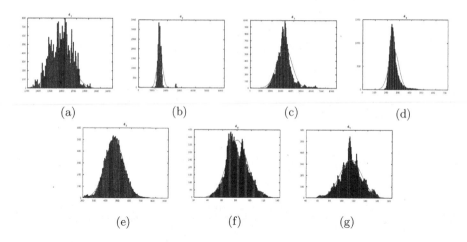

Fig. 4. Statistics histogram for each feature (**a** d_1 distance between floor and head; **b** d_2 distance between floor and shoulders; **c** d_3 area of head surface; **d** d_4 Head circumference; **e** d_5 shoulders circumference; **f** d_6 shoulders breadth; **g** d_7 thoracic anteroposterior depth). The resultant Gaussian curve (in red) is due to the dissimilarity of the analysed subjects. (Color figure online)

4.2   Performance Validation

The *Cumulative Matching Characteristic* (CMC) curve represents the expectation of finding the correct match in the top n matches. It is equivalent of the ROC curve in detection problems. This performance metric evaluates recognition problems, by some assumptions about the distribution of appearances in a camera network. It is considered the primary measure of identification performance among biometric researchers.

As well-established in recognition and in re-id tasks, for each testing item we ranked the training gallery elements using standard distance metrics. We examined the effects of 3 distance measures as the matching distance metrics: the L1 City block, the Euclidean Distance and the Cosine Distance.

To evaluate our dataset, the performance results are reported in terms of recognition rate, using the CMC curves, illustrated in Fig. 5. In particular, the horizontal axis is the rank of the matching score, the vertical axis is the probability of correct identification.

Considering our dataset, we depict a comparison among *TVH* and *TVD* in terms of CMC curves, to compare the ranks returned by using these different descriptors.

Figure 5a provides the CMC obtained for *TVH*. Figure 5b represents the CMC obtained for *TVD*. We compare these results with the average obtained by *TVH* and *TVD*. The average CMC is displayed in Fig. 5d.

It is observed that the best performance is achieved by the combination of descriptors. In Fig. 5d, it can be seen that the combination of descriptors improve the results obtained by each of the descriptor separately. This result is due to the

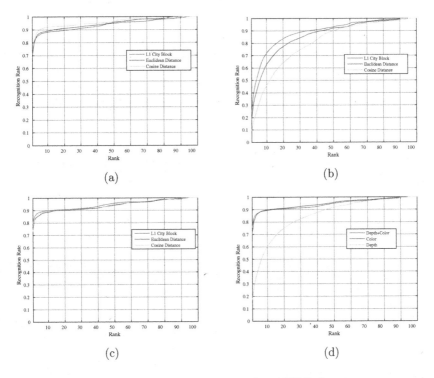

Fig. 5. The CMC curves obtained on TVPR dataset.

depth contribution that can be more informative. In fact, the depth outperform the color, giving the best performance for rank values higher than 15 (Fig. 5b). Its better performance suggests the importance and potential of this descriptor.

5   Conclusions and Future Works

Person re-identification is a critical problem in video analytics applications such as surveillance and security. In this paper, we have proposed a novel dataset for the person re-identification (TVPR) with a features set extracted from colour and depth images.

We use an RGB-D camera to detect, track and describe individuals crossing a monitored area. We chose the top-view configuration for a greater suitability, i.e. more robustness, to a series of tasks like those reported in Table 1.

Further investigation will be devoted to the study of more sophisticated features. The CMC curves have suggested that for the different distance metric approaches the depth descriptor has strong discriminative power. The integration of more features in the model seems to improve the identity discrimination. This aspect is of great importance important, in order to perform a classification model.

Future works would include the integration of this re-identification system with an audio framework and the use of other types of RGB-D sensors, such as time of flight (TOF) ones. The system can additionally be integrated as a source of high semantic level information in a networked ambient intelligence scenario, to provide cues for different problems, such as detecting abnormal speed and dimension outliers, that can alert of a possible uncontrolled circumstance.

References

1. Baltieri, D., Vezzani, R., Cucchiara, R.: Learning articulated body models for people re-identification. In: Proceedings of the 21st ACM International Conference on Multimedia, pp. 557–560. ACM (2013)
2. Barbosa, I.B., Cristani, M., Bue, A., Bazzani, L., Murino, V.: Re-identification with RGB-D sensors. In: Fusiello, A., Murino, V., Cucchiara, R. (eds.) ECCV 2012. LNCS, vol. 7583, pp. 433–442. Springer, Heidelberg (2012). doi:10.1007/978-3-642-33863-2_43
3. Bazzani, L., Cristani, M., Murino, V.: Symmetry-driven accumulation of local features for human characterization and re-identification. Comput. Vis. Image Underst. **117**(2), 130–144 (2013)
4. Castrillón-Santana, M., Lorenzo-Navarro, J., Hernández-Sosa, D.: People semantic description and re-identification from point cloud geometry. In: 2014 22nd International Conference on Pattern Recognition (ICPR), pp. 4702–4707. IEEE (2014)
5. D'Angelo, A., Dugelay, J.-L.: People re-identification in camera networks based on probabilistic color histograms. In: IS&T/SPIE Electronic Imaging, p. 78820K. International Society for Optics and Photonics (2011)
6. Frontoni, E., Mancini, A., Zingaretti, P.: RGBD sensors for human activity detection in AAL environments. In: Longhi, S., Siciliano, P., Germani, M., Monteriú, A. (eds.) Ambient Assisted Living: Italian Forum 2013, pp. 127–135. Springer, Heidelberg (2014)
7. Gheissari, N., Sebastian, T.B., Hartley, R.: Person re-identification using spatiotemporal appearance. In: 2006 IEEE Computer Society Conference on Computer Vision and Pattern Recognition, vol. 2, pp. 1528–1535. IEEE (2006)
8. Gong, S., Cristani, M., Yan, S., Loy, C.C.: Person Re-identification. Advances in Computer Vision and Pattern Recognition, 1st edn. Springer, London (2014)
9. Gray, D., Tao, H.: Viewpoint invariant pedestrian recognition with an ensemble of localized features. In: Forsyth, D., Torr, P., Zisserman, A. (eds.) ECCV 2008. LNCS, vol. 5302, pp. 262–275. Springer, Heidelberg (2008). doi:10.1007/978-3-540-88682-2_21
10. Kepski, M., Kwolek, B.: Fall detection using ceiling-mounted 3d depth camera. In: 2014 International Conference on Computer Vision Theory and Applications (VISAPP), vol. 2, pp. 640–647. IEEE (2014)
11. Kouno, D., Shimada, K., Endo, T.: Person identification using top-view image with depth information. In: 2012 13th ACIS International Conference on Software Engineering, Artificial Intelligence, Networking and Parallel & Distributed Computing (SNPD), pp. 140–145. IEEE (2012)
12. Liciotti, D., Contigiani, M., Frontoni, E., Mancini, A., Zingaretti, P., Placidi, V.: Shopper analytics: a customer activity recognition system using a distributed RGB-D camera network. In: Distante, C., Battiato, S., Cavallaro, A. (eds.) VAAM 2014. LNCS, vol. 8811, pp. 146–157. Springer, Cham (2014). doi:10.1007/978-3-319-12811-5_11

13. Liciotti, D., Massi, G., Frontoni, E., Mancini, A., Zingaretti, P.: Human activity analysis for in-home fall risk assessment. In: 2015 IEEE International Conference on Communication Workshop (ICCW), pp. 284–289. IEEE (2015)

14. Madden, C., Piccardi, M.: Height measurement as a session-based biometric for people matching across disjoint camera views. In: Image and Vision Computing New Zealand, pp. 282–286. Citeseer (2005)

15. Messelodi, S., Modena, C.M.: Boosting fisher vector based scoring functions for person re-identification. Image Vis. Comput. **44**, 44–58 (2015)

16. Migniot, C., Ababsa, F.: 3D human tracking from depth cue in a buying behavior analysis context. In: Wilson, R., Hancock, E., Bors, A., Smith, W. (eds.) CAIP 2013. LNCS, vol. 8047, pp. 482–489. Springer, Heidelberg (2013). doi:10.1007/978-3-642-40261-6_58

17. Pala, F., Satta, R., Fumera, G., Roli, F.: Multimodal person reidentification using RGB-D cameras. IEEE Trans. Circ. Syst. Video Technol. **26**(4), 788–799 (2016)

18. Prosser, B., Zheng, W.-S., Gong, S., Xiang, T., Mary, Q.: Person re-identification by support vector ranking. In: BMVC, vol. 2, p. 6 (2010)

19. Schwartz, W.R., Davis, L.S.: Learning discriminative appearance-based models using partial least squares. In: 2009 XXII Brazilian Symposium on Computer Graphics and Image Processing (SIBGRAPI), pp. 322–329. IEEE (2009)

20. Tu, P.H., Doretto, G., Krahnstoever, N.O., Perera, A.A., Wheeler, F.W., Liu, X., Rittscher, J., Sebastian, T.B., Yu, T., Harding, K.G.: An intelligent video framework for homeland protection. In: Defense and Security Symposium, p. 65620C. International Society for Optics and Photonics (2007)

21. Vera, P., Monjaraz, S., Salas, J.: Counting pedestrians with a zenithal arrangement of depth cameras. Mach. Vis. Appl. **27**(2), 303–315 (2016)

22. Wang, X.: Intelligent multi-camera video surveillance: a review. Pattern Recognit. Lett. **34**(1), 3–19 (2013)

23. Wang, X., Doretto, G., Sebastian, T., Rittscher, J., Tu, P.: Shape and appearance context modeling. In: IEEE 11th International Conference on Computer Vision (ICCV 2007), pp. 1–8. IEEE (2007)

24. Wateosot, C., Suvonvorn, N.: Top-view based people counting using mixture of depth and color information. In: The Second Asian Conference on Information Systems (ACIS) (2013)

25. Zhang, X., Yan, J., Feng, S., Lei, Z., Yi, D., Li, S.Z.: Water filling: unsupervised people counting via vertical kinect sensor. In: 2012 IEEE Ninth International Conference on Advanced Video and Signal-Based Surveillance (AVSS), pp. 215–220. IEEE (2012)

26. Zheng, W.-S., Gong, S., Xiang, T.: Person re-identification by probabilistic relative distance comparison. In: 2011 IEEE conference on Computer vision and pattern recognition (CVPR), pp. 649–656. IEEE (2011)

Pervasive System for Consumer Behaviour Analysis in Retail Environments

Daniele Liciotti[(✉)], Emanuele Frontoni, Adriano Mancini,
and Primo Zingaretti

Dipartimento di Ingegneria dell'Informazione, Università Politecnica delle Marche,
Via Brecce Bianche, 60131 Ancona, Italy
{d.liciotti,e.frontoni,a.mancini,p.zingaretti}@univpm.it

Abstract. In the context of retailing, the monitoring of consumer behaviours is particularly important for supporting vendors in their management and marketing decisions. Many studies have been carried out about various aspects and consequences of different behaviours. However, only recently the potential of computing systems is being used for automated data collection and processing. In this work, we present a novel pervasive system able to automatically monitor consumer behaviour in front of shelves in an intelligent retail environment (IRE). Data collected are stored into a cloud server for data analysis and insights, ready to be used by a Decision Support System (DSS).

The completely autonomous and low cost system proposed in this paper is based on a software infrastructure connected to a video sensor network. A set of computer vision algorithms, embedded in the distributed RGB-D cameras, provides information concerning customer behaviour, in particular, user-shelf interactions described with temporal and spatial features. This large number of analytics allows insight deductions. The use of distributed vision sensors inside a retail environment is novel and produces really valuable data for brands and retailers.

The feasibility and the effectiveness of the proposed architecture and approach have been tested on real retail environments.

Keywords: Ambient intelligence · Computer vision · Embedded sensors · Pervasive systems · Consumer behaviour · Retail

1 Introduction

In literature, there are several researches that study the behaviour of consumers in retail environments, for example, [7,15] and references therein. In particular, Puccinelli et al. [15] identified seven topic areas of consumer behavior research in retail environments: (*1*) goals, schema and information processing, (*2*) memory, (*3*) involvement, (*4*) attitudes, (*5*) affect, (*6*) atmospherics and (*7*) consumer attributions and choices. For each topic, they highlighted the most important issues necessary to be further investigated.

K. Nasrollahi et al. (Eds.): VAAM 2016/FFER 2016, LNCS 10165, pp. 12–23, 2017.
DOI: 10.1007/978-3-319-56687-0_2

A common characteristic of all these studies is to do not use automated approaches for data acquisition and information retrieval. They mainly focus on consumer research and retailing from the social, psychological and marketing point of views. On the contrary, the potential of computing to improve all aspects of retail is firstly studied in deep in [9]. In particular, computer vision systems appear very useful in retail environments (as well as in other application fields), mainly for the huge amount of data and the possibility of an automatic data collection. Obviously, an increasing number of these applications [13, 19] have been and are possible thanks to the strengthening of information systems, the development of more stable and efficient vision algorithms and also the higher speed and the lower price of current hardware.

Focusing on computer vision approaches of consumer attributions and choices, Chandon et al. [2] and Strandvall [16] both used eye tracking methods for measuring the value of point-of-purchase. Määttä et al. [12] classified shopper motion into four behaviour classes, distinguishing if their movement is neutral or repetitive. Another approach for video-based extraction of customer movements at the point of sale is described in [8]: their human behaviour analysis is based on the measurement of the customer trajectories inside the store and on the time spent by each person in each zone of the store. According to [14], newer video surveillance applications, not necessarily related to security issues, were developed for shopping, not only to identify anomalous activities, but also to identify people and to analyse consumer behaviour.

At the same time, other pervasive computing approaches were adopted to solve problems in retail environments. Another system developed for the retail store is "SmartStore" [6], which analyses the customer interest immediately, gathers the sensing data from large-scale area and attaches massive tiny sensors to shopping items.

Our research focuses on the implementation of a software infrastructure coupled with a hardware technology to build a pervasive computing intelligent system for detecting and analysing the human behaviour in real retail stores.

By means of video cameras and computer vision algorithms, our pervasive system detects human motion and then describes human behaviour by quantitative parameters. More in detail, the main objective is to analyse the interactions between customers and products on the shelves. Therefore, our system detects and monitors people when they are in front of a shelf, using a distributed video sensor network. This allows us to better detail the activities of consumers when they stop in a zone of the store, e.g., the objects of the shelf that are touched by each person.

The installation of the system in several parts of the store provides large volumes of multidimensional data on which to perform statistics and deduce insights. The analysis of these data offers a unique possibility to better understand several crucial aspects of a retail ambient, e.g., the appealing of a product, a good positioning of different products on a shelf, the human traffic in front of each shelf.

Just because the sensor installation should be repeated in several zones of the shop to collect a significant large amount of data, we developed a system that can be easily scaled, from a single shelf installation to a large widespread grid of sensors.

Our system is able to detect all the objects on the shelf that interact with the customer using only one RGB-D sensor for each shelf, while in [7] the activity recognition needs an RFID sensor mounted on each object to be performed.

We developed a software infrastructure that is able to automatically detect, measure and store crucial information for a retail ambient. In particular, our pervasive system does not need to interact with customers to retrieve the desired information, as for the cases of the interactive display [17] or the mobile phone [5], where direct customer interactions with the systems are used to exchange information between shoppers and the retail ambient. In our case, information are collected automatically through the computer vision algorithms that we developed.

Summarizing, the paper presents a smart and low-cost embedded sensor network for intelligent retail environments (IREs) able to identify customers and to analyse their behaviour and shelf interactions. Major characteristics of this system are the general and easily scalable architecture really focused on the retail environment application and the very precise and reliable computer vision algorithms, which are able to run efficiently in low cost hardware and to collect automatically several relevant information.

The paper is organized as follows: in Sect. 2 we describe the IRE architecture and application requirements; Sect. 3 describes the implemented computer vision algorithms, focusing on people monitoring and detection of user-shelf interactions; experimental setup and results are presented in Sects. 4 and 5, respectively; finally, conclusions and future works are presented in Sect. 6.

2   IRE Architecture and Application Requirements

The hierarchical architecture of the proposed pervasive retail environment is shown in Fig. 1 along with the information provided at each abstraction layer. Sensor nodes, able to measure autonomously a part of the environment, are logically connected to the concept of shelf, multiple shelves are part of a store and, finally, several stores are part of a retailer chain. The general idea is based on several aggregation layers that provide to the system different information, from raw data to high level data analytics and insights.

At the single camera node level only raw data are available; a first data processing to provide interaction maps occurs at the shelf level. Multi camera analysis is also functional to perform flow comparisons in different areas of the store. At the top level general insights, store comparisons, store optimizations and re-design can be performed by retailers.

The functional requirements of the system, concerning what the system is able to do, its expected behaviour and which are its input/output functions, are:

1. counting the number of people "passing by" the camera vision area;

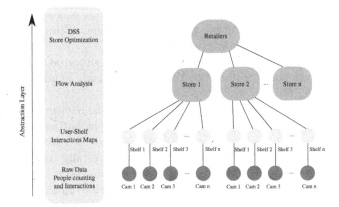

Fig. 1. The hierarchical architecture and the information provided at each abstraction layer of an intelligent retail environment.

2. for each person detected by the camera, storing the input/output position and the permanence time in the camera vision area;
3. storing all the interactions with the shelf:
   (a) who performed the action;
   (b) which product was touched;
4. sending and saving data in a remote database (cloud) available for statistical analysis;
5. from any remote location, controlling RGB-D camera parameters:
   (a) video streaming visualization;
   (b) redefinition of shelf area;
   (c) software upgrade;
6. restoring data from a backup.

Non-functional requirements establish constraints on the system or on its development process, defining how it should be achieved. For the implementation of the system, precise constraints have been imposed:

1. vision sensors should be ceiling mounted, which limits both their size and the total weight of all components to be supported by the structure;
2. cameras should be connected to a main router via a wireless network and accessible from outside of the store for remote control;
3. the whole system should be low cost and scalable.

3   Computer Vision Algorithms

The whole system can be seen as a big sensor network where each node is a micro system that analyses the consumer behaviour in front of a specific shelf of a store. Each node consists of an embedded system that includes an RGB-D sensor, ceiling mounted and looking to the scene from the top, and a software component to send the calculated information to the cloud. Adding a new node/shelf does not require structural modifications of the entire system, so that it is possible to install several RGB-D sensors in every store.

In this section we focus the attention on the two vision algorithms that we have already developed, processed by every node: people monitoring and user-shelf interactions.

To build a system able to detect automatically all the relevant data for a retail environments other algorithms are being developed. In particular, our current researches concern also person re-identification, in order to create an architecture comprehensive of highly-integrated systems able to totally monitor consumer behaviour in a retail environment. The first problem, even if highly studied in the literature [1], is not as much treated for top-view images, where the re-identification of each visitor is made using features like height, colors of hairs and clothes of people that are in the camera field. The second research, on the base of our previous work on Ambient Assisted Living field [11], intends to propose an audio framework able to recognize voice commands by continuously monitoring the acoustic retail environment. Echo and interference cancellation algorithms guarantee a reliable keyword extraction, which is a very important aspect from the store point of view, since it allows to know and follow customer preferences.

3.1   People Monitoring

In this part we describe our algorithm for people monitoring, which consists of two steps: background subtraction and people detection.

As regard background subtraction, in this work we implemented the algorithm of Zivkovic [20], because it ensures a lower computation time than the method we used in [10, 18].

For people detection we used the segmentation algorithm named Multi-Level Segmentation, which has in input the foreground depth image (the output of the background subtraction algorithm) and in output the highest point of each person. The algorithm is explained in detail in the pseudo-code Algorithm 1. The MULTILEVELSEGM function has in input the foreground image $(f(x, y))$. First of all, FINDPOINTMAX function calculates the highest point of whole image (max) and its coordinates $(point_{max})$. In line 3, the *level* counter assumes the *threshold* value, that is a fixed value corresponding to average height of a human head (we adopted the value 10 cm). So, the number of segmentations is strictly related to the height of the tallest person. The output condition of the while loop is when the segmentation level becomes negative (above the floor). The SEGM function yields in output a binary image with blobs representative of moving objects that are above the segmentation level $(max - level)$. This binary image is the input of FINDCONTOURS, an OpenCV function that returns a vector of points for each blob. Then, the FILTERCONTOURS function deletes noise (blobs with a little dimension and/or a bad shape). The **for** loop from line 8 to line 14 inserts in the vector *points* the highest point/depth value (FINDPOINTMAX function) of each blob identified by means of the FILTERMASK function. Finally,

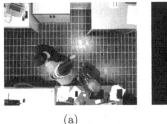 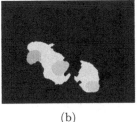 

(a) (b) (c)

Fig. 2. Head recognition (2b): different colors of the blob highlight the head of the people detected in the scene (2a). Parameters defining a shelf zone (2c) (green area). (Color figure online)

MULTILEVELSEGM function returns a vector with all maximum local points. The length of this vector indicates the number of people that are in the image.

The Multi-Level Segmentation algorithm intends to overcome the limitations of the binary segmentation method proposed in [10] in case of collisions among people. In fact, using a single-level segmentation, in case of a collision, two people become a single blob (person), without distinguishing between head and shoulders of the person. By using this new approach, when a collision occurs, even if two people are identified with a single blob, the head of each person is anyway detected, becoming the discriminant element. Figure 2 highlights the head of each person obtained by the Multi-Level Segmentation algorithm: different colors highlight the head of a person detected by the camera. In case of collisions (Figs. 2a and b) the yellow blob contains two people and both heads are also detected.

3.2 Detection of User-Shelf Interactions

In this subsection, we focus on the algorithm for the detection of interactions with the shelf. A shelf zone is the part of the store interested by an interaction

---

Algorithm 1. Multi-Level Segmentation algorithm

```
1:  function MULTILEVELSEGM(f(x, y))
2:      (max, point_max) = FINDPOINTMAX(f(x, y))
3:      level = threshold
4:      while (max − level) > 0 do
5:          f_level(x, y) = SEGM(f(x, y), (max − level))
6:          contours = FINDCONTOURS(f_level(x, y))
7:          FILTERCONTOURS(contours)
8:          for each contour i ∈ contours do
9:              f_mask(x, y) = FILTERMASK(f_level(x, y), i)
10:             (v_max, p_max) = FINDPOINTMAX(f_mask(x, y))
11:             if p_max ∉ points then
12:                 points.PUSHBACK(p_max)
13:             end if
14:         end for
15:         level = level + threshold
16:     end while
17:     return points
18: end function
```

between the hand of the shopper and a product in the shelf. As described in [4], it is defined by the user during the installation phase and it is characterized by the following tree parameters, written in a configuration file: the maximum distances of the left (x_{dl}), right (x_{dr}) and frontal (y_d) shelf sides from the image borders (see Fig. 2c). This setting is valid for most of the shelves of a store, but it is possible to define other areas of interest (e.g., in the case of a circular island when a cylinder-shaped configuration is needed).

The Multi-Level Segmentation algorithm, described in the previous paragraph, allowed us to detect the head and the body contours of each person. The contour of the head is used to track the movements of a person within the scene. The contour of entire body is used to identify interactions with the shelf. The three vertical planes built at the distances x_{dl}, x_{dr}, y_d from the image border and defining the shelf zone are used to detect interactions. When the contour of entire body intersects at least one of the three planes we establish that a contact occurs and so determine the 3D coordinates of the contact point.

The Contact Detection algorithm is explained in detail in the pseudo-code Algorithm 2. The FINDINTERACTIONS function has in input the depth image of the sensor and the contour vector. Each point of each contour is analysed (from line 2 to line 4) to find contact points with *shelf zone*. If a contact occurs the PUSHBACK method inserts in the vector *vec* the 3D contact point, where the third dimension corresponds to the depth value. Finally, the function returns vector *vec* with all the contact points.

4   Experimental Setup and Data Stored

The system setup is based on state of the art and low cost RGB-D sensors. For the development of this framework a single board computer is used since it is sufficiently small, suited to manage all functions and low consuming.

The camera sensor captures depth images with dimensions of 320×240 pixels at a rate up to 30 frames per second. The depth value is stored using 16 bits allowing a spatial resolution of few millimeters.

In addition to the RGB-D sensor, a Wi-Fi module is connected to the board to transmit the elaborated data to a cloud server by the home wireless network. Image-processing elaborations and transmission of only synthetic data are performed on the single board computer to respect privacy regulation.

Algorithm 2. Contact detection algorithm

```
 1: function FINDINTERACTIONS(d(x, y), peopleVec)
 2:     for each contour i ∈ peopleVec do
 3:         for each point p ∈ i.GETCONTOURS( ) do
 4:             if d(p.x, p.y) ∈ shelfzone then
 5:                 vec.PUSHBACK(d(p.x, p.y))
 6:             end if
 7:         end for
 8:     end for
 9:     return vec
10: end function
```

With this hardware setup the proposed algorithms are able to process the two video flows at 20 fps on the described low cost hardware. The cameras have been installed on panels in the suspended ceiling of the store. Each system yields as output a significant amount of data that are stored in the cloud, so that they can be successively analysed to extract useful indicators. The final tests in real stores have been realized installing RGB-D cameras for a time period of 3 months, in order to obtain statistically significant data.

A ground truth for algorithm accuracy evaluation was collected both in the laboratory and in some days of the real environment tests.

The indicators adopted to evaluate shopper behaviour and preferences can be:

- Number N_v of "passing by" people, that is people crossing camera field of view;
- Number V_z of visitors in each zone in which the image is subdivided;
- Number V_s of "passing by" people interacting with the shelf, where $V_s \subset N_v$;
- Number I_s of interactions for each person, with $I_s = I/V_s$, where I is the number of the interactions;
- Average visit time $\bar{T} = \sum_{i=1}^{N_v} \Delta t_i / N_v$, where the visit time Δt_i is the permanence of each person in the camera view;
- Number N of products touched;
- Duration of interactions $T_I = \sum_{i=1}^{I} \delta t_i$, where $\delta t_i = t_{i,end} - t_{i,init}$ is the difference between final and initial instant of interaction i;
- Average interaction time $\bar{T}_I = T_I / I$.

5   Results

Table 1 summarizes the results obtained by monitoring 7 stores using a total of 15 cameras and for a working period equivalent to 45 months by a single camera. The values in the table refer to the most significant indicators introduced in Sect. 4. They reveal that the average visit time in front of the shelf is 6.21 s, while the average interaction time is 1.23 s. Moreover, the number of interactions for each person is higher than the number of products touched, corresponding to 1.45 interactions for each person.

5.1   Efficiency and Reliability of Algorithms

The two main requirements/capabilities that the software has to satisfy are: (i) to monitor people; (ii) to understand the occurrence of an interaction between a shopper and a shelf.

Table 1. Values of indicators for experiments in real stores.

Indicator	N_v	V_s	I_s	$\bar{T}$	N	$\bar{T}_I$
Value	87885	17762	1.45	6.21 s	25710	1.23 s

Table 2. People detection confusion and user-shelf interaction matrices.

	TP	FN	FP	Total	TPR
People detection	1110	29	11	1150	0,9902
User-shelf interaction	1050	233	254	1537	0,8052

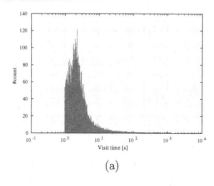

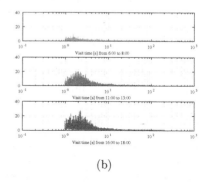

(a)   (b)

Fig. 3. Visit time histogram related to the overall studied period (3a). Visit time histogram related to three different time slots: (i) 6.00 to 8.00 (*green line*). (ii) 11.00–13.00 (*red line*) (iii) 16.00–18.00 (*blue line*) (3b). (Color figure online)

To compare results we considered the sensitivity or true positive rate $TPR = TP/P$, where TP is the number of true positives, calculated by counting the real number of people "passing by" the camera and $P = (TP + FN)$, where FN is the number of false negatives, corresponding to the "passing by" people that the camera has not detected. The same evaluation method has been applied for establishing the correctness of the user-shelf interaction.

Table 2 shows the results of our performance analysis on 4 out of the 7 stores where the system was installed. We have checked the passages and the interactions of consumers measured by the system with the ground truth. More in detail, Table 2 corresponds to the confusion matrices of the people detection and contact detection algorithms. Since our system is built to detect only positive events (detection of people), we can not provide a value for true negative events. Also the number of negative events is unknown. For these reasons, typical confusion matrix parameters (e.g., specificity) are not listed. The sensitivity obtained was 99.02% and 80.52% for the people detection and the hand detection algorithm, respectively.

5.2   Shopper-Shelf Interaction

Once we have demonstrated the high efficiency and robustness of our algorithms, their outputs can be used for statistical analysis.

For example Fig. 3a shows the histogram of the visit time Δt_i related to the overall testing period. Each bin corresponds to an elapsed time of 1 s. The plot shows that there are several counts (47% of the total) with a visit time smaller than 3 s, which can be easily interpreted as not-interacting people. The mean visit time higher than 3 s is equal to 6.46 s. This value, when compared to similar results related to other shelves, can describe the appealing of the shelf to shoppers. Namely, the larger is the mean value higher is the shelf attractiveness. At the same time, the total number of counts indicates if the shelf is located or not in a populated place of the shop.

Since our system detects the precise date/time when each shopper appears in the camera field of view, it is possible to make the same histogram of Fig. 3a for different time slots. Figure 3b shows an example of this for three different time slots: (*i*) from 6.00 to 8.00; (*ii*) 11.00–13.00; (*iii*) 16.00–18.00. During the first slot the shop is closed, hence the data refer only to shop operators. From the remaining slots we can evince that the morning time slot is more populated than the afternoon one. Such information can be very useful to better organize, for example, the staff of the shop according to the time slot with the maximum flux of buyers.

Going into the detail of the products hosted by the shelf, our system is able to storage all the interactions between the shopper and the shelf. Together with this, we can discriminate among three different types of interaction: *neutral* if the hand exceeds the threshold without taking anything; emphpositive when the object is picked up; *negative* when the object is put back after a pickup.

As expected the most interacted zone of the shelf is the central one, but looking at the width distribution of the interactions (Fig. 4a, top panel) it is possible to discriminate at least another peak around shelf width equal to 800 mm, that probably corresponds to an appealing product.

Figure 4 shows maps of the contact points, identified by colored zones, generated during the processing. In particular, Fig. 4a, b, c show respectively, positive, negative and neutral interactions.

Furthermore, Fig. 4 represents some example of a planogram, that is a detailed visual map that establishes the position of the products in a shelf. So to obtain the contact map, the system automatically compares the coordinates

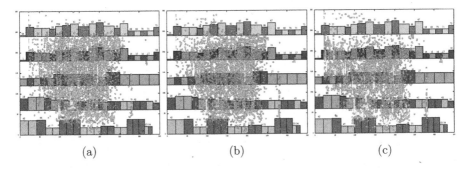

(a)   (b)   (c)

Fig. 4. Maps of interactions produced by the software in a test conducted by our research in a real environment. 2D plots showing the shelf along its width (*x axis*) and height (*y axis*) in millimetres. (Color figure online)

of contact points with ancillary information provided by the planogram management software. The planogram management software and the smart camera hardware are described in [3].

6   Conclusions and Future Works

We developed a pervasive, intelligent vision system for retail applications. It consists in a software infrastructure coupled with a low cost hardware that: (i) receives images from an RGB-D camera; (ii) elaborates the images with computer vision algorithms; (iii) extracts information and collects them into a database for statistical analysis and for being used by a DSS.

The implemented computer vision algorithms: (i) detect the people in the camera field of view; (ii) measure the visit time of each person; (iii) detect occurrences of interactions between shoppers and products on the shelf.

The system has been installed in real retail stores. The long life and real environment tests show the effectiveness of the described system and, in general, the feasibility of the proposed architecture and approach.

The efficiency of the system is defined by its capability in detecting people and shelf interactions. Results show that the people detection algorithm has a very high sensitivity (99%), while the hand detection algorithm shows a good sensitivity slightly above 80%.

The collected information can be used for several useful statistical analyses, since they enhance, e.g., the knowledge of shopper-shelf interactions and the product appeal, as shown in Subsect. 5.2.

The system can be used as part of a sensor network focused on retail reality mining, with the purpose of better understanding customer interactions in retail environments.

Our future projects are directed towards a detailed study of person re-identification using top-view images, a task necessary to assign a single and robust ID to each buyer, and audio recognition. Among several other information, this will allow us to better describe the client behaviour inside the entire shop and not only in front of a single shelf.

References

1. Bedagkar-Gala, A., Shah, S.K.: A survey of approaches and trends in person re-identification. Image Vis. Comput. **32**(4), 270–286 (2014)
2. Chandon, P., Hutchinson, J., Bradlow, E., Young, S.H.: Measuring the value of point-of-purchase marketing with commercial eye-tracking data. INSEAD Business School Research Paper (2007/22) (2006)
3. Frontoni, E., Mancini, A., Zingaretti, P.: Embedded vision sensor network for planogram maintenance in retail environments. Sens. (Switz.) **15**(9), 21114–21133 (2015)
4. Frontoni, E., Raspa, P., Mancini, A., Zingaretti, P., Placidi, V.: Customers' activity recognition in intelligent retail environments. In: Petrosino, A., Maddalena, L., Pala, P. (eds.) ICIAP 2013. LNCS, vol. 8158, pp. 509–516. Springer, Heidelberg (2013). doi:10.1007/978-3-642-41190-8_55

5. Güven, S., Oda, O., Podlaseck, M., Stavropoulos, H., Kolluri, S., Pingali, G.: Social mobile augmented reality for retail. In: PerCom, pp. 1–3. IEEE Computer Society (2009)
6. Iwai, M., Mori, M., Touda, H.: A marketing analysis using massive tiny sensor nodes. In: 2009 Sixth International Conference on Networked Sensing Systems (INSS), pp. 1–4. IEEE (2009)
7. Kourouthanassis, P., Roussos, G.: Developing consumer-friendly pervasive retail systems. IEEE Pervasive Comput. **2**(2), 32–39 (2003)
8. Krockel, J., Bodendorf, F.: Customer tracking and tracing data as a basis for service innovations at the point of sale. In: 2012 Annual SRII Global Conference (SRII), pp. 691–696. IEEE (2012)
9. Krüger, A., Schöning, J., Olivier, P.: How computing will change the face of retail. IEEE Comput. **44**(4), 84–87 (2011)
10. Liciotti, D., Contigiani, M., Frontoni, E., Mancini, A., Zingaretti, P., Placidi, V.: Shopper analytics: a customer activity recognition system using a distributed RGB-D camera network. In: Distante, C., Battiato, S., Cavallaro, A. (eds.) VAAM 2014. LNCS, vol. 8811, pp. 146–157. Springer, Cham (2014). doi:10.1007/978-3-319-12811-5_11
11. Liciotti, D., Ferroni, G., Frontoni, E., Squartini, S., Principi, E., Bonfigli, R., Zingaretti, P., Piazza, F.: Advanced integration of multimedia assistive technologies: a prospective outlook. In: 2014 IEEE/ASME 10th International Conference on Mechatronic and Embedded Systems and Applications (MESA), pp. 1–6. IEEE (2014)
12. Määttä, T., Härmä, A., Aghajan, H., Corporaal, H.: Collaborative detection of repetitive behavior by multiple uncalibrated cameras. Inf. Fusion **21**, 68–81 (2015)
13. Moeslund, T.B., Granum, E.: A survey of computer vision-based human motion capture. Comput. Vis. Image Underst. **81**(3), 231–268 (2001)
14. Moeslund, T.B., Hilton, A., Krüger, V.: A survey of advances in vision-based human motion capture and analysis. Comput. Vis. Image Underst. **104**(2), 90–126 (2006)
15. Puccinelli, N.M., Goodstein, R.C., Grewal, D., Price, R., Raghubir, P., Stewart, D.: Customer experience management in retailing: understanding the buying process. J. Retail. **85**(1), 15–30 (2009)
16. Strandvall, T.: Eye tracking as a tool in package and shelf testing. White Paper (Toby technology) (2008)
17. Strohbach, M., Martin, M.: Toward a platform for pervasive display applications in retail environments. IEEE Pervasive Comput. **10**(2), 19–27 (2011)
18. Sturari, M., Liciotti, D., Pierdicca, R., Frontoni, E., Mancini, A., Contigiani, M., Zingaretti, P.: Robust and affordable retail customer profiling by vision and radio beacon sensor fusion. Pattern Recogn. Lett. **81**, 30–40 (2016)
19. Wang, L., Hu, W., Tan, T.: Recent developments in human motion analysis. Pattern Recogn. **36**(3), 585–601 (2003)
20. Zivkovic, Z.: Improved adaptive Gaussian mixture model for background subtraction. In: 2004 Proceedings of the 17th International Conference on Pattern Recognition, ICPR 2004, vol. 2, pp. 28–31. IEEE (2004)

Estimation of Task Difficulty and Habituation Effect While Visual Manipulation Using Pupillary Response

Asami Matsumoto[✉], Yuta Tange, Atsushi Nakazawa, and Toyoaki Nishida

Institute of Informatics, Kyoto University,
Yoshida-Honmachi, Sakyo-ku, Kyoto 606-8501, Japan
matsumoto@ii.ist.i.kyoto-u.ac.jp

Abstract. In this paper, we show the relationship between pupil dilation and visual manipulation tasks to measure the magnitude of individual habituation effect and task difficulty. Our findings show that pupil dilation can be used as a new physiological signal in the application of audience measurement, affective computing, affective communications, and user interface design. We built a pointer maze game where a subject moves a pointer from start to end positions on a straight pathway, and we observe the subject's pupil size while changing the pathway width and performing the game repeatedly. Through the two experiments, we found the maximum pupil size increases during the game when the pathway narrows. The first experiment indicates the difficulty of the task (narrower pathway) is related to the larger pupil diameter. On the basis of these results, we built models relating to (1) pupil size and pathway width, (2) pupil size and duration, and (3) pathway width and duration. The second experiment indicates the pupil constriction is related to the habituation effect of the users. While a similar effect has already been reported, the magnitude of pupil dilation during our task was about ten times as high as that in other tasks, so our confidence in the model is high.

Keywords: Pupil dilation · Physiological signal · Concentration · Task difficulty · Habituation effect

1 Introduction

Estimating individual task difficulty and habituation is an important topic for audience measurement, affective computing, affective communications, behavioral analysis of drivers, user interface design, and gaze behavior analysis. Through these signals, we can obtain the status of human concentration which plays an important role in the applications of gaze analysis, which currently uses the duration of the gaze points ('heat-map' representation) as the ground-truth of the saliency. However, duration does not always reflect the importance of the gaze target, e.g. one looks at the target inattentively such as when one is disturbed. Thus, other measurements for obtaining human concentration are necessary for further gaze analysis.

© Springer International Publishing AG 2017
K. Nasrollahi et al. (Eds.): VAAM 2016/FFER 2016, LNCS 10165, pp. 24–35, 2017.
DOI: 10.1007/978-3-319-56687-0_3

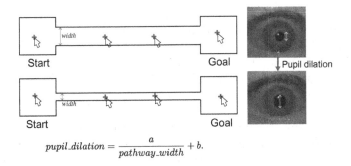

$$pupil\_dilation = \frac{a}{pathway\_width} + b.$$

Fig. 1. Pointer maze task, and the model of pupil dilation and path width.

In this paper, we aim to use human pupillary response to estimate the magnitude of human mental effects, such as concentration and habituation effect, to solve these issues. Though a person's pupil size changes in response to visual coordination such as adjustment to incoming light [20], visual focusing (accommodation reflex) [7], viewing distance [14], optical aberrations and diffraction [4,15,18]. It also reflects people's internal states such as cognitive workloads [11], memory recall [13,17], stress [1], and interest in visual targets [3,10], since the pupillary muscle is coordinated by the autonomic nervous systems (ANS).

We designed a point mange gaze which is designed to control the task difficulty with a physical parameter (pathway length and width) and observe a pupil size during the task, and then build a model relating to the task difficulty and pupil dilation (Fig. 1). Since a user requires stronger concentration to complete a more difficult task, we can estimate the status of concentration through the user's pupil size.

Our findings provide the following contributions to physiology and engineering.

First, our visual manipulation task (*pointer maze game task*) can effectively make a subject concentrate strongly, so we can easily observe the relationship between a person's internal state (concentration, cognitive workload, etc.) and pupil dilation even from a single trial. Our experimental setup produces a much larger magnitude of pupil dilation than existing visual tasks including *object detection* and *target pointing*. In addition, we experimentally prove the elapsed time of the pointer maze game is proportional to the length of the pathway and inversely correlates to the pathway width. These findings indicate the difficulty of the pointer maze game can be defined by the length and width of the pathway.

Second, through the experiments involving ten subjects, we build a model of the pupil dilation during the pointer maze game. Specifically, the pupil diameter increases when the pathway lengthens and/or widens. This model contributes to estimate (a) the magnitude of one's concentration during the task and (b) the difficulty of the manipulation task, using the pupillary response.

Third, we show that the personal dependency of the task difficulty can be measured by the pupillary response. Namely, our experimental results show that (1) if the pupil constricts while the task, the task is difficult to the subject and (2) if the size of pupil does not change while the task, the task is easier to the subject. Since the task difficulty is related to the concentration, we can measure the subject's magnitude of concentration for the particular visual manipulation/observation tasks from the pupillary response.

From the engineering point of view, our method has a potential to be a new physiological signal and enable a person's concentration and task difficulty to be estimated. Unlike other physiological signals such as skin conductivity (SCR) or heart rate (HR), the pupillary response can be measured without body-attached sensors. In particular, this signal suits the simultaneous observation of the eye-tracking systems because we can use the same camera for both measurements. Moreover, the sensors (cameras) are cost effective and easy to combine with other systems such as PCs and wearable systems.

In the rest of this paper, we first describe the method for the experimental setup and task, then show the results, analysis, and the model of the pupil dilation, and finally give a brief discussion and conclusion.

2   Related Work

Pupil diameter (iris size) is controlled by two muscles, the sphincter pupillae and dilator pupillae. The sphincter pupillae is basically related to the parasympathetic nervous system (PSNS) that activate when the body is at rest. On the other hand, the dilator pupillae is related to the sympathetic nervous system that activates fight-or-flight response (acute stress response). Therefore, although pupil response is primarily related to control the optical factors in human visual system, such as retinal irradiance, viewing distance, but it also influenced by the cortical response including alertness and cognitive load. Since pupil dilation has the potential to be used as a physiological signal to sense cognitive load without using body-attached device, several efforts have been conducted. Hess and Polt produced a pioneering work investigating the relationship between image contents and pupillary response. The results indicate a relationship between pupillary response to image contents and gender [9–11]. Similarly, Steinhauer showed the relationship between emotional visual contents and pupil reactions: highly pleasant pictures cause more pupil dilation [19]. It is reported that pupil dilation is related to memory storage and recall. Kahneman and Beatty had subjects perform a task of remembering and recalling several digits and showed that the number of digits in the task is related to the magnitude of pupil dilation [13]. Extending this work, Beatty showed the pupil dilation is also related to the difficulty of memorization in a calculation task [2]. Similar findings relating to task difficulty and pupillary responses have also been reported [8].

Several researchers have focused on pupil dilation during practical tasks. Marshall developed the index of task difficulty (ITD), which uses high-frequency pupil response to measure the cognitive workload. Because high frequency pupillary response is less affected by light intensity, it can be used to robustly estimate cognitive state [16]. Jiang et al. showed that the magnitude of pupil dilation during a target pointing (TP) task follows Fitts' law [12]. In their experiment, users were asked to move a cursor from start to goal regions. In the results, the magnitude of pupil dilation D followed Fitts' law [6]. Their work provides considerably interesting evidence of the potential to build a mathematical model for pupillary response. However, the magnitude of the response during one TP task is quite small, so they required 40 repetitions of the task to obtain enough response.

3   Methods

3.1   Pointer Maze Game and Task Difficulty

We designed a *pointer maze game* as the task for finding the relationship between the magnitude of human concentration during a visual manipulation task and pupil dilation. In this game, a subject moves a pointer from start to goal positions without it touching the boundary of the pathway drawn by two parallel lines (Fig. 1). If the pointer touches the boundary, the subject must start over again from the start point.

We can control the task difficulty through two physical parameters: the width and length of the pathway. As the task becomes more difficult (i.e. when the pathway becomes narrower and/or longer), the subject must concentrate more.

3.2   Pupil Observation Using a Corneal Imaging Camera

Corneal Imaging Camera

To measure pupil size accurately, we developed and used a specially designed eye observation camera system (Fig. 2). This system consists of a head rig, a camera module with a infrared filter (IDS UI-1241LE-C-HQ, 1/1.8" CMOS, 1280×1024 pixel), and an infrared light source (LED) attached to the side of the camera. The camera has a 12 mm lens ((H, V) = (33.3, 24.8) deg), and the internal IR-cut filter is removed. The device can capture close-up images of an eye with an iris diameter of about 400–450 pixel at a distance of 70–110 mm. The cameras are connected to a PC, where images are captured at 30 fps.

Figure 3(a) and (b) show eyes under normal and infrared lighting, respectively. In Fig. 3(a), the pupil size is difficult to confirm because the scene is reflected on the ocular surface. On the other hand, the pupil can be clearly observed in the image under the infrared light (dark pupil method). Therefore, the pupil area is easily determined using binarization.

In the followings, we describe the method to measure the pupil size.

Pupil Measurement

We used the dark-pupil method under IR illumination to obtain the pupil size from the captured images (Fig. 3). First, we performed a grayscale conversion and applied a smoothness filter to remove the small image noises (Fig. 3(c)), and then applied the binary thresholding and obtained the contours of darker areas (Fig. 3(d) and (e)). From the extracted regions, we obtained the circular level

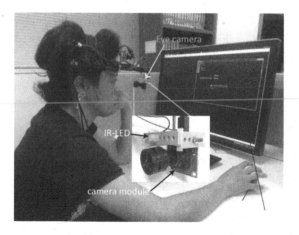

Fig. 2. An experimental scene using a cornel imaging camera

using the following equation and found the image that shows the highest value
for the pupil.

$$circular\_level = 4\pi \frac{area}{perimeter^2}. \tag{1}$$

Here *area* is the area of the region and *perimeter* is the length of the contour.
After finding the pupil region, we performed ellipse fitting using RANSAC-based
method [5] and obtains the major axis (longer axis) as the pupil size.

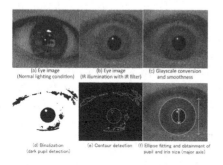

Fig. 3. Processing flow of measuring
pupil diameter

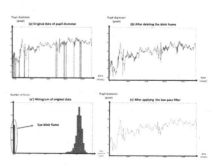

Fig. 4. Process of noise removal

3.3 Data Processing

After obtained iris and pupil size, we perform following step to obtain the amount
of pupil diameter change and the mean of pupil from original data.

Noise Removal.

Figure 4 shows the process of noise removal for the time-series data of pupil diameter. As shown in Fig. 4(a), the original data is noisy, and the noise makes it difficult to obtain the correct maximum/minimum value. The noise is thought to be due to blinking and high-frequency noise of the ellipse fitting. Thus, the following process is performed to remove noise.

1. Determine the threshold for the blink frame in the histogram (Fig. 4(a)) and delete the subthreshold frame (Fig. 4(b))
2. Remove high-frequency noises over the cutoff frequency of 1 Hz by using a low-pass filter (Fig. 4(c))

In step 2, cutoff frequency is set to 1 Hz because the frequency of the pupillary light reaction is 0.5 Hz. After this filtering, we confirmed that noise is removed and data is changing smoothly (Fig. 4(c)).

Normalization by the Pupil Diameter.

Afterward, we perform the pupil size by the iris diameter for the purpose to eliminate the effect of eye-camera distance. Since the size of the cornea is constant for each subject, we can obtain an invariant value with respect to the face-camera distance and individuals by the normalization of the pupil diameter by the corneal size. In reality, we ask subjects to face forward in order to measure the corneal diameter at the start of measurement.

4   Experiments

We performed two experiments. The first experiment is to find out the relationship between the physical conditions of the task and the pupil size, namely, we observe the change of pupil size while the maze task while changing the width of the pathway. The second experiment is for observing the habituation effect of the users. We observe the pupil size while the repetitive maze task game.

4.1   Experiment 1: The Relation Between the Physical Conditions and Pupil Size

Ten undergraduate or graduate students (seven males and three females) participated in the study. Each subject played the pointed maze game about 30 times. Path width randomly changed in 15 steps among 4 and 18 pixels (0.25 mm per pixel) with a constant length of 500 pixels (250 mm). The display screen was 400.8×641.28 mm (1600×2560 pixels), and the distance between the monitor and the subject was about 500 mm. Therefore, the view angle of path width was between about $0.1° - 0.5°$.

Pupil Change-Ratio.

Figure 5 shows an example of a noise-removed graph of pupil diameter during the task. Usually, the pupil contracts immediately and reaches a minimum size at about 1 s (Fig. 5(a)) after the task starts. This contraction is commonly observed among subjects. Then, the pupil gradually expands to reach the maximum size (Fig. 5(b)). We obtain the difference between the minimum and maximum sizes while the game, and the difference is normalized by the minimum size, that we use as the *pupil change-ratio* (Fig. 5).

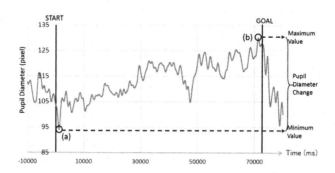

Fig. 5. Pupil diameter during the pointer maze game (after noise removal)

4.2   Results

Figure 6 shows the relations between (a) path width and duration, (b) path width and pupil change ratio and (c) duration and pupil change ratio. Different colors represent different subjects.

According to the figure, we can observe a relationship either logarithmically or inversely proportion between the path width and duration. This indicates that the narrower the path, the longer the duration, therefore as the path width becomes narrower, the task difficulty increases. We can also find that as the wider the path width, the pupil change ratio becomes linearly smaller. Thus, we observe the positive relationship between the path width (task difficulty) and pupil size. Based on these findings, we develop following formulas:

1. **The model of the pupil size, duration and task difficulty.**

$$T = l \cdot log_2(\frac{D}{W} + 1) + k \tag{2}$$

$$ID = log_2(\frac{2D}{W}) \tag{3}$$

$$T = c \cdot log_2(1 + \frac{1}{W}) + d \tag{4}$$

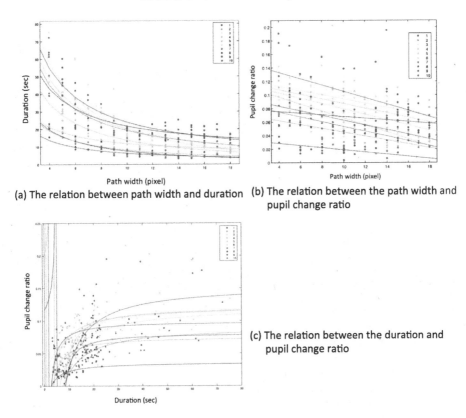

(a) The relation between path width and duration

(b) The relation between the path width and pupil change ratio

(c) The relation between the duration and pupil change ratio

Fig. 6. The relations between (a) path width and duration, (b) path width and pupil change ratio and (c) duration and pupil change ratio.

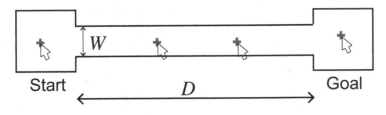

Fig. 7. The pointer maze game and parameters.

where T, W and D are the duration, path width and target distance (Fig. 7). l, c and d are the constants depending of the individuals, and ID is the task difficulty.

2. **Pupil size and path width model.**

In case the distance D is constant, the task difficulty (ID) of the pointer maze game is defined as $ID = \frac{1}{W}$. Then, the relationship between the pupil change ratio P and task difficulty can be formulated as follows using individual parameters a, b.

$$P = -\frac{a}{ID} + b \tag{5}$$

3. Pupil size and duration model.

According to the two formulations described above, we can compute the relationship between the pupil change ratio and duration by using individual parameters a, b (Eq. 5), c, and d (Eq. 4).

$$P_i = -\frac{a_i}{2^{\frac{T_i - d_i}{c_i}} - 1} + b_i \tag{6}$$

$$\sim -a_i \frac{c_i}{T_i - d_i} + b_i$$

In Fig. 6(a)–(c), the fitting results are overlaid onto the plots.

4.3   Experiment 2: Estimation of the Habituation Effect from Pupil Observation

Five graduate students (five males) participated in the study. Each subject continued to play the pointed maze game until succeeding the game twenty times. Path width and length were 12 pixels and 1200 pixels (0.25 mm per pixel), respectively. The size of display and the distance between the display screen and the subject was same as Experiment 1.

Subjects are asked to repeat the game while they succeeded for 40 times. The subjects start the game from a starting region, stopping for three seconds, then trace the pathway. When the subject fails to the trials such as touching the boundaries of the pathway, they have to start over the game from the starting region again. For the purpose to observe the pure mental effect, we use the average pupil size before the each task starts for three seconds.

4.4   Results

Figure 8 shows the result of the pupil size (y-axis) and the number of trial (x-axis). In the figure, markers 'O' and 'X' indicate successful trials and failed trials, respectively and different color shows the individuals. According to this figure, we can clearly observe the number of trials increases, the pupil size decreases. We think this is due to the habituation effects of the subjects, namely, the repetitive trials affects to lose the concentration therefore pupil size decreases.

We computed the correlation coefficients of subjects individually to confirm the trends for each subject. The Table 1 shows, for each subject, Spearman's rank correlation coefficient (RHO) and p-value between the mean of pupil (P) and the number of trial (N), and the number of failures of the earlier half and the last half of the experiment. Between mean of pupil and the number of trial (RHO(P,N) in Table 1), a significant strong-negative correlation is observed for three subjects in five subjects. In subject A, B, C who negative correlation was

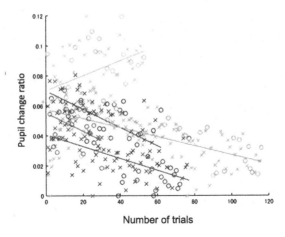

Fig. 8. Model fitting of the number of trial - means of pupil

Table 1. Rank correlation coefficient and p-value of means of pupil (P) and the number of failures (N), and the value of number of failures of each subject

Subject	A	B	C	D	E
RHO(P,N)	−0.5993	−0.653	−0.5947	0.2353	-0.2205
p-value	1.65E−08	2.14E−08	0	9.00E−2	2.41E−1
The number of failures earlier half/last half	49/8=6.125	27/15=1.8	80/16=5	15/18=0.833	4/6=0.667

observed for, number of failures in the last half is less than the one in earlier half, that is, task proficiency was improved through experiment. On the other hand, in subject D, E who negative correlation was not observed for, number of failures in the earlier half is less than the one in last half, moreover, these values are relatively small. This means that their task proficiency had been fully improved from the beginning of experiment.

5   Discussion and Conclusion

With this paper, we show the relationship between the pupil size and mental states. Namely, we show the concentration and habituation effect while a visual manipulation task can be observed through pupil size. We observe (1) the pupil dilates when the difficulty of the visual manipulation task increases, and (2) the pupil constricts when the subject habituate to the task. We also show the models relating between the physical parameter (pathway width and length) and pupil size.

These finding can be used for many tasks that treats mental effect of the subjects, such as the estimation of the level of concentration of the people that performing visual observation tasks (air traffic controllers, security monitoring) and car drivers. Regarding to the visual audience monitoring, our method can be used for evaluating the level of interest of the visual content. As wrote in the introduction, eye tracker or heat map cannot be used for this purpose since it does not evaluate the internal state of the subject. Since pupillometry does not use body-attached devices, it has a lot of potentials for daily use.

There exists several remaining issue for using pupillometry for real applications. The major issue is how to distinguish the effect of light (pupillary light reflex (PLR)) and mental effects. Several models that formulate PLR are reported, however, the persona divination is still large therefore not easy to estimate. We are now trying to develop a method that use the time-synchronicity between the incoming light and pupil size.

References

1. Barreto, A., Zhai, J., Adjouadi, M.: Non-intrusive physiological monitoring for automated stress detection in human-computer interaction. In: Lew, M., Sebe, N., Huang, T.S., Bakker, E.M. (eds.) HCI 2007. LNCS, vol. 4796, pp. 29–38. Springer, Heidelberg (2007). doi:10.1007/978-3-540-75773-3_4
2. Beatty, J.: Task-evoked pupillary responses, processing load, and the structure of processing resources. Psychol. Bull. **91**(2), 276 (1982)
3. Bradley, M.M., Miccoli, L., Escrig, M.A., Lang, P.J.: The pupil as a measure of emotional arousal and autonomic activation. Psychophysiology **45**(4), 602–607 (2008)
4. Campbell, F.W., Green, D.G.: Optical and retinal factors affecting visual resolution. J. Physiol. **181**(3), 576 (1965)
5. Fischler, M.A., Bolles, R.C.: Random sample consensus: a paradigm for model fitting with applications to image analysis and automated cartography. Commun. ACM **24**(6), 381–395 (1981)
6. Fitts, P.M.: The information capacity of the human motor system in controlling the amplitude of movement. J. Exp. Psychol. **47**(6), 381 (1954)
7. Gislén, A., Gustafsson, J., Kröger, R.H.H.: The accommodative pupil responses of children and young adults at low and intermediate levels of ambient illumination. Vis. Res. **48**(8), 989–993 (2008)
8. Goldwater, B.C.: Psychological significance of pupillary movements. Psychol. Bull. **77**(5), 340 (1972)
9. Hess, E.H.: Attitude and Pupil Size. Scientific American (1965)
10. Hess, E.H., Polt, J.M.: Pupil size as related to interest value of visual stimuli. Science **132**(3423), 349–350 (1960)
11. Hess, E.H., Polt, J.M.: Pupil size in relation to mental activity during simple problem-solving. Science **143**(3611), 1190–1192 (1964)
12. Jiang, X., Stella Atkins, M., Tien, G., Zheng, B., Bednarik, R.: Pupil dilations during target-pointing respect fitts' law. In: Proceedings of the Symposium on Eye Tracking Research and Applications, pp. 175–182. ACM (2014)
13. Kahneman, D., Beatty, J.: Pupil diameter and load on memory. Science **154**(3756), 1583–1585 (1966)
14. Kasthurirangan, S., Glasser, A.: Characteristics of pupil responses during far-to-near and near-to-far accommodation. Ophthalmic Physiol. Opt. **25**(4), 328–339 (2005)

15. Liang, J., Williams, D.R.: Aberrations, retinal image quality of the normal human eye. JOSA A **14**(11), 2873–2883 (1997)
16. Marshall, S.P.: Method and apparatus for eye tracking and monitoring pupil dilation to evaluate cognitive activity, 18 July 2000. US Patent 6,090,051
17. Papesh, M.H., Goldinger, S.D.: Memory strength and specificity revealed by pupillometry. Int. J. Psychophysiol. **83**(1), 56–64 (2012)
18. Schwiegerling, J.: Theoretical limits to visual performance. Surv. Ophthalmol. **45**(2), 139–146 (2000)
19. Steinhauer, S.R.: Pupillary responses, cognitive psychophysiology and psychopathology (2002). On line paper
20. Watson, A.B., Yellott, J.I.: A unified formula for light-adapted pupil size. J. Vis. **12**(10), 12 (2012)

Robust Probabilistic Logo Detection in Broadcast Videos for Audience Measurement

P.L. Mazzeo[✉], M. Leo, P. Spagnolo, M. Del Coco,
P. Carcagnì, and C. Distante

Institute of Applied Sciences and Intelligent Systems (ISASI) National Research
Council of Italy (CNR), DHITECH - University Campus of Lecce Via Monteroni s.n.,
73100 Lecce, Italy
pierluigi.mazzeo@cnr.it

Abstract. In the last decades there has been a increasing interest in the development of computer vision strategies to automatically recognize logos in images/videos since several application contexts have arisen in which the logo detection task has also a huge economical relevance. In this paper a logo detection system is presented. The modular architecture consists of a decoder DVB-T/DVB-S, a workstation to drive/control/record and process videos and a console that enables the (even remote) management of various video streams coming from several decoders. The algorithmic pipeline runs on the workstation and it consists of a preliminary key-point detection based on speeded-up key point detection and a matching strategy based on an optimized version of RANSAC. The main advantages of the proposed solution are the capability to detect multiple occurrences in the same image and to keep detection accuracy even under heavy occlusions. Experiments were carried out on a publicly available dataset and on three challenging broadcast videos concerning a music show and two sport events (rugby and rally). The encouraging results make the proposed system a reliable measure of the visibility of logos, whose functionalities could be fully exploited if the cross-check with official audience rating will be carried out.

Keywords: Logo detection · Broadcast videos · Surf · Key-point extraction · Robust estimation

1 Introduction

A logo is a graphic representation or symbol of a company name, trademark, abbreviation, etc., often uniquely designed for ready recognition. Generally a logo contains colors, shapes, textures and text as well. In the last decades there has been a increasing interest in the development of computer vision strategies to automatically recognize logos in images/videos since several application contexts have arisen in which the logo detection task has also a huge economical

© Springer International Publishing AG 2017
K. Nasrollahi et al. (Eds.): VAAM 2016/FFER 2016, LNCS 10165, pp. 36–47, 2017.
DOI: 10.1007/978-3-319-56687-0_4

relevance: automatic identification of products on the web to improve commercial search-engines [15], the verification of the visibility of advertising logos in sports events [4], the detection of near-duplicate logos and unauthorized uses [1]. Special applications of social utility have also been reported such as the recognition of groceries in stores for assisting the blind [7]. The first approaches facing this task used well known pipeline successfully exploited for object detection. These pipelines mainly relied on color and edge features [16] and experienced satisfying performance for document retrieval [10]. Unfortunately they did not perform well on images/videos of real world since logos often appear in indoor or outdoor scenes superimposed on objects of any geometry, shirts of persons or jerseys of players, boards of shops or billboards and posters in sports play-fields. In most of the cases they are subjected to perspective transformations and deformations, often corrupted by noise or lighting effects, or partially occluded. Such images - and logos thereafter have often relatively low resolution and quality. Regions that include logos might be small and contain few information. Last but not least, attention has to be paid on the efficiency of the algorithm, which is critical for obtaining real-time response, meaning that the algorithm must be fast enough to keep up with the frame rate of the video.

For these reasons specialized solutions appeared in literature. Most of them exploited spatial locality following the idea in [14] where description task is moved from global appearance of the image to a set of interest points detected and described by local visual descriptors like SIFT [9], that have been proved to be able to capture sufficiently discriminative local elements with some invariant properties to geometric or photometric transformations and are robust to occlusions. For a more effective performance, some recent works [12] have attempted to combine the shape and SIFT together for context sensitive feature representation. In a recent work [13] the definition of a "Context-Dependent Similarity" (CDS) kernel directly incorporates the spatial context of local features and this way the geometric layout of local regions can be compared across images which show contiguous and repeating local structures as often in the case of graphic logos. One of the main challenges in these set of approaches is to match keypoint descriptors in the test and training images. Different solutions have been proposed but the one that experienced very good results is based on a probabilistic estimation based on RANSAC [3].

In this paper a logo detection system is presented. The modular architecture consists of a decoder DVB-T/DVB-S, a workstation to drive/control/record and process videos and a console that enables the (even remote) management of various video streams coming from several Decoders. The algorithmic pipeline runs on the workstation and it consists of a preliminary key-point detection based on SURF [2] and a matching strategy based on an optimized version of RANSAC [6]. On the one side the use of SURF descriptors allows the research of interest points to be efficiently carried out in a quicker way with respect traditional approaches that lack of scalability and elasticity and for this reason are mainly performed offline instead of on real time video streams [5]. On the other side the use of the modified version of RANSAC assures robustness with respect to outliers and this favorable feature is related to the fact that the devised penalty function does not directly measure the (weighted) mean square error (that as known tends to level out or "low pass" residuals), but only the distribution of the relative squared errors. The main advantages of the proposed solution are the capability to detect multiple occurrences in the same image and to keep detection accuracy even under heavy occlusions. Experiments were carried out on a publicly available dataset [11] and on three challenging broadcast videos concerning a music show and two sport events (rugby and rally). The encouraging results make the proposed system a reliable measure of the visibility of logos, whose functionalities could be fully exploited if the cross-check with official audience rating will be carried out. The rest of the paper is organized as follows: in Sect. 2 the modular hardware architecture of the proposed system is described whereas in Sect. 3 the proposed algorithm for logo detection is detailed. Experimental session is then reported in Sect. 4 and finally Sect. 5 concludes the paper.

2   System Overview

The modular hardware architecture of the proposed system is schematized in Fig. 1. The hardware equipment is composed by

- a stack of decoders DVBT/DVBS that are able to receive and register, locally, broadcast video streamings from different TV channels (satellite or earth transmission) at the same time;
- a CPU farm for driving, controlling, recording and processing videos;
- a remote console that manages different broadcast video streaming from several decoders, using a web platform.

The DVBT/DVBS decoders are linked to the aerial by a coaxial cable and they are connected to the CPU farm with a GIGAbit Ethernet. All the operations are managed by a control console with a web application which is able to remotely pilot all the system operations. The software architecture is composed by two modules for managing and recording the incoming video-streaming and for the logo detection in each video sequence recorded. Both modules are hosted in each workstation in the CPU farm and each one is remotely driven by the console.

3   Logo Detection and Recognition Algorithm

The proposed algorithm for logo detection consists of a pipeline of distinct and independent stages. Recorded videos are processed frame by frame in order to detect occurrences and statistics of predetermined logos. In each processed frame the algorithm extracts the regions containing the logos (if present). This step is carried out by using local descriptors that extract image key-points and then they measure the local appearance similarity by computing vectorial distance for possible matching among detected key-points and those included in the predetermined logos. This way, regions that contains a sufficient number of matched

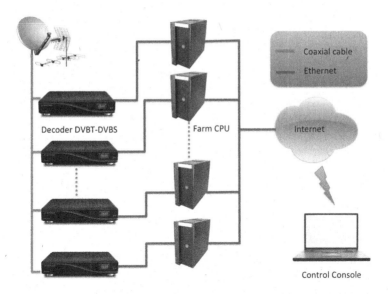

Fig. 1. Block Diagram of System's Hardware components

points are further analyzed by the next algorithmic stage that uses a similarity transformation model in order to robustly find true matchings. The similarity transformation model is estimated by a modified version of RANSAC, described in Subsect. 3.3, and then a voting scheme is applied to detect actual correspondences among the searched logo and the frame processed. This way, the proposed algorithm detects logos in both scale and rotation space, using an object-oriented bounding box. Figure 2 shows the algorithm diagram block and its functional workflow. The following subsections will details how the algorithm detects logos in the current frame and the way in which the algorithm estimates the logo geometry in the scene and the possible multi-occurrences of logos.

3.1   SURF as Local Feature Descriptors

Image Features detection and description is an important task in the proposed pipeline. SURF [2] Speeded Up Robust Features descriptor, is an image feature detector and descriptor inspired by SIFT. SURF approximates or even outperforms previously proposed schemes with respect to repeatability, distinctiveness, and robustness, yet can be computed and compared much faster. This is achieved by: (i) relying on integral images for image convolutions; (ii) Building on the strengths of the leading existing detectors and descriptors (using an hessian matrix-based measure for the detector and a distribution-based descriptor); (iii) simplifying this methods to the essential. SURF belong to the family of scale invariant feature detector and to this end it uses multiscale detection operation called scale space representation. Detected features are assigned to a rotation invariant descriptor computed from the surrounding pixel neighborhood. SURF

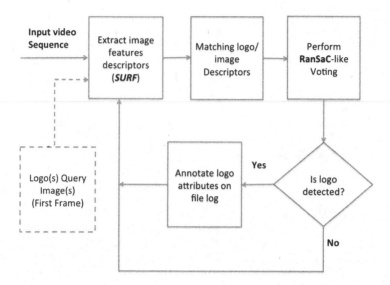

Fig. 2. Block diagram presenting the principal workflow and the functional component of the proposed logo detection algorithm

build on the concepts of SIFT introduces more radical approximations in order to speed up the detection process. Due to the use of integral images the complexity of SURF is greatly reduced, so SURF often achieves superior performance than its predecessor. Another difference is that SURF uses the determinant of the Hessian for feature detection in scale space instead of the Laplacian operator. For the goal of this work the decision to use SURF as local feature descriptors has been taken considering their computational speed-up without significant loss of information with respect other descriptors.

3.2   Matching Logo/Image Descriptors

In order to extract the logo regions in the current frame, we compute ratio likelihood to estimate how much closer are the local frame descriptors to the logo ones. The likelihood ratio threshold λ_L (it has been set to 0.6 in the experiments) concept is strictly linked the familiar matching criterion used in SIFT [9]. The set of ordered couples of matched descriptors between the video sequence frame and the logo image feature template is given by:

$$\mathbb{ML}_t = \mathcal{R}_{\lambda_L}[\mathbb{D}_t, \mathbb{L}] \tag{1}$$

where $\mathbb{ML}_t$ contains $\{(i_1, j_1), (i_2, j_2), \cdots, (i_n, j_m)\}$ a set of couples of descriptor indexes and $\mathbb{D}_t$ is the set of descriptors of the video frame t, $\mathbb{L}$ is the set of descriptors of the image logo and $\mathcal{R}_\lambda$ is defined as:

$$\mathcal{R}_\lambda[A, B] : \{(i, j) | \mathbf{d_i} \in A, \mathbf{d_j} \in B \wedge \|\mathbf{d_i} - \mathbf{d_j}\| < \lambda\} \tag{2}$$

3.3   Logo Geometry Estimation

In this stage we robustly estimate multiple view relations from points correspondences obtained by Eq. 1. We used RANSAC-lel [6] an optimized version of classic RANSAC algorithm, that is well suited to estimate geometric transformation from couples of points data. These are relations among corresponding image points from logo template and current video frame. This way the couple of points features computed by Eq. 1 are sampled using a robust estimation method which implements, in cascade, two algorithms: (i) a Random Sample and Consensus (RANSAC) algorithm and (ii) a novel non- linear prediction error estimator minimizing a cost function inspired by the mathematical definition of Gibbs entropy [6]. The minimization of the nonlinear cost function allows to refine the Consensus Set found with standard RANSAC in order to reach optimal estimates of geometric transformation. Logo voting performed according RANSAC least entropy-like estimator produces better estimates either used in cascade to a weak RANSAC algorithm or to the robust RANSAC-MSAC with a smaller number of $P_{Inliers}$.

4   Experimental Results

We have tested the proposed system on two different types of data. First of all, in order to show the effectiveness of our matching strategy, we evaluate the performances of multiple-logo detection on *FlickrLogos-32* image collection. Figure 3 shows four examples of classes each containing 30 images of a single logo under various views.

We report the results in Fig. 4 compared to bow and msDT [8]. As demonstrated by this figure our method gives very good performance also including a single reference logo and substantially improves both method with more reference images. This way the effectiveness of the proposed approach on this well-know benchmark dataset has been demonstrated.

In the second experimental phase we tested the algorithm on three different broadcast videos acquired during three different events: (a) a music show from Telenorba channel, (b) Italian Rugby match from DMAX channel (c) Rally race from RaiSport channel. In Fig. 5 there are three screen shots of the broadcast videos acquired for logo detection statistics.

Figure 6 contains the six images of the query logos we want to catch in the broadcast videos.

The broadcast video sequences, acquired with a frame rate of 25 frames per second, are interlaced and have HD resolution (1280×720) whereas their lengths measured in term of number of frames is summarized in Table 1. Figure 7 clears up the algorithm behavior when it detects different logo occurrences in the current frame. The yellow lines from the logo template to the logo occurrences represent the descriptor matching couples and they are the results obtained after the matching logo/image step, described in Subsect. 3.2 (note the presence of an outlier). The red bounding box which surrounds each logo occurrence in the image, represents the geometric estimation results explained in Subsect. 3.3. This

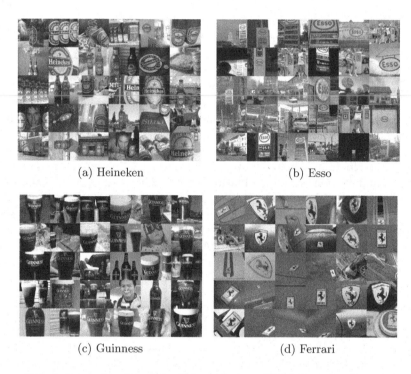

(a) Heineken   (b) Esso

(c) Guinness   (d) Ferrari

Fig. 3. Examples of 4 of the 32 logo classes of FlickrLogos-32 Dataset

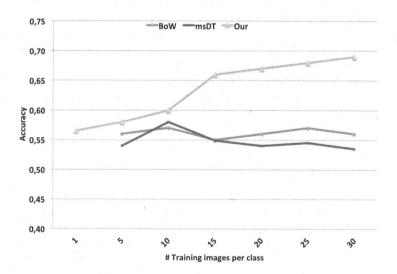

Fig. 4. Comparison of the performance of the proposed approach and those obtained by BoW and msDT [8] methods on the FlickrLogos-32 dataset.

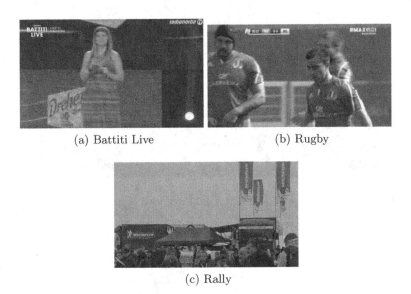

(a) Battiti Live   (b) Rugby

(c) Rally

Fig. 5. Screenshots taken from the broadcast videos considered in the experiments. In each picture is visible at least on instance of the searched logos.

(a) Dreher Lemon   (b) Cariparma   (c) Michelin

(d) Total Erg   (e) Edison   (f) Skoda

Fig. 6. Query logos for broadcast videos

Fig. 7. How the algorithm works to detect multiple logo occurrences in images (Color figure online)

Fig. 8. Example of the the logo detection: the red stars represent inliers whereas the blue ones represent outliers (Color figure online)

way the wrong matches, which represent outliers for the geometric estimation are correctly removed.

Figure 8 better details how the algorithm works: the red stars in the yellow bounding box represents the inliers, contrarily, the blue stars represent the outliers or the wrong descriptors matching.

It is also possible to note how the algorithm is robust against heavy logo occlusions (see Fig. 9).

In Table 1 are reported the detection performance: the lowest detection rate was obtained for the *Skoda* logo (see Fig. 10d). We expected this results because the *Skoda* logo was mainly located on the pilot' sleeves and this means that it was difficult to estimate an in-plane geometric transformation since the features points lie on no-plane surface. Same considerations for the detection rate experienced for *Cariparma* logo that was, often, located on the players shirt. However in that case, the implemented geometric estimator correctly handled this quasi-planar surface, allowing successfull detections of the logo areas (see Fig. 10c).

(a) Dreher Lemon   (b) Cariparma

Fig. 9. Results on heavily occluded logos.

Table 1. Detection results on three broadcast videos

Videos	Query	Minutes	# Frames	Detection Rate
Battivi Live	Dreher Lemon	120	180000	79%
Rugby Match	CariParma	80	120000	65%
	Edison			78%
Rally	Michelin	30	45000	80%
	Skoda			50%
	Total Erg			70%

In order to better highlight the strength of the system, especially if data will be cross-checked with audience rating of TV channels, in Table 2. Table points out the number of occurrences along the video, the total time of the visibility (i.e. 322 s), the maximum frame area covered by the logo (i.e. 7%); how many times the logo is in the center and side position in the processed videos and the number of time the detected logo is partially occluded.

Table 2. In deep statistics relative to the music show broadcast video for Dreher logo

# occurrences	7500
Length	322 s
Max size	7 %
Center position	5007
Side position	2493
Occluded	4011

Finally some considerations about the computational load of the logo detection procedure: it is able to process a video frame in about **0.25** s, running the proposed algorithm in Matlab on a PC equipped with a Intel i7 CPU@2.80 GHz con 8 GB RAM.

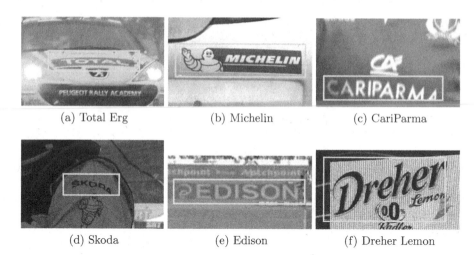

(a) Total Erg   (b) Michelin   (c) CariParma

(d) Skoda   (e) Edison   (f) Dreher Lemon

Fig. 10. Results of different logo detection on the three broadcast videos

5 Conclusion

In this paper a logo detection system prototype has been proposed. The strength of the proposed system can be found in two main aspects: (i) the novelty of the scalable hardware architecture able to drive/control/record and process incoming videos, driven by a remote web-based console; (ii) the novel algorithmic pipeline based on SURF combined with RANSAC-lel, which is able to detect multiple logo occurrences in the same image and to keep detection accuracy even under heavy occlusions. Further works will deal with the refinement of the logo geometry estimation in order to handle out-of-plane logo transformations, and to speed up the computational time of the whole process.

References

1. Anuar, F.M., Setchi, R., kun Lai, Y.: Trademark image retrieval using an integrated shape descriptor. Expert Syst. Appl. **40**(1), 105–121 (2013). http://www.sciencedirect.com/science/article/pii/S095741741200886X
2. Bay, H., Ess, A., Tuytelaars, T., Van Gool, L.: Speeded-up robust features (surf). Comput. Vis. Image Underst. **110**(3), 346–359 (2008)
3. Boia, R., Florea, C., Florea, L., Dogaru, R.: Logo localization and recognition in natural images using homographic class graphs. Mach. Vis. Appl. **27**(2), 287–301 (2016)
4. Constantinopoulos, C., Meinhardt-Llopis, E., Liu, Y., Caselles, V.: A robust pipeline for logo detection. In: ICME, pp. 1–6 (2011)
5. Ding, J., Chao, H., Yang, M.: Real-time logo recognition from live video streams using an elastic cloud platform. In: Cui, B., Zhang, N., Xu, J., Lian, X., Liu, D. (eds.) WAIM 2016. LNCS, vol. 9659, pp. 469–480. Springer, Cham (2016). doi:10.1007/978-3-319-39958-4_37

6. Distante, C., Indiveri, G.: Ransac-lel: an optimized version with least entropy like estimators. In: 2011 18th IEEE International Conference on Image Processing, pp. 1425–1428, September 2011
7. George, M., Mircic, D., Soros, G., Floerkemeier, C., Mattern, F.: Fine-grained product class recognition for assisted shopping. In: Proceedings of the IEEE International Conference on Computer Vision Workshops, pp. 154–162 (2015)
8. Kalantidis, Y., Pueyo, L.G., Trevisiol, M., van Zwol, R., Avrithis, Y.: Scalable triangulation-based logo recognition. In: Proceedings of the 1st ACM International Conference on Multimedia Retrieval, ICMR 2011, pp. 20:1–20:7. ACM, New York (2011). http://doi.acm.org/10.1145/1991996.1992016
9. Lowe, D.G.: Object recognition from local scale-invariant features. In: The Proceedings of the Seventh IEEE International Conference on Computer Vision, vol. 2, pp. 1150–1157 (1999)
10. Pham, T.A., Delalandre, M., Barrat, S.: A contour-based method for logo detection. In: 2011 International Conference on Document Analysis and Recognition, pp. 718–722. IEEE (2011)
11. Romberg, S., Pueyo, L.G., Lienhart, R., van Zwol, R.: Scalable logo recognition in real-world images. In: Proceedings of the 1st ACM International Conference on Multimedia Retrieval, ICMR 2011, pp. 25:1–25:8. ACM, New York (2011). http://www.multimedia-computing.de/flickrlogos/
12. Rusiñol, M., Lladós, J.: Efficient logo retrieval through hashing shape context descriptors. In: Proceedings of the 9th IAPR International Workshop on Document Analysis Systems, DAS 2010, pp. 215–222. ACM, New York (2010). http://doi.acm.org/10.1145/1815330.1815358
13. Sahbi, H., Ballan, L., Serra, G., Del Bimbo, A.: Context-dependent logo matching and recognition. IEEE Trans. Image Process. **22**(3), 1018–1031 (2013)
14. Tao, R., Gavves, E., Snoek, C.G.M., Smeulders, A.W.M.: Locality in generic instance search from one example. In: 2014 IEEE Conference on Computer Vision and Pattern Recognition, pp. 2099–2106, June 2014
15. Wang, M., Li, W., Liu, D., Ni, B., Shen, J., Yan, S.: Facilitating image search with a scalable and compact semantic mapping. IEEE Trans. Cybern. **45**(8), 1561–1574 (2015)
16. Wei, C.H., Li, Y., Chau, W.Y., Li, C.T.: Trademark image retrieval using synthetic features for describing global shape and interior structure. Pattern Recogn. **42**(3), 386–394 (2009). http://www.sciencedirect.com/science/article/pii/S0031320308003324

Saliency Prediction for Visual Regions of Interest with Applications in Advertising

Shailee Jain[(⊠)] and S. Sowmya Kamath

National Institute of Technology Karnataka, Surathkal 575025, India
{shaileejain.13it140,sowmyakamath}@nitk.edu.in

Abstract. Human visual fixations play a vital role in a plethora of genres, ranging from advertising design to human-computer interaction. Considering saliency in images thus brings significant merits to Computer Vision tasks dealing with human perception. Several classification models have been developed to incorporate various feature levels and estimate free eye-gazes. However, for real-time applications (Here, real-time applications refer to those that are time, and often resource-constrained, requiring speedy results. It does not imply on-line data analysis), the deep convolution neural networks are either difficult to deploy, given current hardware limitations or the proposed classifiers cannot effectively combine image semantics with low-level attributes. In this paper, we propose a novel neural network approach to predict human fixations, specifically aimed at advertisements. Such analysis significantly impacts the brand value and assists in audience measurement. A dataset containing 400 print ads across 21 successful brands was used to successfully evaluate the effectiveness of advertisements and their associated fixations, based on the proposed saliency prediction model.

Keywords: Visual saliency · Free eye-gaze estimation · Machine Learning · Advertising · Neural networks · Support Vector Machines

1 Introduction

When humans freely view natural scenes, their eyes are drawn to areas that are more prominent amongst background objects. This property, known as *saliency*, refers to the conspicuity of a particular point or region in an image. Free eye-gaze estimation thus aims at determining saliency, with the help of several predictive models. Employed in a plethora of fields, from graphic-oriented tasks (video compression [1], content-aware image resizing [2]), to complex computer vision problems (seam carving [3], non-photorealistic rendering [4]), visual attention prediction plays a pivotal role in determining a user's focus and possibly, manipulating it. This ability to direct a viewer's focus, by incorporating features that play a consequential role in determining saliency, can be extensively applied to use-cases like 'Effective Advertising'.

In this digital era, consumers are constantly being inundated with copious amounts of advertisements. Businesses are resorting to invasive marketing strategies to promote their products aggressively and gain an edge over competitors.

© Springer International Publishing AG 2017
K. Nasrollahi et al. (Eds.): VAAM 2016/FFER 2016, LNCS 10165, pp. 48–60, 2017.
DOI: 10.1007/978-3-319-56687-0_5

A critical part of such strategies, however, lies in audience measurement. When the company is able to thoroughly evaluate the efficacy of its marketing strategy, it is likely to have a stronger impact on potential customers. Measuring the effectiveness of an advertisement is thus an important task in determining the impact of a product. While this can be traditionally done by collecting manual feedback, free eye-gaze estimation enables companies to instead, predict human fixations.

Employing saliency prediction to measure anticipated audience response to advertisements will enable companies to enhance their designs, during the production phase itself. A thorough analysis of human fixations can thus assist the company in re-designing their advertisements, to ensure maximized attention to critical components such as the product, company logo etc. While saliency prediction is an effective tool for such hands-on market analysis, the applicability of existing models is limited. Advanced models such as Deep Convolution Networks are resource/time intensive, while primitive models do not consider multi-level features appropriately, resulting in weak predictions.

Our work, therefore, has two major contributions. Firstly, we analyze and extract various features from an extensive data-set. The resultant tensors are fed into two different classification models - linear kernel Support Vector Machines and a Multi-layer Neural Network. These approaches are then compared to find a suitable classification model, that can sufficiently predict saliency while also being less resource intensive (appropriate for on-line analysis). Secondly, we present a case-study applying the proposed techniques to print advertisements across various genres to find their salient points. The resultant fixations are thoroughly investigated, to evaluate the focus or attraction of an advertisement, and its success. The correlation highlights the applicability of saliency detection in effective design, attention manipulation, and audience measurement through free eye-gaze estimation.

The rest of the paper is organized as follows. Section 2 discusses existing literature in the problem sphere. Section 3 highlights the methodology adopted to develop a saliency model, with specific attention to feature extraction from images and application of two non-linear classifier models. Section 4 presents the experimental results along with an exhaustive case study on the application of saliency models to advertising data, followed by conclusion and references.

2   Related Work

Saliency detection has several primitive hardware oriented approaches involving the use of Eye-trackers. An Eye-tracker is an expensive and cumbersome device that records *saccades* (a rapid movement of the human eye between fixation points) of the user sitting in front of a computer. Given the dynamic nature of applications like audience measurement for advertising and the expansive nature of visual input, device-oriented approaches that consider raw fixation points can be primitive and impractical [5]. Saliency detection models that provide a probabilistic view of prominent locations in an image can instead be used to predict human fixations, even in arbitrary images. Without the limitations of the eye-tracking data-set and sans the need for expensive equipment, saliency prediction can be addressed through alternative computational models. Conventional saliency models are based on 'bottom-up' approach that extracts several intuitive attributes like color contrast, intensity and image center from the picture. Traditional paradigms [6,7] incorporate such low-level, psychologically-backed features to develop a model. In the "Winner-Take-All' and 'Inhibition of Returns' Approach, various features were considered for constructing a linear combination of each map to give the resultant saliency map. The maximum of the result then corresponds to regions of 'highest saliency', to which the visual focus is directed by optical neurons.

In the Itti-Koch model [6], saliency is detected by considering a 2-dimensional layer of integrate-and-fire neurons - multi-layer neurons that 'fire' or alter weights together (global inhibition/reluctance to alter weights). The weights of a neuron activate the inhibition, such that, the first such 'integrate-and-fire' cell to fire is proclaimed the 'winner'. This generates a sequence of action potentials, resulting the FOA (Attention Focus) to shift to the winning location. As a consequence, all cells in the layer are inhibited, to set network in the original state, and find any remaining points of saliency. However, the 'static' scene causes selection of the same 'winner', at all times. Therefore, inhibitory feedback is taken from the winner, such that, within a radius of the FOA, the point and its neighbors are inhibited, allowing different conspicuous locations to be selected, i.e., 'Inhibition-of-Returns'. Nevertheless, these models are limited to images that have a contrast or orientation bias and do not perform well on highly variable human saccades. Also, in spite of a strong center bias that humans hold, as proved by eye-tracking data collected by Judd et al. [8], various other high-level semantic features considered by humans (such as faces or vehicles) are ignored by these approaches. Bottom-up mechanisms, thus, do not completely determine attention selection, as a result of incomplete semantic analysis of the scene.

Context, therefore, remains the most important feature to predict human visual cognition as a more involved activity than merely seeing low-level features. Infusing this into the scene can enhance saliency. For instance, in a textual image like a magazine article, contrast would out play text, unlike a signboard where the text is crucial. Torralba's saliency model [9] effectively incorporates this context in an image. It uses 'Discriminant Spectral Templates' and simple Bayesian classifiers to distinguish scenes as a whole, acting as a precursor to detecting saliency in images, by including semantics. However, it is still incapable of considering high-level features. Thus, the task of feature selection and appropriately combining the same to arrive at a resultant saliency map has a broad scope for research.

The need to understand the scene through a global context, while also extracting primitive information and intuitive features like contrast, and successfully combining the two, to finally determine if a pixel is salient, makes the problem difficult, and virtually impossible with linear classifiers. Recent developments have thus moved onto complex prediction models, that effectively incorporate the entire scene's context and features, to arrive at fixation points. Multiple classification paradigms satisfactorily achieve this task. The most influential are non-linear classifiers, such as Support Vector Machines in Judd's saliency model [5] and Multi-layer Neural Networks, coupled with stochastic gradient descent. Judd's model proposes a combination of several low-, mid- and high-level features to holistically analyze contributors to saliency. It eventually achieves high accuracy by combining methods proposed by Itti et al. [6], Hou et al. [7] and Oliva et al. [9]. Jain et al. [10] proved that Judd's model with Torralba's context inclusion doesn't improve accuracy, but effectively intertwines center-bias and provides more advanced features like face detection to capture visual attention.

Recent advancements in the field of Machine Learning and Computer Vision have brought forth a highly complex, and non-intuitive model - a *Convolutional Neural network (CNN)*. CNNs have been proven to provide the best results for all image-related tasks and have been aptly applied to saliency detection. They broadly learn complex features, removing the bias due to human intervention while selecting appropriate input parameters. Nevertheless, it is critical that techniques be adopted for optimizing these time and memory intensive networks, for which effective hardware is still under development, and largely inaccessible.

Although Judd's model has limited classification power, and more advanced models have been developed through deep networks [11,12], it sufficiently includes several feature-ranges to accurately capture saliency. Nevertheless, it is computationally expensive in time to train an SVM with stochastic gradient descent primarily due to its search for appropriate support vectors for margin maximization in the cost function. Also, a linear kernel SVM is essentially a single-layer perceptron (neural network) and a kernelized SVM can be viewed as a Multi-layer Neural Network (MNN) that maximizes the margin in hidden layer space [13]. Bengio et al. [14] proved that given such representations, MNNs learn more intelligently as against shallow architectures such as a linear kernel SVM. In light of these findings, we adopt an approach that successfully incorporated saliency features into an MNN to achieve significant improvement in accuracy when compared to non-linear classifiers like SVM. Our approach is also less resource intensive than deep architectures, and encouragingly effective.

3   Proposed Work

To develop an effective computational model for saliency prediction, non-linear classifiers with multi-level features that appropriately consider intuitive aspects and context of the image, along with high-level semantics were used. These features are fed to a classifier model consisting of SVM and MNNs. The process of determining saliency of given images is described in detail next.

3.1   Features Influencing Saliency

Low-level Features. These features primarily focus on intuitive aspects of the image, largely influenced by its composition. Pixels in an image are made of combinations of primary colors represented. A channel in this context is the gray-scale image of the same size as a color image, made of just one of these primary colors. An RGB image, however, has three channels (red, green, blue); which follow the receptors present in the human eye. In our work, the channels pertaining to these image features are calculated as per Itti-Koch's saliency method. We used the *SaliencyToolbox* [6], a collection of Matlab functions for calculating the saliency map for an image and for serially scanning it as per FOA. Simple features such as orientation, color contrast and intensity are also incorporated in bottom-up saliency. Steerable Pyramid filters in various linear orientations and scales serve as an image decomposition technique to capture energy distribution across the image, influencing its low-level composition.

Mid-level Features. As per the analysis done by Judd et al. and Torralba et al., humans have a natural tendency to look along the horizon as most 'familiar' objects lie on the Earth's surface. Keeping with this, we used a horizon line detector from *LabelMe* [15] as a mid-level feature.

High-level Features. Cognitive visual features such as 'faces', 'humans' and 'vehicles' play a crucial role in saliency and affect human fixations, due to their familiarity and the belief that they hold crucial information while being processed in the user's mind. In early stages of free viewing (first few hundred milliseconds), these image-based conspicuous points guide visual attention. High-level factors like events or actions require a relatively involved analysis by the viewer and thus direct eye movements much later. However, false positive rates significantly impact the performance of saliency models that use such object detectors. These were calculated using the Viola-Jones and Felzenszwalb detectors. Viola-Jones algorithm [16] is a real-time face detection system that uses the image for feature computation, Adaboost for feature selection and an attentional cascade for computational resource allocation. *Felzenszwalb Detector* [17] is a learning based system for detection and localization of objects (vehicles, people) in images, by representing objects using deformable part models.

Center Prior. Humans hold a strong center bias while viewing images. This can be partly attributed to the nature of image capturing wherein the object of interest is more often that not framed near the center of the image. In machine vision, this image center is known as the focus of expansion or the center-of-perspective projection. In our model, focus of expansion is incorporated as a feature indicating the distance of each pixel from the center. Thus, pixels located closer to the center are given more weight/priority, in accordance with the bias.

3.2   Classification Models

There exist several advanced classification models that cannot learn the linear mappings between features and associated class labels. Instead, such models have to be trained to recognize complex non-linear decision boundaries that can appropriately map a feature set with its class. One such involved problem is that of 'Saliency Prediction'. To develop a computational model for the same, we used two non-linear classifiers that were trained on the features obtained after feature extraction. A thorough analysis of the same also proved one approach to be superior to the other (discussed in Sect. 4).

Support Vector Machines. These non-linear classifiers construct a linear decision boundary by mapping complex problems to a higher dimension, where the data behaves linearly. The classifier model focuses on finding the 'Maximum-margin Hyperplane' using 'Support Vectors'. However, due to the involved mathematical computation and resource constraints, 'kernels' are used to reduce complexity. As the saliency data-set is comparatively small when compared to the number of features, the linear kernel is most suited, as against Gaussian or Polynomial kernels that require a huge data-set with much fewer features.

Multi-layer Neural Networks (MNN). A neural network is an advanced non-linear classification model, developed around the structure of our brain. Complex learning tasks are accomplished by a collection of nodes/neurons, connected to each other through weights. The computational task is thus to learn these weight values, by constantly updating them as per the required output. The Network is commonly trained using 'Back-propagation' [18], which carries out optimization using stochastic gradient descent.

3.3 Developing the Saliency Model

The proposed saliency models are described next. The process consists of using a *Feature Extraction* process for obtaining saliency features of data-set images and then using *Classification Models* to generate their saliency maps.

Feature Extraction. The following tools/codes were used for extracting the described low-, mid- and high-level features from the data-set images:

- *Steerable Pyramids* - Used to get the subbands of the steerable pyramids and Torralba saliency model's features [9].
- *Itti and Koch Saliency Toolbox* - Used to get color channels as per the Itti and Koch saliency model.
- *Felzenszwalb and Viola-Jones detectors* - Used to find people, cars and faces in images respectively.
- *LabelMe Toolbox* - Needed for the LMgist.m which is used for the horizon code. The values of the RGB channels, their probabilities as features and the probability of each color as calculated from 3D color histograms are treated as a low-level feature for this model.
- *Distance to center* - indicates the distance from each pixel to center, as these pixels have more significance than pixels farther away from image center.

The second phase involved development of the linear kernel SVM. The input features were fed into the model, to arrive at the required saliency image. Each training image was used to feed 10 positive and 10 negative saliency points from the top 20% salient points and bottom 70% salient points from ground-truth human fixations, respectively. The data-set was divided into 903 training and 100 testing images. The SVM parameter 'C' was empirically found to be 1.

The Multi-layer Neural Network consisted of input nodes that represented the pixels' feature set. It had a single hidden layer and one node, that predicted 1 as salient, and 0 as not (Binary Classification). The model used the same training setup as the SVM and was developed using back-propagation (stochastic gradient descent). Negligible training error was the termination criterion. Weights and bias values were randomly initialised, and optimal value of learning rate was found to be 0.3.

4 Results and Analysis

We used MATLAB R2015a [19] version for Windows (64 bit) for feature extraction and for the development of the proposed saliency model. The MIT data-set[1], consisting of 1003 images depicting natural indoor and outdoor scenes was used for the discussed experiments. A separate advertising data-set comprising of 400 images from 21 different companies across 3 genres was collected for the case study. The SVM was developed using the liblinear library. The Multi-layer Neural Network was designed from ground-up, particularly, for the proposed saliency prediction model.

4.1 Saliency Prediction

Figure 1 shows the saliency maps generated for Neural Network and SVM classifiers. Each map shows a saliency gradient wherein white indicates a highly salient pixel, and black indicates an inconsequential one. The salient area is clearly visible, and from the resultant saliency maps, it is evident that Multi-layer Neural Network (MNN) has performed better than the SVM model. While both capture *actual fixations*[2] to a suitable degree of approximation, the SVM model doesn't always depict the entire salient region and instead focuses on particular points that do not draw as much user attention. The MNN model, alternatively, learns the image structure and accurately predicts saliency, as can be concluded from the similarity between fixations and the MNN saliency map.

The accuracy of both classifiers was compared using the area under ROC curves for various test images. From Fig. 2(a), it can be seen that the MNN model outperforms SVM as is evident from the greater area under the ROC curve. This indicates that the True Positive (TP) Rate increases at a faster rate than the False Positive (FP) Rate, which is of utmost importance in a Computer Vision task. For example, pixels that are wrongly labeled salient could have catastrophic consequences in applications like video compression. Table 1

---

[1] Available online at http://people.csail.mit.edu/tjudd/WherePeopleLook.

[2] The salient points shown by actual fixations, i.e., raw user inputs (not normalized), depict wagering user attention and thus, do not completely portray salient locations in the image. Instead, they are used as a rough baseline for comparison.

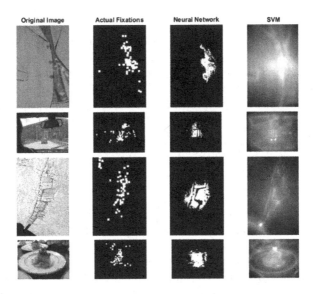

Fig. 1. Saliency Maps generated for MNN and SVM Classifiers

Table 1. Neural network vs. SVM

Method/metric	TPR	FNR	F1 score	Informedness	Markedness
Neural network	0.85	0.36	0.769	0.490	0.513
SVM (Based on [5])	0.74	0.42	0.685	0.320	0.328

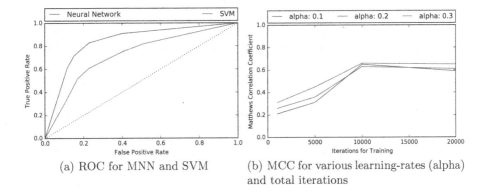

(a) ROC for MNN and SVM

(b) MCC for various learning-rates (alpha) and total iterations

Fig. 2. Comparative results of MNN and SVM

includes the various comparison metrics used for the experimental conditions. The Neural Network is compared against the SVM baseline, on the MIT Saliency Dataset. The previous models indicated in the literature survey include only a subset of these features and use primitive classification techniques, resulting in significantly lower accuracy. Hence, they have been left out of the comparison. Additionally, Matthews Correlation Coefficient (MCC) can be used to gauge effectiveness of binary classification, especially when the class sizes are very different, as in our case (large number of inconsequential points, few salient ones). Figure 2(b) clearly highlights the MCC value for various hyper-parameter values and it can be inferred that appropriate initialization enables high correlation between observation and prediction. Thus, we can conclude that MNN is highly suitable for predicting saliency when compared to the SVM model, while also avoiding the extensive usage of resource and time as is the case of deep networks.

4.2   Case Study: Applying Saliency Prediction in Advertising

Advertisements are the driving force of sales for most of the products that we use today. A substantial amount of money is pumped into ads by companies for marketing and publicity every year. The aim of this case study is to thus find the salient regions in advertisements to check for any correlation between the areas of interest as seen by the consumer (salient regions detected by the model, within acceptable approximation) and positive brand images, for audience measurement. When the regions detected match with the areas of interest, one can presume that the advertisement has the desired effect of publicizing the product. The areas of interest as seen by a majority of consumers generally involves one or more of the following features: *People, Company's Logo and Product, Colorful region or Design*. These features were used for the comparison of areas of interest on the advertisement data-set, which contained print ads of products belonging to different categories like food, lifestyle and electronics. As the proposed MNN saliency detection model performed better in terms of time and accuracy when compared to SVM, it was applied on this data-set for saliency prediction. This map was used as a reference to compare the regions of interest of the advertisement. We present the results for ads for brands in lifestyle (Vans, Rolex), electronics (Nokia, LG) and food (Pepsi, Nestle) here.

Figure 3 depicts the salient zones obtained for the brand samples for Vans shoes and Rolex watches. As can be seen from the results, the saliency predictions show the print ads satisfy the requirements of an effective advertisement, but can be improved. The company's logo in Fig. 3(a) is rendered salient but is not as eye-catching as the other attributes. For example, the text is presented with the highest saliency, probably in accordance with the company's intention to draw attention to the freebie offer. In the saliency map of Rolex (Fig. 3(b)), the company's brand is the area with the least saliency. Rolex, being a luxury brand, is always associated with celebrities, as can be observed by the dominating saliency region in its print ad. Despite this, the combination of other strong attributes, like a well-placed product picture and the celebrity face significantly boost the efficacy of this print ad. Overall, it can be seen that the above advertisement resonates well with the proposed saliency model, highlighting most key features required to hold user's attention.

In Fig. 4(a), the product (Nokia smartphone) is placed such that it is distinct and demands immediate viewer attention. The ad is not particularly focused on

(a) Vans Shoes   (b) Rolex Watches

Fig. 3. Saliency map generation for Lifestyle brands

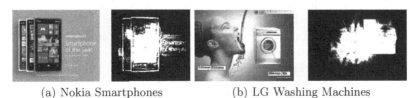

(a) Nokia Smartphones   (b) LG Washing Machines

Fig. 4. Saliency map generation for Consumer Electronics brands

the company's logo but the text is saliently depicted, providing useful information that would draw a user's glance and generate interest. Generally, smartphone manufacturers aim at attracting buyers to their product's appearance and their exemplary features in comparison to competitors, which this particular ad achieves successfully. Similarly, for the LG washing machine (Fig. 4(b)), the product itself is depicted reasonably well. The ad is not particularly focused on the company's logo and the text is also not well-defined on the map. However, the use of a person, along with the eye-catching design, captures viewer's attention. If the company's objective was to capture customer attention through its use of bold art, this advertisement is quite effective, as opposed to primal attributes like text and company logo.

In the case of Pepsi (Fig. 5(a)), the product was accurately depicted as a salient zone on the map and the company's logo was also in a well-defined zone. However, the ad text was found to be quite non-salient in this ad, ensuring that user attention is not unnecessarily diverted. The use of a fit person to advertise

(a) Diet Pepsi   (b) Nestle

Fig. 5. Saliency map generation for Food brands

the product clearly enhances the saliency in this advertisement, which is for a diet product. Overall, this advertisement responds positively by rendering critical points as salient. In comparison, the Nestle ad (Fig. 5(b)) only the product was placed in a highly salient region, drawing majority of the user's attention. The company's logo and the ad text were not salient or eye-catching. However, as Food brands predominantly focus on their product design and visual appeal to intrigue viewers, this advertisement works well.

Figure 6 shows some results obtained for samples from other ad genres. These results clearly show that the salient regions obtained from advertisements have a strong correlation with the areas of interest. These reputed, brand-oriented companies are thus strongly linked to 'effective' advertisements[3] that further propagate their marketing. Such techniques of audience measurement can effectively be used by companies to evaluate their designs in early stages of development, enabling them to appeal to their potential customers better. Improvements can also be done using saliency features, such as bold design on known faces. Consequentially, effective advertisements designed after thorough investigation of probable impact will boost sales and maximize product outreach.

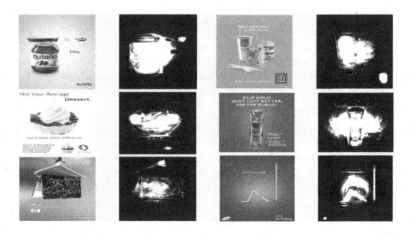

Fig. 6. Saliency Maps for sample ads belonging to other genres

5   Conclusion and Future Work

In this paper, a novel Multi-layer Neural Network approach for the Computer Vision task of saliency prediction was presented. This model comprises of a nonlinear classifier that incorporates multilevel features like intuitive attributes (like contrast), image semantics and face detection. The proposed classifier model is

---

[3] By effectiveness, we mean that the advertisement highlights the product, company etc. and immediately captures consumer attention, sparking interest.

extensively trained, tested and compared to human fixation points. Its effectiveness was also compared with that of a SVM model, in terms of prediction accuracy. The obtained experimental results highlight the success of our approach, while also depicting significant improvements when compared to the SVM. The MNN model also has lower resource usage (does not require specific hardware and has reasonable training time), making it suitable for real-time tasks with time, resource constraints. A case-study to demonstrate the role of saliency in effective advertising and its contribution to successful product/brand images was also presented. Using the proposed MNN saliency prediction model, it was found that there exists a strong correlation between the outreach of an advertisement and its ability to render important attributes salient, such as the product or company name. Advertisement applications can, therefore, be developed significantly along the lines of saliency prediction, for effective marketing.

As part of future work, we intend to explore the possibility of the existence of a correlation between the features incorporated in our saliency model *(hand-engineered)* and those extracted by a Convolution Neural Network *(found using reverse engineering)*. We also intend to extend this study to deep networks on development of appropriate, feasible architectures to analyze further significant improvements in real-time (time constrained) applications like Advertising. This can be used as an alternative to our saliency model while carrying out an extended study to tasks that do not require speedy analysis but need to incorporate a learnable model.

References

1. Wang, Z., Lu, L., Bovik, A.C.: Foveation scalable video coding with automatic fixation selection. IEEE Trans. Image Process. **12**(2), 243–254 (2003)
2. Santella, A., Agrawala, M., DeCarlo, D., Salesin, D., Cohen, M.: Gaze-based interaction for semi-automatic photo cropping, pp. 771–780 (2006)
3. Rubinstein, M., Shamir, A., Avidan, S.: Improved seam carving for video retargeting. ACM Trans. Graph. **27**(3) 16:1–16:9 (2008)
4. DeCarlo, D., Santella, A.: Stylization and abstraction of photographs. ACM Trans. Graph. **21**(3), 769–776 (2002)
5. Judd, T., Ehinger, K., Durand, F., Torralba, A.: Learning to predict where humans look. 2106–2113 (2009)
6. Itti, L., Koch, C., Niebur, E., et al.: A model of saliency-based visual attention for rapid scene analysis. IEEE Trans. Pattern Anal. Mach. Intell. **20**(11), 1254–1259 (1998)
7. Hou, X., Zhang, L.: Saliency detection: a spectral residual approach, pp. 1–8 (2007)
8. Judd, T., Durand, F., Torralba, A.: A benchmark of computational models of saliency to predict human fixations (2012)
9. Oliva, A., Torralba, A.: Modeling the shape of the scene: a holistic representation of the spatial envelope. Int. J. Comput. Vis. **42**(3), 145–175 (2001)
10. Jain, E., Mukerjee, A., Kochhar, S.: Predicting where humans look in a visual search: Incorporating context-based guidance
11. Borji, A., Tavakoli, H.R., Sihite, D.N., Itti, L.: Analysis of scores, datasets, and models in visual saliency prediction. In: IEEE ICCV 2013, pp. 921–928. IEEE (2013)

12. Zhao, R., Ouyang, W., Li, H., Wang, X.: Saliency detection by multi-context deep learning. In: IEEE Conference of Computer Vision and Pattern Recognition (CVPR), pp. 1265–1274 (2015)

13. Collobert, R., Bengio, S.: Links between perceptrons, MLPs and SVMs. In: Proceedings of the Twenty-First International Conference on Machine Learning, ICML 2004, p. 23. ACM, New York (2004)

14. Bengio, Y., LeCun, Y., et al.: Scaling learning algorithms towards AI. Large-scale Kernel Mach. **34**(5), 1–41 (2007)

15. Russell, B.C., Torralba, A., Murphy, K.P., Freeman, W.T.: Labelme: a database and web-based tool for image annotation. Int. J. Comput. Vis. **77**(1), 157–173 (2008)

16. Viola, P., Jones, M.J.: Robust real-time face detection. Int. J. Comput. Vis. **57**(2), 137–154 (2004)

17. Felzenszwalb, P., McAllester, D., Ramanan, D.: A discriminatively trained, multi-scale, deformable part model, pp. 1–8 (2008)

18. Bottou, L., Cortes, C., Denker, J.S., Drucker, H., Guyon, I., Jackel, L.D., LeCun, Y., Muller, U.A., Sackinger, E., Simard, P., et al.: Comparison of classifier methods: a case study in handwritten digit recognition. In: ICPR, pp. 77–87 (1994)

19. The Mathworks, Inc. Natick, Massachusetts: MATLAB version 8.5.0.197613 (R2015a) (2015)

Person Invariant Classification of Subtle Facial Expressions Using Coded Movement Direction of Keypoints

Kosuke Sasaki[1(✉)], Manabu Hashimoto[1], and Noriko Nagata[2]

[1] Graduate School of Computer and Cognitive Sciences, Chukyo University,
101-2 Yagoto Honmachi, Showa-ku, Nagoya-shi, Aichi 466-8666, Japan
{sasaki,mana}@isl.sist.chukyo-u.ac.jp
[2] Graduate School of Science and Technology, Kwansei Gakuin University, 2-1 Gakuen,
Sanda City, Hyogo 669-1337, Japan
nagata@kwansei.ac.jp

Abstract. This paper describes a person invariant method for classifying subtle facial expressions. The method uses keypoints detected by using a face tracking tool called Face Tracker. It describes features such as coded movements of keypoints and uses them for classification. Its classification accuracy was evaluated using the facial images of unlearned people. The results showed the average F-measure was 0.93 for neutral (expressionless) facial images, 0.73 for subtle smile images, and 0.92 for exaggerated smile images. Also, person invariant accuracy was evaluated by using F-measure frequency of unlearned people. The results revealed that the proposed method has higher person invariant accuracy than the previous methods.

Keywords: Subtle facial expression · Person invariant feature · Facial expression classification

1 Introduction

Because people are always looking for ways to improve their quality of life, product makers and service providers desire a system that can estimate human emotions so they can develop products and services that customers will feel positively towards.

One study for estimating human emotions reported a method using a contact sensor like an electroencephalogram (EEG) [1]. However, the sensor is uncomfortable to wear, and this disturbs the expression of natural emotion. To avoid such disturbance, human emotion needs to be estimated in a natural situation. Since facial expressions are closely related to emotions, many researchers have studied facial expressions by acquiring them by using a non-contact sensor like an RGB (red, green, and blue) camera.

Two types of methods for classifying facial expressions have previously been reported. One uses local facial features such as HoG [2], Local Binary Pattern [3], and Gabor wavelets [4]. The other uses a small set of keypoints detected from parts of the face [5, 6]. These methods can classify many facial expressions but cannot recognize

© Springer International Publishing AG 2017
K. Nasrollahi et al. (Eds.): VAAM 2016/FFER 2016, LNCS 10165, pp. 61–72, 2017.
DOI: 10.1007/978-3-319-56687-0_6

very subtle ones. Consequently, Matsuhisa and Hashimoto [7] proposed a method to recognize subtle facial expressions by using Gabor filters and the AdaBoost algorithm. Gabor filters have a response value that is sensitive to subtle changes in facial expression. However, they have difficulty classifying facial expressions of unlearned people because the response value represents a 3D facial shape that is different for each person. Also, Nomiya and Hochin [8] proposed a method to recognize subtle facial expressions by using the geometric features of keypoints. However, this method has the same problem as Matsuhisa and Hashimoto's method because the placement of the facial parts is different for each individual. Thus, Faisal et al. [9] proposed a person-independent method to recognize facial expressions by using Compound Local Binary Patterns. However, this method cannot recognize subtle facial expressions because it selects only features that change significantly.

Thus, previous methods have two problems. First, they cannot recognize subtle facial expressions. Second, identification performance is dependent on using learned people as subjects. To address these problems, we propose a person-independent method for classifying subtle facial expressions. In the proposed method, keypoints are extracted by using a face tracking tool called Face Tracker [11]. The distances and angles of moving keypoints are calculated and coded from neutral (expressionless) facial images to each facial expression image or exaggerated facial expression image. We define them as Coded Movement Direction. In addition, keypoints are selected on the basis of the following two requirements. First, the feature must be highly similar for each person. Second, the feature must differ from one facial expression to another. These factors enable the proposed method to recognize subtle facial expressions of unlearned people.

2 Basic Idea for Designing Person Invariant Feature

Ekman and Friesen [10] reported that primary emotions correspond to facial expressions that all people make regardless of gender, race, or culture. When someone is happy, for example, his/her mouth corners move backward and lower lip moves downward. Because such changes are common to all human beings, we focus on them. However, when a whole facial part is focused on, facial shapes differ because muscles and skeletons differ for each individual. In other words, identification accuracy is susceptible to differences in individual faces. Thus, the proposed method focuses on the local position of each facial part such as eyes and mouth. This feature is common to multiple people because it captures the direction of movement in the local position when the facial expression changes. By using this feature, we achieve person invariant classification of subtle facial expressions.

3 Proposed Method for Classifying Facial Expression

3.1 Overview

Figure 1 shows a block diagram of the method we propose to classify facial expressions.

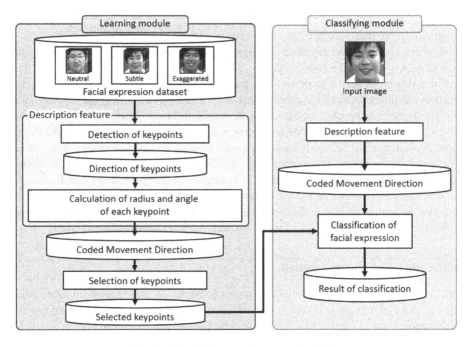

Fig. 1. Block diagram of proposed method.

The proposed method comprises two modules: module 1 for learning and module 2 for classifying. Module 1 detects keypoints from a local position such as an eye tail or corner of mouth by using a Constrained Local Models (CLM) method that is versatile to humans. Figure 2 shows detected keypoints and used keypoints from a facial image.

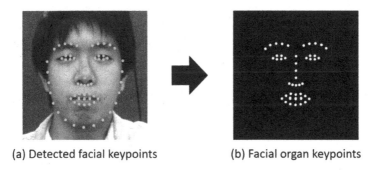

(a) Detected facial keypoints   (b) Facial organ keypoints

Fig. 2. Facial keypoints.

This method detects 66 keypoints in all (Fig. 2 (a)). However, the 17 keypoints of the facial outline are unusable as background information, so we used only 49 keypoints (Fig. 2 (b)). In addition, the size and rotation of a facial image must be corrected to calculate the feature stably. The selected keypoints are corrected by using relationships among keypoints such as the horizontality of the centers of both eyes and the center of the gravity point that is comprised of the centers of both eyes and the upper lip.

The proposed method calculates the movement direction of keypoints from neutral face images to expressive face images. Its angle and distance are coded to enhance the commonality from person to person. We call this feature Coded Movement Direction, which is calculated from all keypoints. Next, the feature is calculated from learning data containing multiple people for each keypoint, and its occurrence probability is generated for each facial expression. The keypoints are selected on the basis of two requirements. First, the feature must be highly similar for each person. Second, the feature must differ from one facial expression to another. The likelihood of each facial expression is calculated by using the occurrence probability of features at selected keypoints. In module 2, the keypoints are detected in the same way as in module 1. The feature is calculated by using the movement distance of keypoints. The input facial image is classified by using its feature and the likelihood of a feature for each facial expression in module 1.

3.2   Coded Movement Direction

The Coded Movement Direction feature enhances the person-independent characteristic because it codes moving keypoint angle and distance from neutral images to expressive facial images. An example of Coded Movement Direction is shown in Fig. 3.

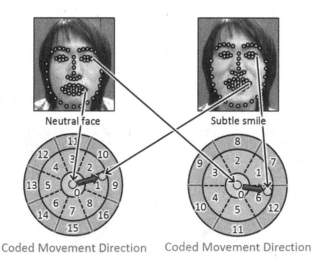

Neutral face   Subtle smile

Coded Movement Direction   Coded Movement Direction

Fig. 3. Coded movement direction.

We calculated the distance and angle for all keypoints, including keypoints of both standard facial images and facial expression images. Raw data of the angle differ between individuals. Since the raw data of the distance are the same for each person, each angle and distance are coded. We call this the Coded Movement Direction and define it as a feature for classifying facial expressions. Each of its codes shows the likelihood of each facial expression. The likelihood is the occurrence probability of a feature for each facial expression and is used to classify facial expressions.

3.3 Automatic Determination of Number of Code

The movement direction of keypoints from a neutral face image to an expressive one is different for every keypoint because muscles are different in every local position of the face. Therefore, the code number needs to be determined by using angle resolution and radius threshold of Coded Movement Direction for each keypoint. We describe the automatic determination of angle resolution and radius threshold.

Automatic Determination of Angle Resolution. The proposed method uses angle distribution to determine the angle resolution for each keypoint. Figure 4 shows the flow for automatically determining angle resolution on the basis of angle distribution.

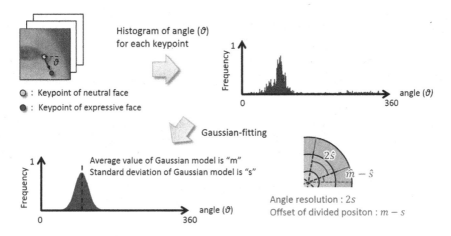

Fig. 4. Automatic decision of angle resolution.

The angle of a keypoint from a neutral face image to an expressive one in learning data is calculated, and the angle histogram is generated for each keypoint. Gaussian models that have an average value (m = 0, 1,..., 359) and standard deviation (s = 0.00, 0.05, 0.10,..., 25.000) are fitted to a histogram generated from learning data. The Gaussian model that has the smallest error is selected in the fitting models. The angle resolution is determined by using the standard deviation range of the selected model. In addition, the value obtained by subtracting the standard value from the average value is added to the calculated angle value because the peak value of the angle distribution should be prevented from being concentrated between codes.

Automatic Determination of Radius's Threshold. Since the radius threshold is determined for each keypoint as the same as the angle resolution, the proposed method uses generated angle distribution for each radius threshold. Figure 5 shows the flow for automatically determining radius threshold.

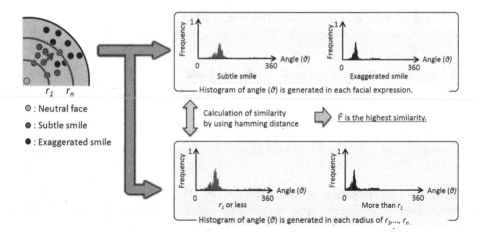

Fig. 5. Automatic determination of radius's threshold.

The histogram of angle frequency is generated for each facial expression in the same way as the angle resolution. Since this histogram is calculated for each facial expression of the learning data, it is comprised of only one facial expression. Also, the histogram separated by any radius threshold is generated from the learning data of a continuum of facial expressions (neutral face and subtle facial expressions, or subtle and exaggerated facial expressions). The similarity between the calculated and generated histograms for each radius threshold ($r = 0.01, 0.02,..., 1.00$) is calculated using the Hamming distance. Since this similarity is calculated for each facial expression, the optimal threshold has the highest sum for similarity of facial expressions on a continuum in the radius threshold.

3.4   Selection of Facial Keypoint

Coded Movement Direction calculates the occurrence probability of each facial expression. Therefore, keypoints for using facial expression classification are selected by using the distribution of the occurrence probability. Figure 6 shows the characteristics of Coded Movement Direction that has selected keypoints.

The keypoints are selected on the basis of two requirements. First, the feature must be highly similar for each person. Second, the feature must differ from one facial expression to another. Therefore, the proposed method focuses on the occurrence probability of the feature of each keypoint. The selected keypoints must have three characteristics. First, the code number that has the maximum occurrence probability of a feature must be different for each facial expression. Second, the frequency of an occurrence probability must be similar for each person. Third, the frequency of an occurrence probability must be high for each person. The proposed method selects keypoints on the basis of the three characteristics and uses them to classify facial expressions.

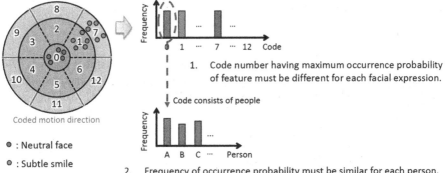

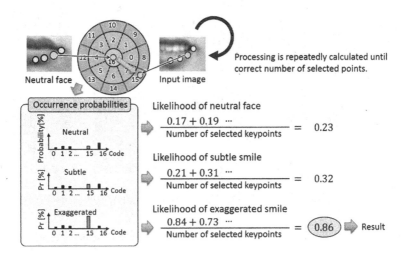

Neutral face   Input image

Fig. 6. Characteristic of coded movement direction having selected keypoint.

3.5 Classification of Facial Expression Using the Likelihood of Each Facial Expression

Figure 7 shows the flow of facial expression classification.

Fig. 7. Flow of facial expression classification.

The proposed method detects facial keypoints from the input image in the same way as the learning image and calculates Coded Movement Direction from keypoints of the input image selected by module 1. Each code of Coded Movement Direction shows the likelihood of each facial expression. The average likelihood of each facial expression is calculated from Coded Movement Direction of each keypoint on an input image. The classification results obtained show the facial expression that has the highest likelihood on average.

4   Experimental Results

4.1   Dataset

We focused on smile as natural emotion in consideration of an ethical problem. We videoed 28 men and women watching a comedy program and used the captured images in an experiment. Five other people watched the taken video at the normal frame rate and typed in the ground truth to the video. They pressed 1, 2, or 3 when a someone made a neutral face, a subtle smile, or an exaggerated smile, respectively. We used the images given the same ground truth by at least four of the five people who watched the video. Figure 8 shows example images of each facial expression in the experiment.

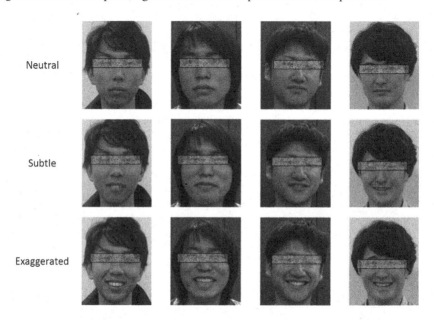

Fig. 8. Example of image of each facial expression.

4.2   Expression Classification Performance for Learned People

The facial expression images of subjects are divided into the learning dataset and classification dataset, and the proposed method classified images in the classification dataset to either neutral, subtle smile, or exaggerated smile. We used 10 learning images and 20 test images to classify the facial expressions of 28 learned people. Figure 9 shows the F-measure of each facial expression obtained for each person.

The results showed the average F-measure was 0.97 for neutral images, 0.89 for subtle smile images, and 0.98 for exaggerated smile images. However, the subtle smile of subject D could not be classified. Since the difference between the neutral face and subtle smile of subject D was less than that of other subjects, there was no great difference

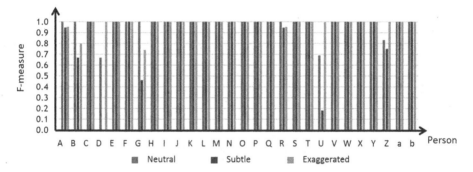

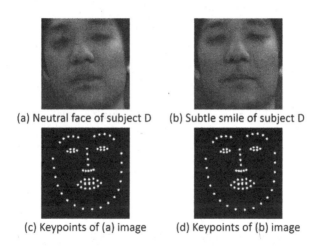

Fig. 9. F-measure of each facial expression for each person.

in Coded Movement Direction of each keypoint. Figure 10 shows facial images and facial keypoints of a neutral face and a subtle smile.

(a) Neutral face of subject D   (b) Subtle smile of subject D

(c) Keypoints of (a) image   (d) Keypoints of (b) image

Fig. 10. Facial image and keypoints of neutral face and subtle smile.

The subtle smile image (Fig. 10 (a)) is compared with the neutral face image (Fig. 10 (b)). We assumed that the subtle smile does not greatly differ from the neutral face. The images of facial keypoints (Fig. 10 (c) and (d)) show the corrected facial key-points. After comparing these images, we assumed that keypoints do not change. Conse-quently, the calculated feature did not appear to differ much be-tween the neutral face and subtle smile. One reason for this problem was that facial expressions seemed to be mixed due to the delayed reactions of people who gave ground truth.

4.3 Expression Classification Performance for Unlearned People

By using a 28-fold cross-validation approach, a classifier was trained by 27 people, and unlearned people were classified by it. Using 30 images for each facial expression, we also compared our method with those reported elsewhere [7–9, 12]. Faisal et al. [9]

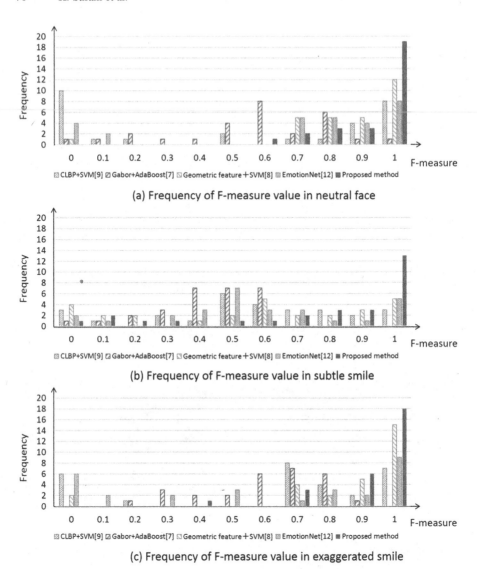

(a) Frequency of F-measure value in neutral face

(b) Frequency of F-measure value in subtle smile

(c) Frequency of F-measure value in exaggerated smile

Fig. 11. Frequency of F-measure of unlearned people.

reported a facial expression classification method that considered person independence. Matsuhisa and Hashimoto [7] and Nomiya and Hochin [8] reported a recognition method for subtle facial expressions. Bradley and Adam [12] proposed EmotionNet that is a method of Convolutional Neural Networks (CNN) to emotion recognition in facial image. We utilized a learning CNN model that generated by the 15000 iterations. Figure 11 shows the F-measure frequency of unlearned people.

Table 1. Experimental comparison of facial expression classification performance.

	Neutral	Subtle	Exaggerated
Proposed method	0.93	0.73	0.92
EmotionNet (CNN) [12]	0.68	0.57	0.57
Geometric feature + SVM [8]	0.85	0.57	0.85
Gabor filter + AdaBoost [7]	0.58	0.43	0.61
CLBP + SVM [9]	0.51	0.56	0.63

This graph shows the classification accuracy becomes person-independent as the distribution is concentrated on the right side. We confirmed that the results of the proposed method were distributed more to the right than those of previous methods. This shows that the proposed method is more person invariant than the previous methods. In addition, Table 1 shows the average of F-measures of each facial expression.

The results showed the average F-measure was 0.93 for neutral images, 0.73 for subtle smile images, and 0.92 for exaggerated smile images. These results are similar to those in Sect. 4.2 and thus demonstrate that our method provides highly flexible identification performance from person to person.

5   Conclusion

In this paper, we proposed two ideas for achieving person invariant classification of facial expression. The first was to use features based on coded movement direction in local positions of a person-independent muscle and skeleton. The second was to select features considering person invariance and identity of facial expression. The person invariant accuracy was evaluated by using the frequency of F-measure of unlearned people. When the proposed method was used, the average F-measure for learned people was found to be 0.97 for neutral images, 0.89 for subtle smile images, and 0.98 for exaggerated smile images. For unlearned people, the respective values were 0.93, 0.73, and 0.92. Also, the F-measure of the proposed method was distributed at higher frequencies than the F-measures of previous methods. These results lead us to conclude that the proposed method can accurately classify subtle expressions and is person-independent.

Acknowledgments. This research is partially supported by the Center of Innovation Program from Japan Science and Technology Agency, JST.

References

1. Kothe, C.A., Makeig, S., Onton, J.A.: Emotion recognition from EEG during self-paced emotional imagery. In: Humaine Association Conference on Affective Computing and Intelligent Interaction (ACII2013), pp. 855–858 (2013)
2. Chen, J., Chen, Z., Chi, Z., Fu, H.: Facial expression recognition based on facial components detection and HOG features. In: Scientific Cooperations International Workshops on Electrical and Computer Engineering Subfields, pp. 64–69 (2014)

3. Shan, C., Gong, S., McOwan, P.: Facial expression recognition based on local binary patterns: a comprehensive study. Image Vis. Comput. **27**(6), 803–816 (2009)
4. Owusu, E., Zhan, Y., Mao, Q.R.: A neural-AdaBoost based facial expression recognition system. Expect Syst. Appl. **41**(7), 3383–3390 (2014)
5. Majumder, A., Behera, L., Subramanian, V.K.: Emotion recognition from geometric facial features using self-organizing map. Pattern Recogn. **47**(3), 1282–1293 (2014)
6. Kotsia, I., Pitas, I.: Facial expression recognition in image sequences using geometric deformation features and support vector machines. IEEE Trans. Image Process. **16**, 172–187 (2007)
7. Matsuhisa, H., Hashimoto, M.: Identifying subtle facial expression changes using optimized gabor features. J. Inst. Image Inform. Telev. Eng. **68**(6), J252–J255 (2014). (in Japanese)
8. Nomiya, H., Hochin, T.: Efficient emotional video scene detection based on ensemble learning. IEICE Trans. Inform. Syst. **J95-D**(2), 193–205 (2012). (in Japanese)
9. Ahmed, F., Bari, H., Hossain, E.: Person-independent facial expression recognition based on compound local binary pattern (CLBP). IAJIT **11**(2), 195–203 (2014)
10. Ekman, P., Friesen, W.V.: Unmasking the Face. Malor Books
11. Saragih, J., Lucey, S., Cohn, J.: Deformable model fitting by regularized landmark mean-shifts. Int. J. Comput. Vision **91**(1), 200–215 (2011)
12. Kennedy, B., Balint, A.: EmotionNet. github. https://github.com/co60ca/EmotionNet

A Two-Directional Two-Dimensional PCA Correlation Filter in the Phase only Spectrum for Face Recognition in Video

Víctor E. Alonso$^{(\boxtimes)}$, Rogerio Enríquez-Caldera, and L. Enrique Sucar

Instituto Nacional de Astrofísica, Óptica y Electrónica,
Luis Enrique Erro 1, Tonantzintla, 72840 Puebla, Mexico
{vic.alonso,rogerio,esucar}@inaoep.mx

Abstract. This paper presents a novel hybrid two-directional, two-dimensional Principal Component Analysis based correlation filter for face recognition. This hybrid $(2D)^2$PCA-correlation filter is capable of simultaneously dealing with several uncontrolled factors that are present in video surveillance cameras making it difficult to properly recognize faces. Such factors are addressed by linking $(2D)^2$PCA in the Fourier domain with correlation filters (CFs) to speed up the process of video-based face recognition. The former method helps to extract and to represent more efficiently the facial features using the original image matrices, while the later method is used to simultaneously handle illumination variations, expression, partial occlusions and spatial shifts. An exploration of the capabilities of this novel method is performed using the Yale-B, AR, and YouTube face databases, showing an improvement in face recognition despite using a subspace of smaller dimensionality.

Keywords: Correlation filters · Frequency domain representation · Phase spectrum · Two-directional two-dimensional PCA · Face recognition

1   Introduction

It is well known that when identifying faces in an automatic way, there exist great difficulties when the images to be processed are coming from a surveillance video system in which there are uncontrolled factors: severe variations of lighting, expression, pose, occlusion and low resolution [4], among other factors. Furthermore, an automatic face detection process does not provide registration accuracy neither does guarantee that the location of the face is perfect, resulting in misalignment errors [3,4,18]. Additionally, the recognition performance is affected by undesirable scene background and faces partially occluded [17].

A method capable of dealing with several simultaneous and unconstrained factors in facial recognition, - such as variable lighting, partial occlusions and shift variations - was proposed by Savvides *et al.* [18]. This method uses a hybrid PCA-correlation filter called Corefaces [18], which performs PCA on the phase-only

© Springer International Publishing AG 2017
K. Nasrollahi et al. (Eds.): VAAM 2016/FFER 2016, LNCS 10165, pp. 73–87, 2017.
DOI: 10.1007/978-3-319-56687-0_7

spectrum of the training images, disregarding the corresponding magnitude spectrum. The resulting linear subspace, called Eigenphases [15], can model the phase variations of a given particular person. Eigenphases essentially computes the eigenvectors of the phase-only spectra for a set of training images, and later the test image phase spectrum is reconstructed by simply using the projection coefficients in that specific subspace, that is, the reconstructed phase spectrum is turned into a correlation filter. However, this method has the following glitch: if the reconstructed phase spectrum is not correctly modelled by the PCA-based subspace, the test image could be misclassified affecting the recognition performance [18].

In this paper a new hybrid $(2D)^2$PCA-correlation filter is proposed with the purpose of further enhancing the quality of the reconstructed phase spectrum, simultaneously modeling the phase spectrum variations of face images in the frequency domain. The main contributions and advantages of this novel method are: *(i)* Performing a two-directional two-dimensional Principal Component Analysis $(2D)^2$PCA [25] on the phase-only spectrum; this procedure not only can represent more efficiently the face images but it is also both, computationally more efficient than its hybrid PCA-correlation filter counterpart and it increases the recognition rate. *(ii)* Extending further the hybrid-$(2D)^2$PCA subspace to achieve shift-invariance. This is done by developing a hybrid $(2D)^2$PCA-correlation filter that performs phase matching with a built-in shift-invariance function: if the test input image is shifted, then the correlation output is also shifted by the same amount of pixels, and therefore the classification decision is not affected by this shifting.

Thus, this hybrid $(2D)^2$PCA-correlation filter inherits and further improves some of the attractive properties from a hybrid PCA-correlation filter such as tolerance to shift, illumination, expression and occlusion variations. The experimental results using the Yale-B, AR, and YouTube face databases show that the proposed method significantly improves the recognition performance over typical eigenphases algorithm and other methods, including PCA, IPCA, $(2D)^2$PCA, FM-$(2D)^2$PCA.

The remainder of this paper is organized as follow. Section 2 reviews spatial domain representations in conjunction with frequency domain representations. Section 3 briefly introduces the phase spectrum under Fourier transform. Section 4 explains hybrid $(2D)^2$PCA-correlation filter designs, and how to compute the eigenvectors of phase-only spectra for training images as well as the procedure to quantitatively assess the reconstructed phase spectrum. Section 5 presents the video-based face recognition system. In Sect. 6 we present the experimental evaluation, including the main findings and comparisons. Finally, Sect. 7 presents the conclusions and future work.

2   Related Work

Several common face recognition methods, such as Principal Component Analysis (PCA), two-dimensional PCA (2DPCA) and Linear Discriminant Analysis (LDA) used in the frequency domain, have proven to be far more robust than their spatial domain counterparts.

By using the PCA subspace of the phase-only spectra, Savvides *et al.* [18] proposed a hybrid PCA-correlation filter for illumination-invariant face recognition from still images. In contrast, Bhagavatula *et al.* [2] proposed to perform PCA and FLDA using the Eigen and Fisher-Fourier Magnitudes, the resulting FM-PCA and FM-FLDA subspaces are shift-invariant and are not prone to register errors of the input image. To achieve higher recognition accuracy of these algorithms, 2DPCA based algorithms such as FM-2DPCA, FM-$(2D)^2$PCA and FM-DiaPCA were proposed by Zeytunlu *et al.* [24]. Ribarić *et al.* [13] presented four phase-information extraction approaches where the MagUn approach achieves the best recognition when illumination variation is present in the dataset. This, however, is not the case when pose and expression variations were present.

Li *et al.* [9] proposed a method which involves using a hybrid-PCA subspace together with illumination tolerant correlation filters to reconstruct and recognize images respectively using a different representation of the face. Sao *et al.* [14] proposed to perform eigenanalysis using the cosine and sine functions of the phase of the Fourier transform and of analytic image to avoid the phase wrapping problem.

Benitez-Garcia *et al.* [1] proposed a sub-block based eigenphases algorithm where face image under analysis is divided into optimal sub-blocks, and then all phase spectra are computed. The resulting hybrid-PCA subspace is obtained by concatenating the phase spectra of all blocks. Inspired by CFA [7,21], an effective feature extraction method also based on multi-subregion, called Multi-Subregion based correlation filter bank (MS-CFB), is proposed by Yan *et al.* [22], which combines the benefits of global based and local-based feature extraction algorithms. However, the multi-block strategy can not handle face recognition with large pose variations, and the mismatching of face subregions between training samples and test samples can occur.

It is evident that, if the subspace of the phase and magnitude spectrums is separately used, then an increase in recognition accuracy can be accomplished over the corresponding subspace in the spatial domain. More specifically, the hybrid $(2D)^2$PCA-correlation filter proposed has proven to be much more robust to illumination variations, partial occlusions and spatial shifts than the PCA only based correlation filter. Furthermore, when performing $(2D)^2$PCA to compute the eigenvectors of the phase-only spectra, the original matrix does not need to be transformed into a 1D long vector beforehand, as it is done in 1D-PCA. Instead, two covariance matrices are directly constructed from both, rows and columns, of the 2D image matrices [6]. Additionally, because the size of both image covariance matrices is just equals to the width and height of the face image, $(2D)^2$PCA not only represents and extracts more efficiently the facial features but also can significantly improve the speed of image feature extraction. In contrast to our method, the recognition accuracy of all the methods mentioned above could not achieve good performance when the test images present large variations in lighting, occlusion, expression, pose and spatial shifts simultaneously.

3   Phase-Only Fourier Synthesis

It has been shown (Oppenheim *et al.* [12]) that the phase information of an image in the Fourier domain is more important than its magnitude. Mathematically, let $f(x, y)$ be the brightness of an image at a spatial point with coordinates (x, y), and if $F(u, v) = |F(u, v)|e^{j\theta(u,v)}$ represents its Fourier transform at the respective spatial frequencies (u, v), with spectral magnitude $|F(u, v)|$ and spectral phase $\theta(u, v)$, then it is possible to define the magnitude-only Fourier synthesis as

$$f_m(x, y) = \mathcal{F}^{-1}\{|F(u, v)|\} \tag{1}$$

as well as to define its corresponding phase-only Fourier synthesis

$$f_\theta(x, y) = \mathcal{F}^{-1}\{M(u, v)e^{j\theta(u,v)}\} \tag{2}$$

where $M(u, v)$ is either unit, average or a spectral magnitude representing the class of signals. In practice, when using the phase-only spectra with the purpose of phase matching, it is necessary to previously perform a pre-whitening step, which correspondingly produces a unity magnitude for all the spatial frequencies of the training and test images.

When calculating the magnitude-only Fourier synthesis, the $f_m(x, y)$ does not resemble the original image, while the phase-only synthesis does retain the necessary information. Thus, a 2D signal constructed from only the phase is intelligible and retains many of the important features of the original. Moreover, by using only the phase information, the original 2D signal can be reconstructed up to a scale factor [5].

The previous idea was exploited in [15], where it was proven that the eigenvectors obtained by performing PCA in the frequency domain alone were the same principal components resulting in its spatial domain counterpart and only differ by a sign change. Moreover, by modelling the subspace of the phase-only spectra of the training images, it yields what is known as Eigenphases, and it simultaneously gives robustness against occlusion and illumination variations. This method assumes that most of illumination variations are in the lower frequency spectrum.

Even though this subspace of eigenphases seems good to represent face images in the minimum mean squared error sense [1,9,14,15], PCA may not capture the variability in a set of training images discriminating one person's face from another, unless this information is explicitly given in this dataset [23]. To overcome such drawbacks, the recognition performance can be improved by building a hybrid-$(2D)^2$PCA subspace, which not only increases the margin of separability between classes, but also keeps the advantage of robustness and efficiency in representing face images of the phase-only synthesis in conditions of variable illumination and partially occluded faces.

The next section shows how such advantages can be achieved.

4   CSS-Based Hybrid (2D)²PCA-Correlation Filter Bank

An overview of the class-specific subspace-based hybrid $(2D)^2PCA$ correlation filter bank for face recognition is shown in Fig. 1. The hybrid-$(2D)^2PCA$ subspaces, based on an individual subspace, are first used to yield a filter bank to make them shift invariant, and thus tolerant to face image registration errors, resulting in a css-based hybrid $(2D)^2PCA$-correlation filter.

During the training stage, a phase spectrum subspace, for every person, is built from the phase-only training images, and used to extract useful discriminatory information for each subject. Each hybrid-$(2D)^2PCA$ subspace is represented by two projection matrices (see Sect. 4.1) of the phase-only spectra, and then used to design a filter bank for all classes; that is, by projecting the test image phase spectrum onto hybrid-$(2D)^2PCA$ subspace, and reconstructing it for each phase spectrum subspace. Thus, we automatically turn each of the reconstructed phase-only test image into a correlation filter. Additionally, to each correlation filter designed, we add the average training phase derived from the phase-only training images corresponding to each subject. During the test stage, the actual test is then cross-correlated with every designed correlation filter derived in the target set, and the resulting product is input to a 2D inverse FFT to produce a correlation output. The PSR value is determined for each correlation output, and selected the one with the largest PSR value to label the test image. As illustrated in Fig. 1, a sharp correlation peak is produced when the input image is from an authentic, and no such discernible peak exist if the input is from an impostor. The location of the correlation peak will depend on the input image, if the input image is translated with respect to training images,

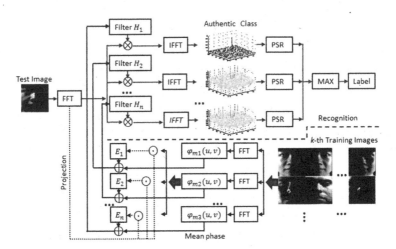

Fig. 1. Schematic representation of the specific class subspace-based hybrid $(2D)^2PCA$-correlation filter bank. The $\otimes$, $\odot$ and $\oplus$ operators represent the correlation, projection and addition respectively.

then the output peak will be also shifted by the same amount without affecting the peak sharpness, neither the recognition performance.

4.1 Using $(2D)^2$ PCA in the Frequency Domain

Given an $m \times n$ image matrix $\mathbf{A}^w$ in the Fourier domain[1] of the phase-only spectra, and a linear transformation that maps the original phase-only matrix $\mathbf{A}^w$ into an m-dimensional phase-only projected vector, then the new phase-only spectra matrix $\mathbf{Y} \in \mathbb{C}^{m \times d}$ is:

$$\mathbf{Y} = A^w \mathbf{V} \tag{3}$$

where $\mathbf{V} \in \mathbb{C}^{n \times d}$ is the phase-only projection matrix with orthonormal columns and $n \geq d$. This other description space is called phase-only feature space.

Now, consider a set of N image samples where the kth training sample is an $m \times n$ space domain matrix $\mathbf{A}_k^s$, chosen from $k = 1 \ldots N$, and consider the total scatter matrix C_f^r of the projected samples defined as:

$$
\begin{aligned}
C_f^r &= \frac{1}{N} \sum_{k=1}^{N} \{\mathbf{T}_{DFT_w}(\mathbf{A}_k^s - \mu)\}^+ \{\mathbf{T}_{DFT_w}(\mathbf{A}_k^s - \mu)\} \\
&= \mathbf{T}_{DFT_w}\mathbf{X}^+\mathbf{X}\mathbf{T}_{DFT_w}^{-1}
\end{aligned}
\tag{4}
$$

where $\mathbf{T}_{DFT_w}$ is the discrete Fourier transform matrix of the phase-only spectra, $\mu \in \mathbb{C}^{m \times n}$ is the mean image of all the samples and the superscript $^+$ represents the conjugate transpose, then the scatter matrix is in fact characterized by the trace of the covariance matrix of the projected feature vectors in the frequency domain. Since Eq. (4) is an $n \times n$ Hermitian nonnegative definite matrix, their eigenvalues will be real and positive.

Note that $\mathbf{X}^+\mathbf{X}$ is the respective spatial covariance matrix C_s^r defined as:

$$C_s^r = \mathbf{X}^+\mathbf{X} = \sum_{k=1}^{N}(\mathbf{A}_k^s - \mu)^+(\mathbf{A}_k^s - \mu) \tag{5}$$

Thus, after applying the previously defined linear transformation, the scatter of the projected feature vectors $\{\mathbf{Y}_1, \mathbf{Y}_2, \ldots, \mathbf{Y}_d\}$ is $\mathbf{V}_f{}^+C_f^r\mathbf{V}_f$. Then, the projection optimal $\mathbf{V}_{opt_f}$ is defined as:

$$\mathbf{V}_{opt_f} = \{\mathbf{V}_{1_f}, \mathbf{V}_{2_f}, \ldots, \mathbf{V}_{d_f}\} = \arg\max \, \mathrm{tr}\left(\mathbf{V}_f{}^+C_f^r\mathbf{V}_f\right) \tag{6}$$

where $\{\mathbf{V}_{1_f}, \mathbf{V}_{2_f}, \ldots, \mathbf{V}_{d_f}\}$ are the orthonormal eigenvectors of C_f^r corresponding to the first d largest eigenvalues. However, one optimal projection axis is not enough to accurately represent the data [23], and therefore a set of projection axes are needed.

---

[1] A pre-whitening step is performed to yield a phase-only spectrum with a unity magnitude for all spatial frequencies (u, v).

Note that the size of image covariance matrix C_f^r is $n \times n$ which allows us to efficiently compute its eigenvectors [23, 25]. Likewise as PCA, the number of eigenvectors of d is chosen by setting a threshold:

$$\frac{\sum_{i=1}^{d} \lambda_i}{\sum_{i=1}^{n} \lambda_i} \geq \theta. \tag{7}$$

where $\lambda_{1_f}, \lambda_{2_f} \ldots \lambda_{n_f}$ are n largest eigenvalues of C_f^r and θ is a pre-set threshold value.

Equation (4) can be considered as the original 2DPCA which is working in the images row direction [23]. An alternative way of 2DPCA can be obtained by applying 2DPCA on the image columns [25] as follows:

$$C_f^c = \frac{1}{N} \sum_{k=1}^{N} \{\mathbf{T}_{DFT_w} (\mathbf{A}_k^s - \mu)\} \{\mathbf{T}_{DFT_w} (\mathbf{A}_k^s - \mu)\}^+$$
$$= \mathbf{T}_{DFT_w} \mathbf{X}\mathbf{X}^+ \mathbf{T}_{DFT_w}^{-1} \tag{8}$$

where $\mathbf{X}\mathbf{X}^+$ is the space domain covariance matrix C_s^c defined as:

$$C_s^c = \mathbf{X}\mathbf{X}^+ = \sum_{k=1}^{N} (\mathbf{A}_k^s - \mu)(\mathbf{A}_k^s - \mu)^+ \tag{9}$$

The projection $\mathbf{U}_{opt_f}$ is chosen to maximize the trace of the scatter matrix:

$$\mathbf{U}_{opt_f} = \{\mathbf{U}_{1_f}, \mathbf{U}_{2_f}, \ldots, \mathbf{U}_{q_f}\} = \arg\max \operatorname{tr} \left(\mathbf{U}_f^+ C_f^c \mathbf{U}_f\right) \tag{10}$$

where $\{\mathbf{U}_{1_f}, \mathbf{U}_{2_f}, \ldots, \mathbf{U}_{q_f}\}$ are the orthonormal eigenvectors of C_f^c corresponding to the first q largest eigenvalues. The number of eigenvectors of q can also be selected by setting a θ threshold value using Eq. (7). Likewise as in Eq. (3), the new phase-only feature matrix $\mathbf{B} \in \mathbb{C}^{q \times n}$ is defined by the following linear transformation:

$$\mathbf{B} = \mathbf{U}^+ \mathbf{A}^w \tag{11}$$

where $\mathbf{U} \in \mathbb{C}^{m \times q}$ is the phase-only projection matrix with orthonormal columns, with $m \geq q$. In the above Eqs. (3) and (11), the phase-only projection matrices are computed off-line.

4.2 Hybrid $(2D)^2$PCA-Correlation Filter

Once both row-based and column-based optimal linear subspaces have been computed for the phase-only spectra of the training images, then the reconstructed phase spectrum $e^{\phi_R(u,v)}$ is computed as:

$$e^{\phi_R(u,v)} = U_{f_j(u,v)} e^{\phi_T(u,v)} V_{f_i(u,v)}^+ \tag{12}$$

where $e^{\phi_T(u,v)}$ is the test image phase spectrum projected onto the frequency domain eigenvectors U_{f_j} and V_{f_i}. Note that the subscripts i and j denote the ith and jth projection vectors.

This $(2D)^2$PCA-based subspace of the phase-only spectra not only improves the reconstruction accuracy but also increases the recognition performance, as it will be shown in the next section. Figure 2 shows a training face image synthesized from the Fourier transform phase with unity magnitude, where the phase spectrum was reconstructed under similar compression ratios [25]. It can be shown that the $(2D)^2$PCA based phase-only Fourier synthesis yields face images with higher quality while preserving the edge information.

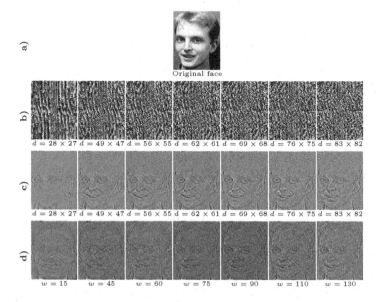

Fig. 2. Phase-only synthesis from the reconstructed phase spectrum of a face image by using the inverse Fourier transform under similar compression ratios. (a) Original face, (b) 2D^{2}PCA based eigenvectors of the phase-only spectra (phase angles between the imaginary and real part of each frequency), (c) Inverse Fourier transform of the phase-only synthesis based on 2D^{2}PCA and (d) Inverse Fourier transform of the phase-only synthesis based on PCA.

In spite of yielding illumination-tolerant images synthesized from Fourier transform discriminating one person of each other, reconstruction errors in the frequency domain can be produced because if the input image is shifted then a linear term is added to the phase [18]. Thus, by using a similarity measure such as the Frobenius norm between the reconstructed image and the test image, the recognition performance will degrade [13,24].

However, in order to achieve shift-invariance along with tolerance to illumination and occlusion, as it was done in [18], a hybrid $(2D)^2$PCA-correlation filter was developed from the reconstructed phase spectrum. To examine how well this phase spectrum is reconstructed, i.e., if the reconstructed phase spectrum is identical to the test phase spectrum, the phase-only correlation between the conjugate of the reconstructed phase spectrum and the phase spectrum of the test image at all possible shifts is computed as follows:

$$C(u,v) = e^{-\phi_R(u,v)}e^{\phi_T(u,v)} = e^{\phi_T(u,v)-\phi_R(u,v)} \tag{13}$$

$$C_T(x,y) = \sum_{u=0}^{m-1}\sum_{v=0}^{n-1} e^{\phi_T(u,v)-\phi_R(u,v)} e^{\frac{j2\pi ux}{m}} e^{\frac{j2\pi vy}{n}} \tag{14}$$

thus, as expected, a constant flat spectrum is obtained cancelling out all phases by adding their opposites.

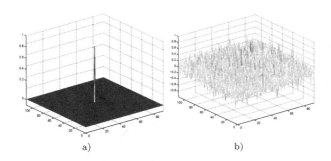

a)   b)

Fig. 3. Correlation plane corresponding to the genuine and impostor class. (a) Sharp correlation peak belonging to a face from the same person and (b) Correlation output belonging to a face from a different person.

Thus, by using the inverse Fourier transform, a sharp peak appeared in the correlation output plane C_T. Figure 3(a) shows a sharp correlation peak resulting from the $(2D)^2$PCA filter cross-correlated with a face from the same person whose filter was made for. Meanwhile, Fig. 3(b) shows a shapeless correlation output resulting from the filter cross-correlated with a face image from a different person to whom the filter was made. An appropriate measure to compute the peak sharpness and its location along with the shift in the input image is the Peak-to-Sidelobe Ratio (PSR) metric [18], which allows us to decide whether a test image belongs or not to the authentic class. The PSR is defined as follows:

$$PSR = \frac{peak - \mu_{area}}{\sigma_{area}} \tag{15}$$

where μ_{area} and σ_{area} are the mean and standard deviation of a small region centered at, but excluding the peak.

5   Video-Based Face Recognition System

we extended the css-based hybrid $(2D)^2$PCA-correlation filter bank to video-based face recognition, by developing a still-to-video face recognition system, where the gallery consists of high-quality face images of different subjects as reference, and the test set consists of video sequences, captured by CCTV cameras, of face images of a person moving at an office building. In this scenario, we assume that the frames obtained by video cameras, although the subject may not be cooperative, are similar views to the corresponding views in the training set, and can be used as evidence to recognize the identity of the test subject.

The proposed still-to-video face recognition system is based on the still image based face recognition block diagram shown in Fig. 1, where a single correlation filter per person is designed from the css-based hybrid-$(2D)^2$PCA subspace of the phase spectrum of the cropped training images. Our idea is to accumulate evidence (the PSRs values generated in each phase spectrum subspace, and used as partial evidences) from multiples frames to take a better face identification decision. Finally, we compute a sum of matching scores to decide the identity, thus if video sequence with the highest score coincides with the same class, it has correctly identified, otherwise a misclassification is recorded.

6   Experimental Results

In this section the performance for both the hybrid $(2D)^2$PCA-correlation filter bank and the hybrid PCA-correlation filter bank are evaluated experimentally, and for both methods, the Logarithm transformation [16], of the intensity values for face image enhancement, is used. Additionally, other state-of-the-art algorithms such as IPCA [10], PCA [19], FM-$(2D)^2$PCA [24] and $(2D)^2$PCA [25] are used as *baseline*. With the purpose of exploring the face identification performance, experiments were carried out on three face databases: Yale-B [8], AR [11], and YouTube [20]. The Yale-B database is used to examine the performance under 64 different lighting conditions and various facial expressions. The AR database is employed to test the performance when there are different lighting conditions; partial occlusions and facial expressions. The YouTube database is used to evaluate the unconstrained video performance under motion blur, occlusions, lighting conditions, and pose.

The face images used for the Yale-B and YouTube databases are of a fixed size 64×64 pixels while for the AR database are of a fixed size 32×32. The number of projection coefficients used in PCA or its case IPCA (see Eq. 7) is controlled by the value θ, set to 0.95 for all the datasets. Given this dimension, the number of projection vectors is computed for both PCA and $(2D)^2$PCA based correlation filters for representing face images under similar compression ratios [25]. The computational time for each of these methods, which includes both training and recognition stages, is measured for all face databases. Additionally, all the experiments are based on the rank-1 recognition rates and tested on a Core i5 2.5 GHz CPU, 8 Gb memory computer.

6.1   Experiments on the Yale-B Database

The performance of the proposed approach was evaluated using 64 frontal face images under different lighting conditions, from negative azimuth to positive

Fig. 4. Face images exhibiting little or extreme illumination from Yale-B face database.

Table 1. Face recognition performance comparison of PCA, $(2D)^2$PCA, FM-$(2D)^2$PCA, IPCA, the PCA-based filter and the $(2D)^2$PCA-based filter for the Yale-B database, where training images for both Set 1 and Set 2 were captured under illumination directions in both negative and positive azimuth, respectively.

Yale-B database							
Training images	PCA	$(2D)^2$PCA	FM-$(2D)^2$PCA	IPCA	H-PCA	H-$(2D)^2$PCA	Method [14]
	% Rec	% Rec	% Rec	% Rec	% Rec	% Rec	% Rec
Set 1	47.3%	50.3%	61.0%	67.6%	100.0%	100%	95.0%
Set 2	51.1%	52.5%	59.1%	78.0%	98.6%	99.5%	97.0%
Average time (s)	5.28	2.82	3.17	3.54	8.02	4.75	–

azimuth, of 10 people. Examples of cropped images of one subject are shown in Fig. 4. Two different experiments, by forming two sets of training images, were compared with [14]. The first set contains 350 images of negative azimuth (with 35 images per person), and the second set contains 290 images of positive azimuth (with 29 images per person). Table 1 shows the performance as well as average running times of the proposed approach along with other standard methods using Set 1 and Set 2 as training and testing sets, respectively. A significant improvement on the recognition accuracy and robustness of the $(2D)^2$PCA-based filter against the other methods can be easily noticed. In both cases correlation filter methods overcome other methods, however, the proposed method slightly improved the performance, but the running time used (4.75 s) is still lower that its PCA-based correlation filter counterpart.

6.2 Experiments on the AR Database

In this section, we evaluate the recognition performance using a subset with 1150 images of 50 different subjects (25 males and 25 females), and each subject has 23 different face images. Three different experiments was performed by dividing the dataset into two different sets.

In the first experiment, we evaluated the performance of all 6 methods against illumination variations and facial expressions applying the Set 1 (see Fig. 5(a)), where they were trained using seven different images without occlusions. In the second experiment, the performance was evaluated using the Set 2 (see Fig. 5b) along with another set chosen arbitrarily. We use a total of 20 different images including lighting variations; facial expressions and partial occlusions (sunglasses and scarf). We trained the face subspace with only six face images per person

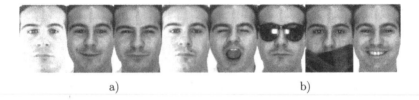

a)   b)

Fig. 5. Example of cropped face images exhibiting different illumination conditions, facial expressions and partial occlusions included in (a) Set 1 and (b) Set 2.

(i.e. three persons with neutral expression, one with illumination variation, one with sunglasses, and one using scarf).

In the last experiment, we trained just as the second experiment, however in the testing stage we used another subset of eight images per person, which includes images with partial occlusions. Table 2 shows that the proposed method presents an improvement in recognition accuracy over the PCA-based correlation filter and the other methods, and shows that is more tolerant to lighting variations, facial expressions, and partial occlusions. Also, the average time of recognition is significantly lower that its PCA-based correlation filter counterpart. By training the subspace algorithms with the Set 1, IPCA performs better than most of presented methods, however, its performance was severely degraded when test images with partial occlusions and facial expressions were present.

Table 2. Face recognition performance comparison of PCA, $(2D)^2$PCA, FM-$(2D)^2$PCA, IPCA, the PCA-based filter and the $(2D)^2$PCA-based filter for the AR database.

AR database						
Training images	PCA	$(2D)^2$PCA	FM-$(2D)^2$PCA	IPCA	H-PCA	H-$(2D)^2$PCA
	% Rec	% Rec	% Rec	% Rec	% Rec	% Rec
Set 1	87.7%	88.0%	87.1%	95.7%	93.1%	95.0%
Set 2	38.3%	39.2%	41.0%	54.6%	88.3%	91.0%
Set 3	27.0%	30.0%	33.0%	44.0%	77.0%	80.5%
Average time (s)	6.9	5.6	5.2	7.2	12.6	10.7

6.3   Experiments on the YouTube Database

To evaluate the proposed still-to-video face recognition system, a subset of video sequences of 12 subjects is used. For each subject, 50 frames are used as a test video sequence, and 20 frames as a training video sequence, as shown in Fig. 4.

To separate the classes as much as possible, we synthesize two filters by using the hybrid-PCA and hybrid-$(2D)^2$PCA subspaces. Our objectives are to maximize correlation outputs for the authentic class using the $2D^2$PCA-based filter, and minimize correlation outputs for impostors with the PCA-based filter.

a)   b)

Fig. 6. Example frames in the YouTube faces dataset, including occlusions, lighting conditions, pose, and motion blur used for (a) Training and (b) Testing.

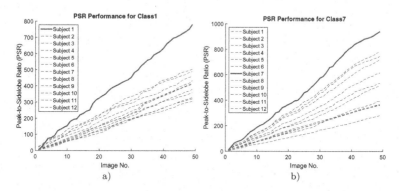

a)   b)

Fig. 7. The accumulated scores over frame index number of subject (a) 1 and (b) 7

Such an integration produces a higher margin of separability between genuine and impostor classes, and is able to exploit video sequence information. The performance of the joint filters is shown in Fig. 7, where the identification decision is based on the video sequence, but at each frame we use the joint correlation filters to accumulate partial evidences (the PSR values). In the experiments, the 12 subjects were correctly labeled. Since correlations filter designs are based on different subspaces, the combination of two filters can yield a better score for a decision final, improving the identification performance. In the experiments, a sequence with the highest score is correctly classified if it has the same class label, otherwise it is misclassified (Fig. 7).

6.4   Discussion

Observations from performed evaluations support that the $(2D)^2$PCA-based filter improves recognition accuracies in less time, and can deal with faces with strong illumination variations, partial concussions, and facial expressions better than its PCA-based filter counterpart.

Based on recognition rates, if dimensionality is reduced, the recognition accuracy of the PCA-based filter can be degraded, while the $(2D)^2$PCA-based filter performance may be increased. However, by increasing the dimensionality and having as limit the similar compression ratios, the resulting hybrid-$(2D)^2$PCA subspace could not discriminate among faces, decreasing the performance. Furthermore, by increasing both the number of eigenvectors and the training images, it is evident that recognition rates may be improved, but it may incur in an increase of processing time because the training, projection, reconstruction and face matching stages are time consuming.

7   Conclusions and Future Work

This paper introduced a new hybrid $(2D)^2$PCA-correlation filter which allows to get a far better representation than its hybrid PCA-correlation filter counterpart of the reconstructed phase spectrum for face images.

Experimental results show that by linking $(2D)^2$PCA in the Fourier domain with correlation filters, the proposed method clearly improves significantly the face recognition accuracy in the frequency domain, and overcomes algorithms in the space domain. Additionally, it is able to identify subjects using a video test sequence by combing the hybrid-PCA and $(2D)^2$PCA subspaces. Future research work is to incorporate face super-resolution for its application in video surveillance system, handle pose variations, and extend the experiments in video.

Acknowledgments. This work is supported by the National Science and Technology Council of Mexico (CONACyT), project #215546, scholarship #328839; and INAOE.

References

1. Benitez-Garcia, G., Olivares-Mercado, J., Sanchez-Perez, G., Nakano-Miyatake, M., Perez-Meana, H.: A sub-block-based eigenphases algorithm with optimum sub-block size. Knowl. Based Syst. **37**, 415–426 (2013)
2. Bhagavatula, R., Savvides, M.: Eigen and Fisher-Fourier spectra for shift invariant pose-tolerant face recognition. In: Singh, S., Singh, M., Apte, C., Perner, P. (eds.) ICAPR 2005. LNCS, vol. 3687, pp. 351–359. Springer, Heidelberg (2005). doi:10.1007/11552499_40
3. Chellappa, R., Wilson, C., Sirohey, S.: Human and machine recognition of faces: a survey. Proc. IEEE **83**(5), 705–741 (1995)
4. Chen, S., Mau, S., Harandi, M.T., Sanderson, C., Bigdeli, A., Lovell, B.C.: Face recognition from still images to video sequences: a local-feature-based framework. J. Image Video Process. **2011**, 11:1–11:14 (2011)
5. Hayes, M., Lim, J., Oppenheim, A.: Signal reconstruction from phase or magnitude. IEEE Trans. Acoust. Speech Signal Process. **28**(6), 672–680 (1980)
6. Kong, H., Wang, L., Teoh, E.K., Li, X., Wang, J.G., Venkateswarlu, R.: Generalized 2D principal component analysis for face image representation and recognition. Neural Netw. **18**(56), 585–594 (2005)
7. Vijaya Kumar, B.V.K., Savvides, M., Xie, C.: Correlation pattern recognition for face recognition. Proc. IEEE **94**(11), 1963–1976 (2006)
8. Lee, K., Ho, J., Kriegman, D.: Acquiring linear subspaces for face recognition under variable lighting. IEEE Trans. Pattern Anal. Mach. Intell. **27**(5), 684–698 (2005)
9. Li, Y., Savvides, M., Bhagavatula, V.: Illumination tolerant face recognition using a novel face from sketch synthesis approach and advanced correlation filters. In: IEEE International Conference on Acoustics, Speech and Signal Processing, vol. 2, p. II (2006)

10. Liu, X., Chen, T., Vijaya Kumar, B.V.K.: Face authentication for multiple subjects using eigenflow. Pattern Recogn. **36**(2), 313–328 (2003)
11. Martinez, A.M., Kak, A.C.: PCA versus LDA. IEEE Trans. Pattern Anal. Mach. Intell. **23**(2), 228–233 (2001)
12. Oppenheim, A., Lim, J.: The importance of phase in signals. Proc. IEEE **69**(5), 529–541 (1981)
13. Ribaric, S., Maracic, M.: Eigenphase-based face recognition: a comparison of phase-information extraction methods. In: Proceedings of IEEE ERK, pp. 233–236 (2010)
14. Sao, A.: Combining analytic phase and Fourier phase for face recognition. In: International Conference on Image Information Processing, pp. 1–4 (2011)
15. Savvides, M., Vijaya Kumar, B.V.K., Khosla, P.: Eigenphases vs eigenfaces. In: 17th International Conference on Pattern Recognition, vol. 3, pp. oo810–oo813 (2004)
16. Savvides, M., Vijaya Kumar, B.V.K.: Illumination normalization using logarithm transforms for face authentication. In: Kittler, J., Nixon, M.S. (eds.) AVBPA 2003. LNCS, vol. 2688, pp. 549–556. Springer, Heidelberg (2003). doi:10.1007/3-540-44887-X_65
17. Savvides, M., Vijaya Kumar, B.V.K., Khosla, P.K.: Robust shift-invariant biometric identication from partial face images. Proc. SPIE **5404**, 124–135 (2004)
18. Savvides, M., Vijaya Kumar, B.V.K., Khosla, P.K.: "Corefaces" - robust shift invariant PCA based correlation filter for illumination tolerant face recognition. In: IEEE Computer Society Conference on Computer Vision and Pattern Recognition, vol. 2, pp. II-834–II-841 (2004)
19. Sharkas, M., Elenien, M.A.: Eigenfaces vs. fisherfaces vs. ICA for face recognition; a comparative study. In: 9th International Conference on Signal Processing, pp. 914–919 (2008)
20. Wolf, L., Hassner, T., Maoz, I.: Face recognition in unconstrained videos with matched background similarity. In: IEEE Conference on Computer Vision and Pattern Recognition, pp. 529–534 (2011)
21. Xie, C., Savvides, M., Vijaya Kumar, B.V.K.: Redundant class-dependence feature analysis based on correlation filters using FRGC2.0 data. In: IEEE Computer Society Conference on Computer Vision and Pattern Recognition, p. 153 (2005)
22. Yan, Y., Wang, H., Suter, D.: Multi-subregion based correlation filter bank for robust face recognition. Pattern Recogn. **47**(11), 3487–3501 (2014)
23. Yang, J., Zhang, D., Frangi, A.F., Yang, J.: Two-dimensional PCA: a new approach to appearance-based face representation and recognition. IEEE Trans. Pattern Anal. Mach. Intell. **26**(1), 131–137 (2004)
24. Zeytunlu, A., Ahmad, M., Swamy, M.: Two-dimensional face recognition algorithms in the frequency domain. In: 25th IEEE Canadian Conference on Electrical Computer Engineering, pp. 1–4 (2012)
25. Zhang, D., Zhou, Z.H.: Two-directional two-dimensional PCA for efficient face representation and recognition. Neurocomputing **69**(1–3), 224–231 (2005)

End to End Deep Learning for Single Step Real-Time Facial Expression Recognition

Bhargava Reddy, Ye-Hoon Kim$^{(\boxtimes)}$, Sojung Yun, Junik Jang, and Soonhyuk Hong

Samsung Electronics, Seoul, South Korea
{tb.reddy,yehoon.kim,sojung15.yun,ji.jang,
soonhyuk04.hong}@samsung.com

Abstract. In recent years, a lot of research has been carried out in face detection and facial expression recognition. Very few of them are capable of achieving these at real time with a very high accuracy. In this paper we present a real time end to end, single step face and facial expression recognition technique which performs at a speed of more than 10 fps (frames per second). We use an end-to-end deep learning approach for localization and expression classification. On the CK+ [1] dataset we get a 10-fold validation accuracy of 94.8% on 640 * 480 images. We have also created a webcam interface, which classifies the emotion of a person at 10 fps, which proves our claim that facial expression recognition has approached real time speed with very decent accuracy.

Keywords: Facial expression recognition · Emotion recognition · Real time classification · Deep learning

1 Introduction

Video based facial expression recognition is challenging because of the variance involved in different people expressing the same emotion in a myriad different ways. Sometimes two different people might understand a particular expression in two different ways. The CK+ dataset [1] was published in 2010 and was the first benchmark to categorize emotion recognition algorithms. Various other competitions started from 2012 which concentrated on emotion recognition, example: emotiW [2] focuses on emotion recognition in the wild, which includes semi-automated clips from various movies. AVEC [3] is another such competition which concentrates on emotion recognition from audio and video samples together. The latter datasets are very hard to work with because of the various illumination conditions, non-frontal faces, low resolution, etc. To obtain decent accuracies in these datasets, many researchers used combination of various machine learning approaches [6, 7] or fusion of deep neural nets. Most of the earlier papers took traditional machine learning approaches, with few recent papers concentrating on deep learning and face recognition along with facial landmark recognition as two different steps [23, 24]. Most of these papers either did not specify the run time or a run time which make them unusable in real-time situations. In this paper our main motive is to make an accurate real time facial expression recognition tool.

© Springer International Publishing AG 2017

K. Nasrollahi et al. (Eds.): VAAM 2016/FFER 2016, LNCS 10165, pp. 88–97, 2017.

DOI: 10.1007/978-3-319-56687-0_8

2   Earlier Approaches

Most of the approaches prior to 2015 on emotion recognition use traditional machine learning techniques. The first part of the algorithm involves face detection and face landmark recognition. Face is extracted from the raw image using any standard face detection software such as opencv or dlib [19] and then facial landmark is applied to this to obtain the location of eyes, mouth, nose etc. Researchers used Facial Action Coding System (FACS) and tried to classify which action units are active [4]. Various approaches also followed the Arousal-Valence space giving a 2D map of the emotion [5]. These features are analyzed and trained with a traditional machine learning algorithm such as AdaBoost or multi-layer perceptron model, and finally the image is classified. Researchers also used combinations of multiple features each involving a different machine learning approach, example: combinations of HOG, dense SIFT [6] or sometimes SIFT features with an SVM classifier [7]. In more recent approaches, researchers used deep CNNs to classify the subject's facial expression [8]. In the all these approaches, the face is extracted using a traditional face recognition algorithm and then this is resized to 227 * 227 image and fed into a deep learning classifier.

3   Our Approach - Design

We used the technique as mentioned in the faster-RCNN paper by Girshick et al. [9]. The paper uses a deep learning approach which does image localization and classification in a single neural network. It classifies up to 20 different classes on PASCAL VOC [10] dataset with a mAP of 70. The faster-RCNN technique has also been used in KITTI [11] vehicle and pedestrian detection for ADAS (Autonomous Driving Assistant System) and achieved a very high accuracy of approximately 80% in car, pedestrian and cycle detection. The faster-RCNN architecture consists of three important networks merged together.

The first network is the convolutional map which uses a standard convolutional maps such as VGG16 [12] or alexnet [13] or ResNet [14] (technically any network of our choice), after these convolutional maps, it has a region proposal network which proposes the region at which the object is present and then Fully Connected layers to classify the object and also adjust the localization parameters.

Faster-RCNN concentrates more on generic object detection, and as per our survey, it has never been used in face detection and classifying into categories in research papers. This motivated us to use faster-RCNN in our facial expression recognition project, since it can detect multiple faces in an image in less than 10 ms, which is much faster than any other face detection software available.

For the current experiment we use VGG16 architecture, since it provides an optimal balance between speed and accuracy. Alexnet would provide very high speed but low accuracy, whereas ResNet would provide more accuracy but non-real time speeds. We get two different types of outputs from the neural network. First one being the localized coordinates named as bbox_prediction which contains 4 numbers representing the top left coordinate and the bottom right coordinate. The second one is the class probability for the bounding box, indicating which facial expression is being shown by the subject. The following Figs. 1, and 2 show the architecture of the neural network.

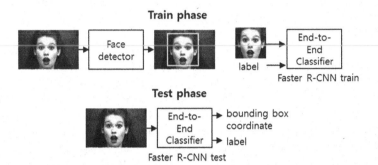

Fig. 1. The train and test phases of the classifier

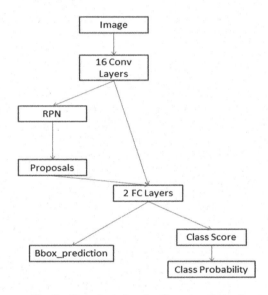

Fig. 2. Flowchart showing the network used

3.1 Dataset

We used CK+ [1] dataset to evaluate the accuracy of the proposed model. CK+ dataset is a publically available dataset. It has been used as one of the basic benchmark for facial expression recognition [20, 21]. The dataset consists of 593 sequences out of which 327 has been classified as classifiable emotions. Each video have frames starting from a neutral expression to emotional high. The dataset consists of 7 expressions Angry, Contempt, Disgust, Fear, Happy, Sad and Surprise. Each video lasts about 10–60 frames. Each frame is a 640×480 or 640×490 image which can be an RGB image or a Grayscale image. The dataset has a total of 123 subjects. The following image sequences (Fig. 3) show a sample of the dataset.

Fig. 3. Sample frames from the CK + dataset

We also used the AFEW-2015 [2] dataset to evaluate the robustness of our method in uncontrolled settings. The AFEW dataset is known for its very high difficulty in classification because of very hard face recognition and equally challenging classification because each image has a different illumination and background. AFEW dataset provides both the video data and the audio data. AFEW dataset is released for the EmotiW competition which takes place annually at ACM ICMI.

The dataset consists of 678 video sequences for training and 350 video sequences for testing and validation. The dataset has 7 classes namely 1 = Angry, 2 = Disgust, 3 = Fear, 4 = Happy, 5 = Neutral, 6 = Sad, 7 = Surprise. The following image sequences show a sample of the dataset (Fig. 4).

3.2 Preparing the Training Data and Testing Data

Preparing the training set is a non-trivial task; we cannot provide the image and its corresponding expression as the only two inputs. We also need to calculate the localized coordinates of the face. To calculate the localized coordinates, we used the dlib's facial recognition software [19]. We extract the top (x, y) coordinates of the top left facial crop and the bottom right facial point, thus giving us 4 numbers to localize the face. We create an xml file for each image, describing its coordinates and facial expressions along with its size in PASCAL VOC [10] xml format.

Fig. 4. Sample frames from the AFEW dataset

The complete dataset has been divided into 10 different subsets $(S_0, S_1, \ldots, S_9)$. Two different sets have no common subject, which makes sure that there is no data overlap in train and test. The data is split almost equally, each subset containing around 32-33 videos in each subset. In the 10-fold evaluation each subset S_i is separately used to test the train result of the remaining subsets other than S_i.

Before proceeding to training, we need to make sure that all the images are either RGB or grayscale, so we converted all the images to grayscale.

3.3   Pre-training

Before starting to train the whole dataset, we perform some pre-training operations to boost the accuracy. We will use VGG16 neural network pre-trained with ImageNet [25] as our base model. Pre training on ImageNet makes the convergence easy for further training. To boost the accuracy of facial expression recognition we pre-train the model with FER dataset. FER-2013 [15] is a dataset containing about 28 k images in the train set along with 4 k images in the validation set. It consists of 7 expressions namely 0 = Angry, 1 = Disgust, 2 = Fear, 3 = Happy, 4 = Neutral, 5 = Sad and 6 = Surprise. Each image is of size 48 × 48. The following images show samples of the FER-2013 dataset (Fig. 5).

Since the VGG16 takes only 227 × 227 images as input, we have resized all the images from 48 × 48 to 227 × 227 and trained the already pre-trained (with ImageNet) VGG16 model. This step is very crucial since it can boost accuracies up to 5–10%. Since this dataset has many robust images from the internet.

The total data is trained for 40 epochs, with a base learning rate of 0.001 and momentum value of 0.9, the learning rate drops 0.1 times every 10 epochs. The weight decay is set at 0.0005. The pre-training took a total of 4 h using CUDA 8.0 and cuDNN v5.0

Fig. 5. 48 × 48 images showing expressions of anger, disgust, neutral and surprise

3.4 Training

We have used the open source py-faster-rcnn [16] library which was developed by Ross Girshick et al. The network consists of a region proposal network and a convolutional network combined with fully connected layers. We used alternating optimization training for our complete network.

The complete training took a total of approximately 7 h for each subset. It took a total of 70 GPU hours for the training to complete.

The training method is as follows [17]:

Assume that F0 is the FER-2013 pre-trained VGG16 network

1. Train an RPN initialized from F0, now obtain F1
2. Generate training proposals P1 using the RPN F1
3. Train the classifier network (Fast-RCNN)F2 on P1 initialized from F0
4. Train RPN F3 from F2 without changing the conv layers
5. Generate training proposals P2 from F3
6. Train the classifier network (Fast-RCNN) with frozen convolutional layers and generate F4
7. Copy the F3's RPN layers to Fast R-CNN F4

The table below (Table 1) shows the parameter settings used in different phases of training.

Table 1. Parameters used in various training stages

Stage	Base learning rate	Gamma	Step size (Epochs)	Momentum	Weight decay
1	0.001	0.1	10	0.9	0.0005
3	0.001	0.1	5	0.9	0.0005
4	0.001	0.1	10	0.9	0.0005
6	0.001	0.1	5	0.9	0.0005

3.5 Hardware

Throughout our experiments we used GTX 1080 GPU with CUDA v8.0, and cuDNN v5.0, Intel i7-4770 processor with 1 TB HDD and 16 GB of RAM. All the experiments are performed on Ubuntu 14.04 Linux machine.

4   Validation and Results

4.1   Experiments on CK+ Dataset

As stated earlier, we have done the 10-fold validation on the complete dataset. The train: test split being in the ratio of 9:1. The test time for each frame using the proposed network is approximately 0.1 s. A particular test video is taken and split into frames at 20 fps, Now these frames are send into the network one after the other, and the corresponding facial expression is calculated, if there is a face present in the frame.

After all the frames are processed, a majority voting is taken for the expression calculated by the model, which will be our final expression class for the video.

The total accuracy for 10-fold validation on 7 classes for CK+ data as calculated by our model is 94.8%. The table (Table 2) shows the confusion matrix across the 7 categories.

Table 2.   Confusion Matrix for CK+ data (all 7 classes of the dataset)

	Angry	Contempt	Disgust	Fear	Happiness	Sadness	Surprise
Angry	97.8						
Contempt		91.2					
Disgust			93.4				
Fear				91.2			
Happiness					100		
Sadness						95.6	
Surprise							100

The following images (Fig. 6) show the GUI of face detection + facial expression classification.

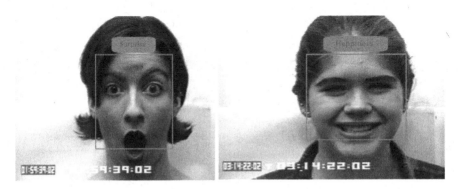

Fig. 6.   GUI showing the results on CK+ validation

4.2 Experiments on AFEW Dataset

The same technique has also been used for AFEW-2015 [2] dataset, which consists of audio + video sequences of various movie clips. We have done similar processing for images as described in the CK+ dataset. And we have ignored the audio in all the video sequences and only the frames are taken in consideration. The state of art accuracy for only video sequences is 39.6% [18] (audio is not considered).

In our faster-RCNN model instead of the VGG16 network, we have inserted the ResNet-50 which consists of 50 layers. This gave us an accuracy of 37.2%.

Since we used a very deep neural network, we got test time of 0.2 s per frame which is approximately 5 fps, not real time but almost near real time. If instead of ResNet-50 if we used VGG16, we got an accuracy of 34.5% with a speed of 0.1 s per frame which is approximately 10 fps, almost near real time. Having a deep network helps better in wild video frames, since the classification becomes a tougher problem. The table below (Table 3) shows the confusion matrix of all the 7 classes in the dataset.

Table 3. Confusion matrix for ResNet50 with faster-RCNN on emotiW-2015 dataset

	Angry	Disgust	Fear	Happy	Neutral	Sad	Surprise
Angry	52.1		4.7	20.3	10.9	6.3	4.7
Disgust	15	25	7.5	20	17.5	10	5
Fear	43.5	6.5	8.7	26.1	8.7	4.3	2.2
Happy	11.1		3.2	63.5	11	7.9	3.2
Neutral	14.3	6.3	6.3	28.5	34.9	29.5	9.8
Sad	13.1	13.1		21.3	11.5	29.5	9.8
Surprise	8.3	8.3	16.7	16.7	25	8.3	16.7

From the result we can understand that the classification is very tough when compared to CK+ dataset, which shows the difficulty of the problem. Only Happiness and Anger gave more than 50% accuracy. And Fear is shown as the most difficult expression to classify.

4.3 Real-Time Demonstration

We have also created a real-time facial expression recognition program in python which does the recognition at nearly 0.1 s per frame. We have used the CK+ data trained model of faster-RCNN. The complete video is available at the following link: https://www.youtube.com/watch?v=3nKoXcExWM0. The images below (Fig. 7) show the frames in the original video.

Fig. 7. Images showing real time demo of author's face

5   Conclusion and Future Plans

In this paper, we have presented a framework to process facial expression recognition in real time, one-step end to end process. We have reported accuracies of upto 94.8% for CK+ data and 37.2% for emotiW data. Faster-RCNN can also be used for human face detection and thus can be further used in classification, which makes the overall task very fast.

In future we will design more faster methods by trying to use dark knowledge [22] to reduce the size of the network without any decrease in accuracy, so as to do the expression recognition at nearly 25 fps.

References

1. Lucey, P., Cohn, J.F., Kanade, T., Saragih, J., Ambadar, Z.: The extended Cohn-Kanade dataset (CK+): a complete dataset for action unit and emotion-specific expression. In: Proceedings of the 3rd IEEE Workshop on CVPR for Human Communication Behaviour Analysis, San Francisco, CA, USA (2010)
2. Video and image based emotion recognition challenges in the wild: EmotiW 2015. In: ACM International Conference on Multimodal Interaction (ICMI) (2015)
3. Audio/visual emotion challenge and workshop: AVEC 2016. In: Proceedings of ACM Multimedia (2016)
4. Tian, Y.-L., Kanade, T., Cohn, J.: Recognizing action units for facial expression analysis. IEEE Trans. Pattern Anal. Mach. Intell. **23**(2), 97–115 (2001)
5. Zhang, L., Tjondronegoro, D., Chandran, V.: Representation of facial expression categories in continuous arousal-valence space: feature and correlation. Image Vis. Comput. **32**(12), 1067–1079 (2014)
6. Liu, M., Wang, R., Li, S., Shan, S., Huang, Z., Chen, X.: Combining multiple kernel methods on Riemannian manifold for emotion recognition in the wild. In: Proceedings of the 16th International Conference on Multimodal Interaction, ICMI 2014, pp. 494–501. ACM, New York (2014)
7. Sun, B., Li, L., Zuo, T., Chen, Y., Zhou, G., Wu, X.: Combining multimodal features with hierarchical classifier fusion for emotion recognition in the wild. In: Proceedings of the 16th International Conference on Multimodal Interaction, ICMI 2014, pp. 481–486. ACM, New York (2014)
8. Ng, H.-W., Nguyen, V.D., Vonikakis, V., Winkler, S.: Deep learning for emotion recognition on small datasets using transfer learning. In: Proceedings of the 2015 ACM on International Conference on Multimodal Interaction, pp. 443–449. ACM (2015)

9. Ren, S., He, K., Girshick, R., Sun, J.: Faster R-CNN: towards real-time object detection with region proposal networks. In: NIPS (2015)

10. Everingham, M., Van Gool, L., Williams, C.K.I., Winn, J., Zisserman, A.: The PASCAL visual object classes challenge 2007 (VOC 2007) results (2007)

11. Geiger, A., Lenz, P., Ortasun, R.: Are we ready for autonomous driving? The KITTI vision benchmark suite. In: CVPR (2012)

12. Simonyan, K., Zisserman, A.: Very deep convolutional networks for large-scale image recognition. In: ILSVRC (2014)

13. Krizhevsky, A., Sutskever, I., Hinton, G.E.: ImageNet classification with deep convolutional neural networks. In: NIPS (2012)

14. He, K., Zhang, X., Ren, S., Sun, J.: Deep residual learning for image recognition. In: CVPR (2016)

15. Challenges in Representation Learning: Facial Expression Recognition Challenge. Kaggle Inc.

16. https://github.com/rbgirshick/py-faster-rcnn

17. https://www.dropbox.com/s/xtr4yd4i5e0vw8g/iccv15_tutorial_training_rbg.pdf?dl=0

18. Ebrahimi Kahou, S., Michalski, V., Konda, K., Memisevic, R., Pal, C.: Recurrent neural networks for emotion recognition in video. In: Proceedings of the 2015 ACM on International Conference on Multimodal Interaction, pp. 467–474. ACM (2015)

19. http://dlib.net/

20. Jung, H., Lee, S., Park, S., Lee, I., Ahn, C., Kim, J.: Deep temporal appearance-geometry network for facial expression recognition (2015). arXiv:1503.01532v1

21. Ghimire, D., Lee, H., Li, Z.-N., Heong, S., Park, S.H., Choi, H.S.: Recognition of facial expressions based on tracking and selection of discriminative geometric features. Int. J. Multimedia Ubiquit. Eng. **10**(3), 35–44 (2015)

22. Korattikara, A., Rathod, V., Murphy, K., Welling, M.: Bayesian dark knowledge. In: NIPS (2015)

23. Yu, Z., Zhang, C.: Image based static facial expression recognition with multiple deep network learning. In: Proceedings of the 2015 ACM International Conference Multimodal Interaction, pp. 435–442. ACM

24. Kim, B.-K., Lee, H., Roh, J., Lee, S.-Y.: Hierarchical committee of deep CNNs with exponentially-weighted decision fusion for static facial expression recognition. In: Proceedings of the 2015 ACM on International Conference on Multimodal Interaction, ICMI 2015, pp. 427–434. ACM, New York (2015)

25. Russakovsky*, O., Deng*, J., Su, H., Krause, J., Satheesh, S., Ma, S., Huang, Z., Karpathy, A., Khosla, A., Bernstein, M., Berg, A.C., Fei-Fei, L.: ImageNet large scale visual recognition challenge. IJCV **115**, 211–252 (2015). (* = equal contribution)

Comparative Study of Human Age Estimation Based on Hand-Crafted and Deep Face Features

C. Belver[1], I. Arganda-Carreras[1,2], and F. Dornaika[1,2(✉)]

[1] University of the Basque Country UPV/EHU, San Sebastian, Spain
fadi.dornaika@ehu.es
[2] IKERBASQUE, Basque Foundation for Science, Bilbao, Spain

Abstract. This paper introduces a comparative study of age estimation based on the analysis of facial images. The main contributions are as follows. First, we provide performance evaluation of eight face descriptors which are given by three hand-crafted features as well as by five pre-trained deep Convolutional Neural Networks (CNNs). Second, we show that the use of deep features provided by pre-trained CNNs can transfer the power of the net to new domains and datasets that were not available at the training phase. This leads to an efficient and stable solution to the problem of cross-database by only retraining the regressor instead of the whole network. The experiments are conducted on two public databases: MORPH II and PAL.

Keywords: Age estimation · Hand-crafted features · Deep features · Transfer

1 Introduction

In the last decade, with the increasing interest in social robotics and video-based security systems, research on the numerical analysis of human faces (including face detection, face recognition, classification of gender, and recognition of facial expression) has attracted attention in the communities of computer vision and pattern recognition [1–5]. In connection with these investigations, estimating the age of a person from the numerical analysis of his face image is a relatively new topic. Age estimation by numerical analysis of the face image has many potential applications such as the development of intelligent human-machine interfaces and improving safety and protection of minors in various and diverse sectors (transport, medicine, etc.). It can be very useful for advanced video surveillance, demographic statistics collection, business intelligence and customer profiling, and search optimization in large databases. The age attribute could also be used in the verification of the face and enriching the tools used in police investigations. In general, automatic age estimation by a machine is useful in applications where the objective is to determine the age of an individual without identifying him. The age estimator can use a machine learning approach to train a model for extracted features and make age prediction for query faces with the

K. Nasrollahi et al. (Eds.): VAAM 2016/FFER 2016, LNCS 10165, pp. 98–112, 2017.
DOI: 10.1007/978-3-319-56687-0_9

trained model. Generally speaking, age estimation can be viewed as a multi-class classification problem, a regression problem or a composite of these two.

The anthropometry-based approach mainly depends on measurements and distances of different facial landmarks. Kwon and Lobo [6] published the earliest paper on age classification based on facial images by computing ratios to distinguish babies from others. In [7], the authors designed a neural network to locate facial features and calculate several geometric ratios and differences which are used for estimating the age from a facial image. The anthropometry-based approaches might be useful for babies, children, and young adults, but they are impractical for adults since their facial skin appearance is the main source of information about ethnicity, gender, and age. Estimating human age from a facial image requires a great amount of information from the input image. Extraction of these features is important since the performance of an age estimation system will heavily rely on the quality of extracted features. Lots of research on age estimation has been conducted towards aging feature extraction. Examples include: the active appearance model (AAM) [8], age manifold [1], AGing pattern Subspace (AGES) [9], biologically inspired features (BIF) [10]. Image-based age estimation approaches view the face image as a texture pattern. Many texture features have been used like Local Binary Patterns (LBP) [11], Histograms of Oriented Gradients (HOG) [12], BIF, Binarized Statistical Image Features (BSIF) [13] and Local Phase Quantization (LPQ) in demographic estimation works. BIF and its variants are widely used in age estimation works such us [14–16]. Han et al. [16] used selected BIF features on order to estimate the age, gender and ethnicity attributes.

Due to their significant performance improvement in facial recognition domain, deep learning approaches have been recently proposed for age estimation (e.g. [3,5]). Deep learning approaches claim to have the best performances in demographic classification (ethnicity, gender and age). However, this claim cannot be always true. It is known, that deep learning can provide impressive results within a single database. However when another database is used with the trained deep net, the age estimation performance can drop significantly. In this paper, we provide a comparative study of age estimation based on hand-crafted and deep features. The paper also shows that the full power of a pre-trained net can be exploited by simply using its deep features and only training an age regressor. This regressor training is much more efficient than retraining or fine-tuning the whole deep net using a sheer number of images. Experiments will show that this scheme for age estimation can be more accurate than the one obtained by the end-to-end deep net solution.

The rest of the paper is organized as follows: face alignment is briefly introduced in Sect. 2. In Sect. 3, we summarize three classic image features and five deep features. The experimental setup is described in Sect. 4 and the evaluation of the results is given in Sect. 5. In Sect. 6 we give the conclusion and the future plans.

Original MORPH-II   Face alignment
image   + cropping

Fig. 1. Face alignment and cropping associated with one original image in MORPH II database.

2   Face Alignment

Face alignment is one of the most important stages in image-based age estimation. In our experiments, the eyes of each face are detected using the Ensemble of Regression Trees (ERT) algorithm [17] which is a robust and very efficient algorithm for facial landmarks localization. Once we have the 2D positions of the two eyes, we use them to compensate for the in-plane rotation of the face. To this end, within the detected face region, the positions of right and left eyes are located as (R_x, R_y) and (L_x, L_y), respectively. Then, the angle of in-plane rotation is calculated by $\theta = artan(\frac{R_y - L_y}{R_x - L_x})$, and the input face region is rotated by the that angle. After rotation correction, we use a global scale for the face image, this scale normalizes the inter-ocular distance to a fixed value l. After performing the rotation and rescaling, the face region should be cropped (aligned face). To this end, a bounding box is centered on the new eyes location (on the transformed face image) and then stretched to the left and to the right by $k_0 \cdot l$, and to top by $k_1 \cdot l$ and to bottom by $k_2 \cdot l$. Finally, in our case, k_0, k_1, k_2 and l are chosen such that the final face image has a size of 50×50 pixels for the MORPH II database and 200×200 for the PAL database.

3   Face Features

In order to make the paper self-contained, this section will briefly describe some features that are very often used for extracting face features. We present three hand-crafted features as well as five deep features that can be obtained from pre-trained deep CNNs.

3.1   Local Binary Patterns (LBP)

The original LBP operator labels the pixels of an image with decimal numbers, which are called LBPs or LBP codes that encode the local structure around each pixel [11, 18]. The basic operator proceeds as follows. Each pixel is compared with its eight neighbors in a neighborhood by subtracting the central pixel value; the resulting strictly negative values are encoded with 0, and the others with 1. For each given pixel, a binary number is obtained by concatenating all these binary values in a clockwise direction, which starts from the one of its top-left neighbor. The corresponding decimal value of the generated binary number is then used for labeling the given pixel. The histogram of LBP labels (the frequency of occurrence of each code) calculated over a region or an image can be used as a texture descriptor. It should be noticed the LBP descriptors can be either an LBP image or a histogram of that image.

In our work, we used the classic LBP operator that provides a histogram of 256 bins for a given face image.

3.2 Histogram of Oriented Gradients (HOG)

The essential thought behind the histogram of oriented gradients descriptor [12] is that local object appearance and shape within an image can be described by the distribution of intensity gradients or edge directions. The image is divided into small connected regions called cells, and for the pixels within each cell, a histogram of gradient directions is compiled. The descriptor is then the concatenation of these histograms. For improved accuracy, the local histograms can be contrast-normalized by calculating a measure of the intensity across a larger region of the image, called a block, and then using this value to normalize all cells within the block. This normalization results in better invariance to changes in illumination and shadowing.

3.3 Binarized Statistical Image Features (BSIF)

This descriptor [13] can be used in texture recognition tasks in a similar manner as LBPs. Each element (i.e. bit) in the binary code string is computed by binarizing the response of a linear filter with a threshold at zero. Each bit is associated with a different filter and the desired length of the bit string is determined by the number of filters used. The set of filters is learnt from a training set of natural image patches by maximizing the statistical independence of the filter responses. Hence, statistical properties of natural image patches determine the BSIF descriptors.

3.4 Visual Geometry Group (VGG) Face Features

This CNN comprises 11 blocks, each containing a linear operator followed by one or more non-linearities such as ReLU and max pooling [19]. The first eight such blocks are said to be convolutional as the linear operator is a bank of linear filters (linear convolution). The last three blocks are instead called Fully Connected (FC); they are the same as a convolutional layer, but the size of the filters matches the size of the input data, such that each filter senses data from the entire image. All the convolution layers are followed by a rectification layer (ReLU). The first two FC layers output are 4,096 dimensional vectors. This multi-way CNN is trained to discriminate between the 2,622 identities using about 2.6 M images. The deep features of this network are extracted by taking the 4 K dimensional features and removing the last classification layer. The resulting vector is L2 normalized.

3.5   ImageNet VGG-F Features

The Fast (VGG-F) architecture [20] is similar to the one used by Krizhevsky *et al.* [21]. It comprises 8 learnable layers, 5 of which are convolutional, and the last 3 are fully-connected. The input image size is 224 × 224. Fast processing is ensured by the 4 pixel stride in the first convolutional layer. The main differences between this architecture and that of Krizhevsky are the reduced number of convolutional layers and the dense connectivity between convolutional layers (Krizhevsky used sparse connections to enable training on two GPUs). The network was trained on ILSVRC-2012 using gradient descent with momentum. The hyper-parameters are the same as used by Krizhevsky. The authors applied data augmentation in the form of random crops, horizontal flips, and RGB color jittering. We extracted the deep features from the 4 K dimensional feature vector after removing the last classification layer. The resulting vector is L2 normalized. The only image pre-processing consists on resizing the input images to the network input size and subtracting the average image (provided by the authors in the network metadata).

3.6   ImageNet VGG-verydeep-16 Features

This network is part of the evaluation of networks of increasing depth carried out by Simonyan and Zisserman [22] that proved to be very performant at the ImageNet 2014 challenge. The configuration is quite different from the ones used in the top-performing entries of the 2012 and 2013 competitions. Rather than using relatively large receptive fields in the first convolutional layers, they used very small 3 × 3 receptive fields throughout the whole net, which are convolved with the input at every pixel. More specifically, the convolution stride is fixed to 1 pixel; the spatial padding of convolutional layer input is such that the spatial resolution is preserved after convolution, i.e. the padding is 1 pixel for 3 × 3 convolutional layers. Spatial pooling is carried out by 5 max-pooling layers, which follow some of the convolutional layers (not all the convolutional layers are followed by max-pooling). Max-pooling is performed over a 2 × 2 pixel window, with stride 2. In total, the network we used has 13 convolutional layers and 3 FC. The only preprocessing we do is subtracting the mean RGB value of the input image. The 4 K features are collected from the last FC layer and L2 normalized.

3.7   DEX-IMDB-WIKI and DEX-ChaLearn-ICCV2015 Features

The Deep EXpectation (DEX) on apparent age method [23,24] uses the VGG-16 architecture for its networks, which are pre-trained on ImageNet for image classification. In addition, the authors explored the benefit of fine-tuning over crawled Internet face images with available age. In total, they collected more than 500,000 images of celebrities from IMDb and Wikipedia. The networks of DEX were fine-tuned on the crawled images and then on the provided images with apparent age annotations from the ChaLearn LAP 2015 challenge on apparent age estimation. We extracted the features provided by two networks: DEX-IMDB-WIKI and DEX-ChaLearn-ICCV2015. The first one was trained on real age estimation using the cropped and aligned faces of the IMDB-WIKI dataset, while the second one is a fine-tuned version of the previous model, trained on apparent age using the challenge images. An ensemble of these models led to 1st place at the challenge (115 teams). The 4 K features are collected from the previous to the last FC layer.

4   Experimental Setup

Our study concerns three hand-crafted features and five deep features. The deep features were obtained by pre-trained CNNs. Two CNNs were trained on images of objects for the purpose of image categorization (ImageNet VGG-F and ImageNet VGG-verydeep-16). One net was trained on face images for the purpose of face identification (VGG-Face). The last two nets (DEX-IMDB-WIKI and DEX-ChaLearn-ICCV2015) were trained on face images for the purpose of age estimation. One can also notice that the first one was trained on real ages and the second one was trained on apparent age. With regards to feature sizes, the LBP,

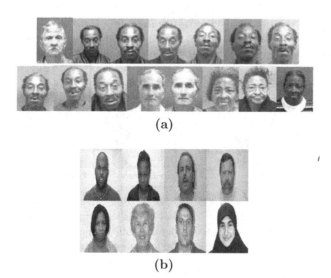

(a)

(b)

Fig. 2. Database images. (a) Sample images from MORPH II database. (b) Sample images from PAL database.

HOG and BSIF descriptors have 256, 832/1872/4212[1], and 256, respectively. All deep features are given by 4096 elements.

4.1 Datasets

In our study, two public datasets are used.

MORPH (Album 2). The MORPH (Album 2), or simply MORPH II, database from the University of North Carolina Wilmington [25] contains ~55,000 unique images of 13,618 individuals (11,459 male and 2,159 female) in the age range of 16 to 77 years old. The average number of images per individual is 4. The MORPH (Album 2) database can be divided into three main ethnicities: African (42,589 images), European (10,559 images) and other ethnicities (1,986 images). Some samples are illustrated in Fig. 2a. We use a 5-fold cross-validation evaluation, the folds are selected in such a way to prevent algorithms from learning the identity of the persons in the training set by making sure that all images of individual subjects are only in one fold at a time.

PAL. The Productive Aging Lab Face (PAL) database from the University of Texas at Dallas [26] contains 1,046 frontal face images from different subjects (430 males and 616 females) in the age range of 18 to 93 years old. The PAL database can be divided into three main ethnicities: African-American subjects (208 images), Caucasian subjects (732 images) and other subjects (106 images). The database images contain faces having different expressions. Some samples are illustrated in Fig. 2b. For the evaluation of the approach, we conduct again a 5-fold cross-validation. In the experiments, we considered three cases: (i) original images, (ii) aligned images with loose crop (face plus some background), and (iii) aligned/cropped images. These cases are illustrated in Fig. 3. The corresponding sizes are 230×350 pixels, 200×200 pixels, and 200×200 pixels, respectively.

Original PAL image   Face alignment   Face alignment
                        + loose cropping   + cropping

Fig. 3. Three types of PAL images. The left one is the original face image. The middle and right images correspond to the aligned and cropped face. The middle image correspond to a loose face cropping and the left one to a tight face cropping.

---

[1] For original and aligned MORPH II images and PAL images respectively.

4.2   Evaluation Protocol

Figure 4 illustrates the training and testing processes used for evaluating the performances of the eight face features. The procedure is the same whether the features are hand crafted or provided by the pre-trained CNNs. We used five-fold cross-validation that allows to test every test image in the considered database. In our experiments, we used the Partial Least Square (PLS) regressor [27]. This is a statistical method that retrieves relations between groups of observed variables X and Y through the use of latent variables. It is a powerful statistical tool which can simultaneously perform dimensionality reduction and classification/regression. It estimates new predictor variables, known as components, as linear combinations of the original variables, with consideration of the observed output values.

It is worthy to notice that, for deep features, the training phase concerns only the regressor. We use two measures that are very common in the literature

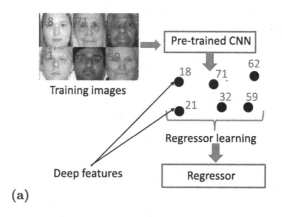

(a)

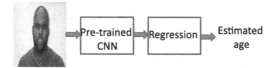

(b)

Fig. 4. (a) In the training phase, the training images are fed to a given pre-trained CNN in order to obtain the deep features. The deep features are used for learning an age regressor. (b) For a test face, the age is estimated by using the learned regressor using the corresponding deep features.

for evaluating the performance of automatic age estimators. The first measure is the Mean Age Error (MAE) (expressed in years) which is given by the average of absolute age error between the ground-truth ages and the predicted ones. The second measure is given by the Cumulative Score (CS). The Cumulative Score reflects the percentage of tested images for which the age estimation error is less than a threshold.

5   Experimental Results

Table 1 illustrates the MAE obtained on the MORPH II database using the eight face features. In this table, we considered two cases: original images and the aligned/cropped images. We can observe that with face alignment and cropping the performances obtained with the hand-crafted features have increased. This is very intuitive since the hand-crafted features need to focus on the face region

Table 1. Mean Age Error (years) obtained with different face features on MORPH II database.

Face features	Original images	Aligned+cropped
LBP	7.20	6.53
HOG	6.26	4.84
BSIF	7.34	6.69
VGG-FACE	4.72	4.79
IMAGENET-VGG-F	5.11	5.04
IMAGENET-VERY-DEEP-16	5.53	5.47
DEX-CHALEARN	**3.67**	4.77
DEX-IMDB-WIKI	3.77	**4.76**

Table 2. MAE (years) obtained with different state-of-the-art approaches on MORPH II database.

Publication	Approach	MAE (years)
Guo and Mu (2011) [28]	BIF[a]+KPLS[b]	4.2
Chang et al. (2011) [29]	BIF[a]	6.1
Geng et al. (2013) [30]	BIF[a]	4.8
Guo and Mu (2013) [31]	BIF[a]	4.0
Huerta et al. [3]	CNN[c]	3.9
Han et al. (2015) [16]	DIF[d]	**3.6**
Proposed scheme	Deep features+transfer	3.67

[a] Biologically Inspired Features.
[b] Kernel Partial Least Squares.
[c] Convolutional Neural Networks.
[d] Demographic Informative Features.

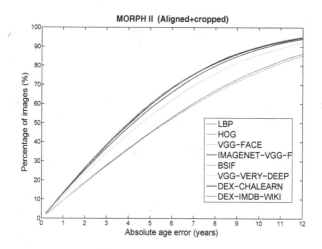

Fig. 5. Cumulative scores obtained with eight face features for MORPH II database (aligned and cropped images).

Table 3. Mean Age Error (years) obtained with different face features on PAL database.

Face features	Original images	Aligned+Loose crop	Aligned+crop
LBP	11.40	11.16	10.99
HOG	8.68	7.61	7.00
BSIF	10.71	11.26	10.09
VGG-FACE	5.91	5.13	5.23
IMAGENET-VGG-F	6.89	6.81	7.14
IMAGENET-VERY-DEEP-16	8.04	8.64	8.41
DEX-CHALEARN	**3.97**	**3.79**	5.12
DEX-IMDB-WIKI	4.04	**3.79**	**4.90**

only. On the other hand, for the last two deep features, the use of the original images provided better performance. This can be explained by the fact that these ones were trained on face images having significant background. Whether the original images or the aligned and cropped images were used, the deep features provided by DEX-IMDB-WIKI and DEX-ChaLearn-ICCV2015 nets provided the best performances. Moreover, we can observe that among deep features the best performances were obtained with nets that were trained on face images, i.e. VGG-Face, DEX-IMDB-WIKI and DEX-ChaLearn.

The performances of some state-of-the-art approaches are shown in Table 2. As can be seen, our deep feature results are comparable to the performance obtained by the work of Han *et al.* (2015) [16]. The latter uses coarse-to-fine and hierarchical age estimation via binary decision trees for classifying non-overlapping age groups and within-group age regressors. In our case, only one single regressor is used. Figure 5 represents the cumulative score associated with the eight face features. As can be seen, for some face features the cumulative scores are similar.

Table 3 illustrates the MEA obtained on the PAL database using the eight face features. In this table, we considered three cases: (i) original images, (ii) aligned images with loose crop (face plus some background), and (iii) aligned/cropped images. We can observe that with face alignment and cropping the performances obtained with the hand-crafted features have increased. The performances obtained by the last two deep features were the best for all three types of cropping. In general, the deep features gave their best results when loose cropping is adopted.

The performances of some state-of-the-art approaches are shown in Table 4. As can be seen, by adopting the proposed scheme, we got a significant improvement in performance. The best state-of-the art MAE was 5.4 years, whereas the best MAE obtained by our adopted scheme was 3.79 years. Figure 6 represents the cumulative score associated with the eight face features. As can be seen, for some face features the cumulative scores are very similar.

Table 4. Mean Age Error (years) obtained with different state-of-the art approaches on PAL database.

Publication	Approach	MAE
Gunay and Nabiyev (2016) [32]	AAM+GABOR+LBP	**5.4**
Nguyen *et al.* (2014) [33]	MLBP+GABOR+SVR	6.5
Bekhouche *et al.* (2014) [34]	LBP+BSIF+SVR	6.2
Choi *et al.* (2010) [35]	GHPF[a]+SVR	8.4
Luu *et al.* (2011) [2]	CAM[b]+SVR	6.0
Proposed scheme	Deep features+transfer	**3.79**

[a]Gaussian High Pass Filter.
[b]Contourlet Appearance Model.
[c]Multi-Quantized Local Binary Patterns.

Table 5. Mean Age Error (years) obtained with two deep CNNs on MORPH II database. For each CNN, the upper row illustrates the MEA obtained by applying the CNN as an end-to-end solution. The lower row depicts the MEA where the net is used to provide only the deep features.

CNN	Scheme	Original	Aligned+crop
DEX-CHALEARN	End-to-end	5.34	11.1
	Deep features	**3.67**	**4.77**
DEX-IMDB-WIKI	End-to-end	5.77	11.6
	Deep features	**3.77**	**4.76**

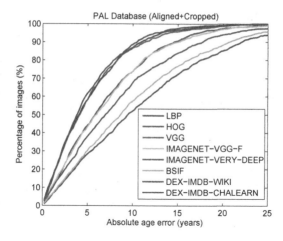

Fig. 6. Cumulative scores obtained with eight face features for PAL database (aligned and cropped images).

Table 6. Mean Age Error (years) obtained with two deep CNNs on PAL database.

CNN	Scheme	Original	Aligned+Loose crop	Aligned+crop
DEX-CHALEARN	End-to-end	7.12	5.43	8.53
	Deep features	**3.97**	**3.79**	**5.12**
DEX-IMDB-WIKI	End-to-end	6.99	4.72	7.98
	Deep features	**4.04**	**3.79**	**4.90**

Table 5 illustrates a comparison between the MAE of the end-to-end CNNs and that obtained by the use of deep features. The table corresponds to the MORPH II database with two different types of images. For each CNN, the upper row illustrates the MAE obtained by applying the net in order to estimate the age. The lower row depicts the MAE where the net is used to provide only the deep features. As can be seen, by adopting the deep features the obtained MAE was better than that of the end-to-end CNN. Table 6 illustrates a comparison between the MAE of the end-to-end CNNs and that obtained by the use of deep features for PAL database. The table corresponds to the database with three different types of images. We can observe a similar behavior to that obtained with the MORPH II database. This tends to confirm that by only retraining the regressor, we are able to transfer the power of the pre-trained CNN without having to retrain the whole network.

Table 7 illustrates the MEA as function of the number of latent component associated with the PLS regressor. We can observe that the use of 20 latent variables for almost all face features provided the best results.

Table 7. MEA as a function of the latent variables used by the Partial Least Square regressor. The results correspond to PAL database.

Features\nb. of PLS components	10	20	30	40
LBP	11.10	**10.84**	11.16	11.16
HOG	**7.02**	7.41	7.61	7.75
BSIF	11.33	**10.91**	11.26	11.34
VGG-FACE	**5.04**	5.07	5.13	5.14
IMAGENET-VGG-F	6.65	**6.45**	6.81	7.10
IMAGENET-VERY-DEEP-16	8.76	**8.54**	8.63	8.74
DEX-CHALEARN	3.79	**3.74**	3.79	3.87
DEX-IMDB-WIKI	3.84	**3.79**	3.79	3.94

6   Conclusion

The paper has addressed the issue of comparing several face features for the task of age estimation from facial images. In the study, we have considered three hand-crafted image features as well as five deep features provides by pre-trained CNNs. The comparison shown is the paper yields several conclusions. First, the solution adopted in the paper shows that efficient and stable age estimation can be obtained from deep features on the premise that the age regressor is retrained. The last process is by far more efficient than re-training the whole deep CNN on the new set of images. Second, the use of deep features gave better results than using hand-crafted features. Third, task accuracy obtained by deep features can be highly correlated to the deep net context (training imaged objects, training objective). Future work would investigate feature fusion provided by deep CNNs.

References

1. Fu, Y., Huang, T.S.: Human age estimation with regression on discriminative aging manifold. IEEE Trans. Multimedia **10**, 578–584 (2008)
2. Luu, K., Seshadri, K., Savvides, M., Bui, T.D., Suen, C.Y.: Contourlet appearance model for facial age estimation. In: 2011 International Joint Conference on Biometrics (IJCB), pp. 1–8 (2011)
3. Huerta, I., Fernández, C., Segura, C., Hernando, J., Prati, A.: A deep analysis on age estimation. Pattern Recogn. Lett. **68**(Pt. 2), 239–249 (2015). Special Issue on Soft Biometrics
4. Levi, G., Hassncer, T.: Age and gender classification using convolutional neural networks. In: 2015 IEEE Conference on Computer Vision and Pattern Recognition Workshops (CVPRW), pp. 34–42 (2015)
5. Ranjan, R., Zhou, S., Chen, J.C., Kumar, A., Alavi, A., Patel, V.M., Chellappa, R.: Unconstrained age estimation with deep convolutional neural networks. In: 2015 IEEE International Conference on Computer Vision Workshop (ICCVW), pp. 351–359 (2015)

6. Kwon, Y.H., da Vitoria Lobo, N.: Age classification from facial images. In: IEEE Conference on Computer Vision and Pattern Recognition, pp. 762–767 (1994)
7. Gunay, A., Nabiyev, V.V.: Automatic detection of anthropometric features from facial images. In: 2007 IEEE 15th Signal Processing and Communications Applications, pp. 1–4 (2007)
8. Cootes, T.F., Edwards, G.J., Taylor, C.J.: Active appearance models. IEEE Trans. Pattern Anal. Mach. Intell. **23**, 681–685 (2001)
9. Geng, X., Zhou, Z.H., Smith-Miles, K.: Automatic age estimation based on facial aging patterns. IEEE Trans. Pattern Anal. Mach. Intell. **29**, 2234–2240 (2007)
10. Guo, G., Mu, G., Fu, Y., Huang, T.S.: Human age estimation using bio-inspired features. In: Computer Vision Pattern Recognition (2009)
11. Bereta, M., Karczmarek, P., Pedrycz, W., Reformat, M.: Local descriptors in application to the aging problem in face recognition. Pattern Recogn. **46**, 2634–2646 (2013)
12. Dalal, N., Triggs, B.: Histograms of oriented gradients for human detection. In: IEEE Conference on Computer Vision and Pattern Recognition (2005)
13. Kannala, J., Rahtu, E.: BSIF: binarized statistical image features. In: 2012 21st International Conference on Pattern Recognition (ICPR), pp. 1363–1366 (2012)
14. Han, H., Jain, A.K.: Age, gender and race estimation from unconstrained face images. Technical report MSU-CSE-14-5, Department of Computer Science, Michigan State University, East Lansing, Michigan (2014)
15. Guo, G., Mu, G.: A framework for joint estimation of age, gender and ethnicity on a large database. Image Vis. Comput. **32**, 761–770 (2014). Best of Automatic Face and Gesture Recognition 2013
16. Han, H., Otto, C., Liu, X., Jain, A.K.: Demographic estimation from face images: Human vs. machine performance. IEEE Trans. Pattern Anal. Mach. Intell. **37**, 1148–1161 (2015)
17. Kazemi, V., Sullivan, J.: One millisecond face alignment with an ensemble of regression trees. In: IEEE Conference on Computer Vision and Pattern Recognition, pp. 1867–1874 (2014)
18. Ahonen, T., Hadid, A., Pietikainen, M.: Face description with local binary patterns: application to face recognition. IEEE Trans. Pattern Anal. Mach. Intell. **28**, 2037–2041 (2006)
19. Parkhi, O.M., Vedaldi, A., Zisserman, A.: Deep face recognition. In: British Machine Vision Conference, vol. 1, p. 6 (2015)
20. Chatfield, K., Simonyan, K., Vedaldi, A., Zisserman, A.: Return of the devil in the details: delving deep into convolutional nets. In: British Machine Vision Conference (2014)
21. Krizhevsky, A., Sutskever, I., Hinton, G.E.: Imagenet classification with deep convolutional neural networks. In: Advances in Neural Information Processing Systems, pp. 1097–1105 (2012)
22. Simonyan, K., Zisserman, A.: Very deep convolutional networks for large-scale image recognition. arXiv preprint arXiv:1409.1556 (2014)
23. Rothe, R., Timofte, R., Gool, L.V.: DEX: deep expectation of apparent age from a single image. In: IEEE International Conference on Computer Vision Workshops (ICCVW) (2015)
24. Rothe, R., Timofte, R., Gool, L.V.: Deep expectation of real and apparent age from a single image without facial landmarks. Int. J. Comput. Vis. (IJCV) (2016)
25. Ricanek, K., Tesafaye, T.: MORPH: a longitudinal image database of normal adult age-progression. In: 7th International Conference on Automatic Face and Gesture Recognition, FGR 2006, pp. 341–345 (2006)

26. Minear, M., Park, D.C.: A lifespan database of adult facial stimuli. Behav. Res. Methods Instrum. Comput. **36**, 630–633 (2004)
27. Rosipal, R., Krämer, N.: Overview and recent advances in partial least squares. In: Saunders, C., Grobelnik, M., Gunn, S., Shawe-Taylor, J. (eds.) SLSFS 2005. LNCS, vol. 3940, pp. 34–51. Springer, Heidelberg (2006). doi:10.1007/11752790_2
28. Guo, G., Mu, G.: Simultaneous dimensionality reduction and human age estimation via kernel partial least squares regression. In: IEEE Conference on Computer Vision and Pattern Recognition, pp. 657–664 (2011)
29. Chang, K.Y., Chen, C.S., Hung, Y.P.: Ordinal hyperplanes ranker with cost sensitivities for age estimation. In: IEEE Conference on Computer Vision and Pattern Recognition, pp. 585–592 (2011)
30. Geng, X., Yin, C., Zhou, Z.H.: Facial age estimation by learning from label distributions. IEEE Trans. Pattern Anal. Mach. Intell. **35**, 2401–2412 (2013)
31. Guo, G., Mu, G.: Joint estimation of age, gender and ethnicity: CCA vs. PLS. In: IEEE International Conference and Workshop on Automatic Face and Gesture Recognition, pp. 1–6 (2013)
32. Günay, A., Nabiyev, V.V.: Age Estimation Based on Hybrid Features of Facial Images. In: Abdelrahman, O.H., Gelenbe, E., Gorbil, G., Lent, R. (eds.) Information Sciences and Systems 2015. LNEE, vol. 363, pp. 295–304. Springer, Cham (2016). doi:10.1007/978-3-319-22635-4_27
33. Nguyen, D.T., Cho, S.R., Shin, K.Y., Bang, J.W., Park, K.R.: Comparative study of human age estimation with or without pre-classification of gender and facial expression. Sci. World J. **2014**, 15 (2014)
34. Bekhouche, S., Ouafi, A., Taleb-Ahmed, A., Hadid, A., Benlamoudi, A.: Facial age estimation using BSIF and LBP. In: International Conference on Electrical Engineering (2014)
35. Choi, S.E., Lee, Y.J., Lee, S.J., Park, K.R., Kim, J.: A comparative study of local feature extraction for age estimation. In: International Conference on Control Automation Robotics Vision, pp. 1280–1284 (2010)

Pose-Selective Max Pooling
for Measuring Similarity

Xiang Xiang[1][(✉)] and Trac D. Tran[2]

[1] Department of Computer Science, Johns Hopkins University,
3400 N. Charles St., Baltimore, MD 21218, USA
xxiang@cs.jhu.edu

[2] Department of Electrical and Computer Engineering, Johns Hopkins University,
3400 N. Charles St., Baltimore, MD 21218, USA

Abstract. In this paper, we deal with two challenges for measuring the similarity of the subject identities in practical video-based face recognition - the variation of the head pose in uncontrolled environments and the computational expense of processing videos. Since the frame-wise feature mean is unable to characterize the pose diversity among frames, we define and preserve the overall pose diversity and closeness in a video. Then, identity will be the only source of variation across videos since the pose varies even within a single video. Instead of simply using all the frames, we select those faces whose pose point is closest to the centroid of the K-means cluster containing that pose point. Then, we represent a video as a bag of frame-wise deep face features while the number of features has been reduced from hundreds to K. Since the video representation can well represent the identity, now we measure the subject similarity between two videos as the max correlation among all possible pairs in the two bags of features. On the official 5,000 video-pairs of the YouTube Face dataset for face verification, our algorithm achieves a comparable performance with VGG-face that averages over deep features of all frames. Other vision tasks can also benefit from the generic idea of employing geometric cues such as 3-D poses to improve the descriptiveness of deep features learned from appearances.

1 Introduction

In this paper, we are interested in measuring the similarity of one source of variation among videos such as the subject identity in particular. The motivation of this work is as followed. Given a face video visually affected by confounding factors such as the identity and the head pose, we compare it against another video by hopefully only measuring the similarity of the subject identity, even if the frame-level feature characterizes mixed information. Indeed, deep features from Convolutional Neural Networks (CNN) trained on face images with identity labels are generally not robust to the variation of the **head pose**, which refers to the face's relative orientation with respect to the camera and is the primary challenge in uncontrolled environments. Therefore, the emphasis of this paper is not the deep learning of frame-level features. Instead, we care about how to

© Springer International Publishing AG 2017
K. Nasrollahi et al. (Eds.): VAAM 2016/FFER 2016, LNCS 10165, pp. 113–126, 2017.
DOI: 10.1007/978-3-319-56687-0_10

improve the video-level representation's descriptiveness which rules out confusing factors (*e.g.*, pose) and induces the similarity of the factor (*e.g.*, identity).

If we treat the frame-level feature vector of a video as a random vector, we may assume that the highly-correlated feature vectors are identically distributed. When the task is to represent the whole image sequence instead of modeling the temporal dynamics such as the state transition, we may use the sample mean and variance to approximate the true distribution, which is implicitly assumed to be a normal distribution. While this assumption might hold given natural image statistics, it can be untrue for a particular video. Even if the features are Gaussian random vectors, taking the mean makes sense only if the frame-level feature just characterizes the identity. Because there is no variation of the identity in a video by construction. However, even the CNN face features still normally contain both the identity and the pose cues. Surely, the feature mean will still characterize both the identity and the pose. What is even worse, there is no way to decouple the two cues once we take the mean. Instead, if we want the video feature to only represent the subject identity, we had better preserve the overall pose diversity that very likely exists among frames. Disregarding minor factors, the identity will be the only source of variation across videos since pose varies even within a single video. Then, following such an disentangling variation idea, we propose a K frame selection algorithm which retains those key frames that preserve the pose diversity. Based on the selection, we further design an algorithm to compute the identity similarity between two sets of deep face features by pooling the max correlation.

Figure 1 shows an example video snippet lasting only a couple of seconds in the YouTube Face (YTF) dataset [23]. A 1-minute video at real time easily gets to two thousands frames. Why bother to send all of them to CNN when they look so similar? Instead of pooling from all the frames, the proposed K frame selection algorithm is highlighted at firstly the pose quantization via K-means and then the pose selection using the pose distances to the K-means centroids. It reduces the number of features from tens or hundreds to K while still preserving the overall pose diversity, which makes it possible to process a video stream at

Fig. 1. Example of the chosen key faces. Top row shows the first 10 frames of a 49-frame YTF sequence of Woody Allen, who looks right and down sometimes. And most of the time his face is slightly slanting. Bottom row are 9 frames selected according to the variation of 3D poses. Disclaimer: the source allows republishing the images.

real time. Thus, this algorithm also samples the video frames (to K images). Once the key frames are chosen, we will pool a single number of the similarity between two videos from many pairs of images. The metric to pool from many correlations normally are the mean or the max. Taking the max is essentially finding the nearest neighbor, which is a typical metric for measuring similarity or closeness of two point sets. In our work, the max correlation between two bags of frame-wise CNN features is employed to measure how likely two videos represent the same person. In the end, a video is represented by a single frame's feature which induces nearest neighbors between two sets of selected frames if we treat each frame as a data point. This is essentially a pairwise max pooling process. On the official 5000 video-pairs of YTF dataset [23], our algorithm achieves a comparable performance with state-of-the-art that averages over deep features.

2   Related Works

Key frame selection has been studied a lot in video-based face recognition, such as frame weighting [17,24], face clustering on Euclidean distances [12], clustering based on geodesic distances on manifolds (LLE [7], Isomap [6]), selection based on difference in face space and image quality [20], selection based on pose and motion blur [14]. In particular, a strategy of the same kind with ours is based on the distance between the class means [24].

The cosine similarity or correlation both are well-defined metrics for measuring the similarity of two images. A simple adaptation to videos will be randomly sampling a frame from each of the video. However, the correlation between two random image samples might characterize cues other than identity (say, the pose similarity). There are existing works on measuring the similarity of two videos using manifold-to-manifold distance [8]. However, the straightforward extension of image-based correlation is preferred for its simplicity, such as temporal max or mean pooling [15]. The impact of different spatial pooling methods in CNN such as mean pooling, max pooling and L-2 pooling, has been discussed in the literature [2,3]. However, pooling over the time domain is not as straightforward as spatial pooling. The frame-wise feature mean is a straightforward video-level representation and yet not a robust statistic. Despite that, temporal mean pooling is conventional to represent a video such as average pooling for video-level representation [1], mean encoding for face recognition [4], feature averaging for action recognition [5] and mean pooling for video captioning [22].

Measuring the similarity of subject identity is useful face recognition such as face verification for sure and face identification as well. Face verification is to decide whether two modalities containing faces represent the same person or two different people and thus is important for access control or re-identification tasks. Face identification involves one-to-many similarity, namely a ranked list of one-to-one similarity and thus is important for watch-list surveillance or forensic search tasks. In identification, we gather information about a specific set of individuals to be recognized (*i.e.*, the gallery). At test time, a new image or group of images is presented (*i.e.*, the probe).

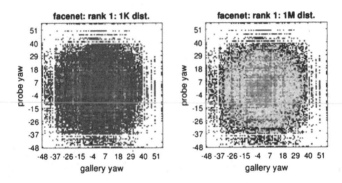

Fig. 2. Analysis of rank-1 identification under varying poses for Google's FaceNet [18] on the recently established MegaFace 1 million face benchmark [10]. Yaw is examined as it is the primary variation such as looking left/right inducing a profile. The colors represent identification accuracy going from 0 (blue, none of the true pairs were matched) to 1 (red, all possible combinations of probe and gallery were matched). White color indicates combinations of poses that did not exist in the test set. (a) 1 K distractors (people in the gallery yet not in the probe). (b) 1 M distractors. This figure is adapted from MegaFace's FaceScrub results (see http://megaface.cs.washington.edu/ results/facescrubresults.html#poseinvariance). (Color figure online)

In this deep learning era, face verification on a number of benchmarks such as the Labeled Face in the Wild (LFW) dataset [11] has been well solved by Deep-Face [21], DeepID [19], FaceNet [18] and so on. The Visual Geometry Group at the University of Oxford released their deep face model called VGG-Face Descriptor [13] which also gives a comparable performance on LFW. However in the real world, pictures are often taken in uncontrolled environment (the so-called in the wild versus in the lab setting). Considering the number of image parameters that were allowed to vary simultaneously, it is logical to consider a divide-and-conquer approach - studying each source of variation separately and keeping all other variations as constants in a control experiment. Such a separation of variables has been widely used in Physics and Biology for multivariate problems. In this data-driven machine learning era, it seems fine to remain all variations in realistic data, given the idea of letting the deep neural networks learn the variations existing in the enormous amount of data. For example, FaceNet [18] trained using a **private** dataset of over 200 M subjects is indeed robust to poses, as illustrated in Fig. 2. However, the CNN features from conventional networks suach as DeepFace [21] and VGG-Face [13] are normally not. Moreover, the unconstrained data with fused variations may contain biases towards factors other than identity, since the feature might characterize a mixed information of identity and low-level factors such as pose, illumination, expression, motion and background. For instance, pose similarities normally outweigh subject identity similarities, leading to matching based on pose rather than identity. As a result, it is critical to decouple pose and identity. If the facial expression confuses the identity as well, it is also necessary to decouple them too. In the paper, the face expression is not considered as it is minor compared with pose. Similarly, if we want to measure the similarity of the face expression, we need to decouple it from the identity. For example in [24] for identification, one class of training data are formed by face videos with the same expression yet across different people.

Moreover, there are many different application scenarios for face verifications. For Web-based applications, verification is conducted by comparing images to images. The images may be of the same person but were taken at different time or under different conditions. Other than the identity, high-level factors such as the age, gender, ethnicity and so on are not considered in this paper as they remain the same in a video. For online face verification, alive video rather than still images is used. More specifically, the existing video-based verification solutions assume that gallery face images are taken under controlled conditions [8]. However, gallery is often built uncontrolled. In practice, a camera could take a picture as well as capture a video. When there are more information describing identities in a video than an image, using a fully live video stream will require expensive computational resources. Normally we need video sampling or a temporal sliding window.

3   Pose Selection by Diversity-Preserving K-Means

In this section, we will explain our treatment particularly for real-world images with various head poses such as images in YTF. Many existing methods such as [24] make a certain assumption which holds only when faces are properly aligned.

By construction (say, face tracking by detection), each video contains a single subject. Each video is formalised as a set $\mathbb{V} = \{\mathbf{x}_1, \mathbf{x}_2, ..., \mathbf{x}_m\}$ of frames where each frame $\mathbf{x}_i$ contains a face. Given the homography $\mathbf{H}$ and correspondence of facial landmarks, it is entirely possible to estimate the 3D rotation angles (yaw, pitch and roll) for each 2D face frame. Concretely, some head pose estimator $p(\mathbb{V})$ gives a set $\mathbb{P} = \{\mathbf{p}_1, \mathbf{p}_2, ..., \mathbf{p}_m\}$ where p_i is a 3D rotation-angle vector $(\alpha_{yaw}, \alpha_{pitch}, \alpha_{roll})$.

After pose estimation, we would like to select key frames with significant head poses. Our intuition is to preserve pose diversity while downsampling the video in the time domain. We learn from Fig. 2 of Google's FaceNet that face features learned from a deep CNN trained on identity-labelled data can be invariant to head poses as long as the training inputs for a particular identity class include almost all possible poses. That is also true for other minor source of variations such as illumination, expression, motion, background among others. Then, identity will be the only source of variation across classes since any factor other than identity varies even within a single class.

Without such huge training data as Google has, we instead hope that the testing inputs for a particular identity class include poses as diverse as possible. A straightforward way is to use the full video, which indeed preserves all possible pose variations in that video while computing deep features for all the frames is computationally expensive. Taking representing a line in a 2D coordinate system as an example, we only needs either two parameters such as the intercept and

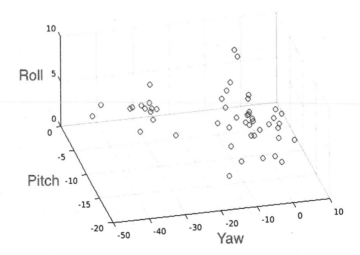

Fig. 3. An example of 3-D pose space. Shown for the 49-frame Woody Allen sequence in YTF. Three axises represent rotation angles of yaw (looking left or right), pitch (looking up or down) and roll (twisting left or right so that the face is slanting), respectively. The primary variation is the yaw such as turning left/right inducing a profile. Pattern exists in pose distribution - obviously two clusters for this sequence so in extreme case for reducing computation we can set $K = 2$.

gradient or any two points in that line. Similarly, now our problem becomes to find a compact pose representation which involves the following two criteria.

First, the pose representation is compact in terms of non-redundancy and closeness. For non-redundancy, we hope to retain as few frames as possible but this criterion is not super critical. For pose closeness, we observe from Fig. 3 that certain patterns exist in the head pose distribution - close points turn to cluster together. That observation occurs for other sequences as well. As a result, we want to select key frames out of a video by clustering the 3D head poses. The widely-used K-means clustering aims to partition the point set into K subsets so as to minimize the within-cluster Sum of Squared Distances (SSD). If we treat each cluster as a class, we want to minimize the intra-class or within-cluster distance.

Second, the pose representation is representative in terms of diversity (*i.e.*, difference, distance). Intuitively we want to retain the key faces that have poses as different as possible. If we treat each frame's estimated 3D pose as a point, then the approximate polygon formed by selected points should be as close to the true polygon formed by all the points as possible. We measure the diversity using the SSD between any two selected key points (SSD within the set formed by centroids if we use the them as key points). And we want to maximize such a inter-class or between-cluster distance.

Now, we put the criteria together in a single objective. There are a limited number of choices for K as we set its upper bound. Then, given a set $\mathbb{P} = \{\mathbf{p}_1, \mathbf{p}_2, ..., \mathbf{p}_m\}$ of pose observations, we aim to partition the m observations into K ($\leq m$) **disjoint** subsets $\mathbb{S} = \{\mathbb{S}_1, \mathbb{S}_2, ..., \mathbb{S}_K\}$ so as to minimize the within-cluster SSD as well as maximize the between-cluster SSD while still minimizing the number of clusters:

$$\min_{K,\mathbb{S}} \frac{SSD_{within}}{SSD_{between}} := \sum_{k=1}^{K} \frac{\sum_{i=1}^{m} \|\mathbf{p}_i - \mu_k\|^2}{\sum_{j=1, j\neq k}^{K} \|\mu_j - \mu_k\|^2} \tag{1}$$

where μ_j, μ_k is the mean of points in $\mathbb{S}_k, \mathbb{S}_k$, respectively. This objective differs from that of K-means only in considering between-cluster distance which makes it a bit similar with multi-class LDA (Linear Discriminant Analysis). However, it is still essentially K-means. To solve it, we do not really need alternative minimization because that K with a limited number of choices is empirically enumerated by cross validation. Once K is fixed, solving Eq. 1 follows a similar procedure of multi-class LDA while there is no mixture of classes or clusters because every point is hard-assigned to a single cluster as done in K-means. Theoretically it can be proven that the pose diversity (induced by Eq. 1's solution) $\sum_{k=1}^{K} \sum_{j=1, j\neq k}^{K} \|\mu_j - \mu_k\|^2 \geq \sum_{k=1}^{K} \sum_{j=1, j\neq k}^{K} \|\mathbf{r}_j - \mathbf{r}_k\|^2$ where $\mathbf{r}_k$ is K randomly sampled pose points which surely include the case given by the standard K-means $\min_{\mathbb{S}} \sum_{k=1}^{K} \sum_{i=1}^{m} \|\mathbf{p}_i - \mu_k\|^2$. The subsequent selection of key poses is straightforward (by the distances to K-means centroids). The selected key poses form a subset $\mathbb{P}_\Omega$ of $\mathbb{P}$ where Ω is a m-dimensional K-**sparse** impulse vector of binary values $1/0$ indicating whether the index is chosen or not, respectively.

The selection of frames will follow the index activation vector Ω as well. Such a selection reduces the number of images required to represent the face from tens or hundreds to K while preserving the pose diversity which is considered in the formation of clusters. Now we frontalize the chosen faces which is called face alignment or pose correction or normalization. All above operations are summarized in Algorithm 1.

Note that not all landmarks can be perfectly aligned. Priority is given to salient ones such as the eye center and corners, the nose tip, the mouth corners and the chin. Other properties such as symmetry are also preserved. For example, we mirror the detected eye horizontally. However, a profile will not be frontalized.

4 Pooling Max Correlation for Measuring Similarity

In this section, we explain our max correlation guided pooling from a set of deep face features and verify whether the selected key frames are able to well represent identity regardless of pose variation.

After face alignment, some feature descriptor, a function $f(\cdot)$, maps each corrected frame $\mathbf{x}_{(i)}^c$ to a $d \times 1$ feature vector $f(\mathbf{x}_{(i)}^c) \in \mathbb{R}^d$ with dimensionality d and unit Euclidean norm. Then the video is represented as a bag of normalized frame-wise CNN features $\mathbb{X} := \{\mathbf{f}_1, \mathbf{f}_2, ..., \mathbf{f}_K\} := \{f(\mathbf{x}_{(1)}^c), f(\mathbf{x}_{(2)}^c), ..., f(\mathbf{x}_{(K)}^c)\}$. We can also arrange the feature vectors column by column to form a matrix $\mathbf{X} = [\mathbf{f}_1|\mathbf{f}_2|...|\mathbf{f}_K]$. For example, the VGG-face network [13] has been verified to be able to produce features well representing the identity information. It has 24 layers including several stacked convolution-pooling layer, 2 fully-connected

---

Algorithm 1. K frame selection.

Input   : face video $\mathbb{V} = \{\mathbf{x}_1, \mathbf{x}_2, ..., \mathbf{x}_m\}$.
Output: pose-corrected down-sampled face video $\mathbb{V}_\Omega^c = \{\mathbf{x}_{(1)}^c, \mathbf{x}_{(2)}^c, ..., \mathbf{x}_{(K)}^c\}$.
(1) Landmark detection: detect facial landmarks per frame in $\mathbb{V}$ so that
correspondence between frames is known.
(2) Homography estimation: estimate an approximate 3D model (say,
homography $\mathbf{H}$) from the sequence of faces in $\mathbb{V}$ with known correspondence
from landmarks.
(3) Pose estimation: compute the rotation angles p_i for each frame using
landmark correspondence and obtain a set of sequential head poses
$\mathbb{P} = \{\mathbf{p}_1, \mathbf{p}_2, ..., \mathbf{p}_m\}$.
(4) Pose quantization: cluster $\mathbb{P}$ into K subsets $\mathbb{S}_1, \mathbb{S}_2, ..., \mathbb{S}_K$ by solving Eq. 1
with estimated pose centroids $\{\mathbf{c}_1, ..., \mathbf{c}_K\}$ which might be pseudo pose
(non-existing pose).
(5) Pose selection: for each cluster, compute the distances from each pose point
$\mathbf{p} \in \mathbb{S}_k$ to the pose centroid c_k and then select the closest pose point to
represent the cluster $\mathbb{S}_k$. The selected key poses form a subset $\mathbb{P}_\Omega$ of $\mathbb{P}$ where Ω
is the index activation vector.
(6) Face selection: follow Ω to select the key frames and form a subset
$\mathbb{V}_\Omega = \{\mathbf{x}_{(1)}, \mathbf{x}_{(2)}, ..., \mathbf{x}_{(K)}\}$ of $\mathbb{V}$ where $\mathbb{V}_\Omega \subset \mathbb{V}$.
(7) Face alignment: Warp the each face in $\mathbb{V}_\Omega$ according to $\mathbf{H}$ so that landmarks
are fixed to canonical positions.

---

layer and one softmax layer. Since the model was trained for face identification
purpose with respect to 2,622 identities, we use the output of the second last
fully-connected layer as the feature descriptor, which returns a 4,096-dim feature
vector for each input face.

Given a pair of videos $(\mathbb{V}_a, \mathbb{V}_b)$ of subject a and b respectively, we want to
measure the similarity between a and b. Since we claim the proposed bag of CNN
features can well represent the identity, instead we will measure the similarity
between two sets of CNN features $Sim(\mathbb{X}_a, \mathbb{X}_b)$ which is defined as the max
correlation among all possible pairs of CNN features, namely the max element
in the correlation matrix (see Fig. 4):

$$Sim(\mathbb{X}_a, \mathbb{X}_b) := \max_{n_a, n_b}(\mathbf{f}_{n_a}^a{}^T \cdot \mathbf{f}_{n_b}^b) = \max\left((\mathbf{X}_a{}^T\mathbf{X}_a)(:)\right) \qquad (2)$$

where $n_a = 1, 2, ..., K_a$ and $n_b = 1, 2, ..., K_b$. Notably, the notation (:) indicates
all elements in a matrix following the MATLAB convention. Now, instead of
comparing $m_a \times m_b$ pairs, with Sect. 3 we only need to compute $K_a \times K_b$ correlations, from which we further pool a single (1×1) number as the similarity
measure. In the time domain, it also serves as pushing from K images to just 1
image. The metric can be the mean, median, max or the majority from a histogram while the mean and max are more widely-used. The insight of not taking
the mean is that a frame highly correlated with another video usually does not
appear twice in a temporal sliding window. If we plot the two bags of features
in the common feature space, a similarity is essentially the closeness between

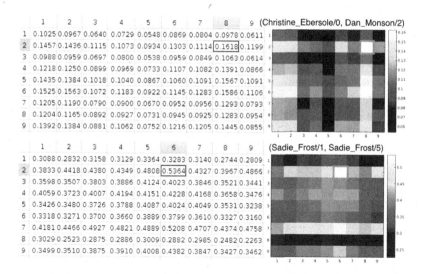

	1	2	3	4	5	6	7	8	9	(Christine_Ebersole/0, Dan_Monson/2)
1	0.1025	0.0967	0.0640	0.0729	0.0548	0.0869	0.0804	0.0978	0.0611	
2	0.1457	0.1436	0.1115	0.1073	0.0934	0.1303	0.1114	0.1618	0.1199	
3	0.0988	0.0959	0.0697	0.0800	0.0538	0.0959	0.0849	0.1063	0.0614	
4	0.1218	0.1250	0.0899	0.0969	0.0733	0.1107	0.1082	0.1391	0.0866	
5	0.1435	0.1384	0.1018	0.1040	0.0867	0.1060	0.1091	0.1567	0.1091	
6	0.1525	0.1563	0.1072	0.1183	0.0922	0.1145	0.1283	0.1586	0.1106	
7	0.1205	0.1190	0.0790	0.0900	0.0670	0.0952	0.0956	0.1293	0.0793	
8	0.1204	0.1165	0.0892	0.0927	0.0731	0.0945	0.0925	0.1283	0.0954	
9	0.1392	0.1384	0.0881	0.1062	0.0752	0.1216	0.1205	0.1445	0.0855	

	1	2	3	4	5	6	7	8	9	(Sadie_Frost/1, Sadie_Frost/5)
1	0.3088	0.2832	0.3158	0.3129	0.3364	0.3283	0.3140	0.2744	0.2809	
2	0.3833	0.4418	0.4380	0.4349	0.4808	0.5364	0.4327	0.3967	0.4866	
3	0.3598	0.3507	0.3803	0.3886	0.4124	0.4023	0.3846	0.3521	0.3441	
4	0.4059	0.3723	0.4007	0.4194	0.4151	0.4228	0.4168	0.3658	0.3476	
5	0.3426	0.3480	0.3726	0.3788	0.4087	0.4024	0.4049	0.3531	0.3238	
6	0.3318	0.3271	0.3700	0.3660	0.3889	0.3799	0.3610	0.3327	0.3160	
7	0.4181	0.4466	0.4927	0.4821	0.4889	0.5208	0.4707	0.4374	0.4758	
8	0.3029	0.2523	0.2875	0.2886	0.3009	0.2882	0.2985	0.2482	0.2263	
9	0.3499	0.3510	0.3875	0.3910	0.4008	0.4382	0.3847	0.3427	0.3462	

Fig. 4. Max pooling from the correlation matrix with each axis coordinates the time step in one video. Top row gives an example of different subjects while the bottom row shows that of the same person. Max responses are highlighted by boxes. Faces not shown due to copyright consideration.

the two sets of points. If the two sets are non-overlapping, one measure of the closeness between two points sets is the distance between nearest neighbors, which is essentially pooling the max correlation. Similar with spatial pooling for invariance, taking the max from the correlation matrix shown in Fig. 4 preserves the temporal invariance that the largest correlation can appear at any time step among the selected frames. Since the identity is consistent in one video, we can claim two videos contain a similar person as long as one pair of frames from each video are highly correlated. The computation of two videos' identity similarity is summarized in Algorithm 2.

Algorithm 2. Video-based identity similarity measurement.

Input   : A pair of face videos $\mathbb{V}_a$ and $\mathbb{V}_b$.
Output: The similarity score $Sim(\mathbb{X}_a, \mathbb{X}_b)$ of their subject identity.
(1) Face selection and alignment: run Algorithm 1 for each video to obtain key frames with faces aligned.
(2) Deep video representation: generate deep face features of the key frames to obtain two sets of features $\mathbb{X}_a$ and $\mathbb{X}_b$.
(3) Pooling max correlation: compute similarity $Sim(\mathbb{X}_a, \mathbb{X}_b)$ according ro Eq. 2.

---

5   Experiments

5.1   Implementation

We develop the programs using OpenCV, DLib and VGG-Face[1].

- Face detection: frame-by-frame detection using DLib's HOG+SVM based detector trained on 3,000 cropped face images from LFW. It works better for faces in the wild than OpenCV's cascaded haar-like+boosting based detector.
- Facial landmark: DLib's model trained via regression tree ensemble.
- Head pose estimation: OpenCV's solvePnP recovering 3D coordinates from 2D using Direct Linear Transform + Levenberg-Marquardt optimization.
- Face alignment: OpenCV's warpAffine by warping to center eyes and mouth.
- Deep face representation[2]: second last layer output (4,096-dim) of VGG-Face [13] using Caffe [9]. For your conveniece, you may consider using MatConvNet-VLFeat instead of Caffe. VGG-Face has been trained using face images of size 224×224 with the average face image subtracted and then is used for our verification purpose without any re-training. However, such average face subtraction is unavailable and unnecessary given a new inputting image. As a result, we directly input the face image to VGG-Face network without any mean face subtraction.

5.2   Evaluation on Video-Based Face Verification

For video-based face recognition database, EPFL captures 152 people facing web-cam and mobile-phone camera in controlled environments. However, they are frontal faces and thus of no use to us. University of Surrey and University of Queensland capture 295 and 45 subjects under various well-quantized poses in controlled environments, respectively. Since the poses are well quantized, we can hardly verify our pose quantization and selection algorithm on them. McGill and NICTA capture 60 videos of 60 subjects and 48 surveillance videos of 29 subjects in uncontrolled environments, respectively. However, the database size are way too small. YouTube Faces (YTF) dataset (YTF) and India Mvie Face Database (IMFDB) collect 3,425 videos of 1,595 people and 100 videos of 100 actors in uncontrolled environments, respectively. There are quite a few existing work verified on IMFDB. As a result, the YTF dataset[3] [23] is chosen to verify the proposed video-based similarity measure for face verification. YTF was built by using the 5,749 names of subjects included in the LFW dataset [11] to search YouTube for videos of these same individuals. Then, a screening process reduced the original set of videos from the 18,899 of 3,345 subjects to 3,425 videos of 1,595 subjects.

---

[1] http://opencv.org/, http://dlib.net/ and http://www.robots.ox.ac.uk/~vgg/software/vgg_face/, respectively.

[2] Codes are available at https://github.com/eglxiang/vgg_face.

[3] Dataset is available at http://www.cs.tau.ac.il/~wolf/ytfaces/.

Fig. 5. Examples of YFT video-pairs. Instead of using the full video in the top row, we choose key faces in the bottom row. Disclaimer: this figure is adapted from VGG-face's presentation (see also http://www.robots.ox.ac.uk/~vgg/publications/2015/Parkhi15/presentation.pptx) and follows VGG-face's republishing permission.

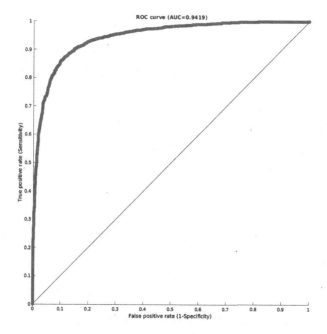

Fig. 6. ROC curve of running our algorithm on the YTF initial official list of 5,000 pairs.

In the same way with LFW, the creator of YTF provides an initial official list of 5,000 video pairs with ground truth (same person or not as shown in Fig. 5). Our experiments can be replicated by following our tutorial[4]. $K = 9$ turns to be averagely the best for the YTF dataset. Figure 6 presents the Receiver Operating Characteristic (ROC) curve obtained after we compute the 5,000 video-video similarity scores. One way to look at a ROC curve is to first fix the level of false positive rate that we can bear (say, 0.1) and then see how high is the true positive

---

[4] Codes with a tutorial at https://github.com/eglxiang/ytf.

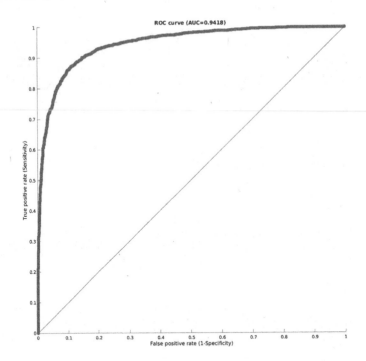

Fig. 7. ROC curve of running our algorithm on the YTF corrected official list of 4,999 video pairs.

rate (say, roughly 0.9). Another way is to see how close the curve towards the top-left corner. Namely, we measure the Area Under the Curve (AUC) and hope it to be as large as possible. In this testing, **the AUC is 0.9419 which is quite close to VGG-Face [13] which uses temporal mean pooling**. However, our selective pooling strategy have much fewer computation credited to the key face selection. We do run cross validations here as we do not have any training.

Later on, the creator of YTF sends a list of errors in the ground-truth label file and provides a corrected list of video pairs with updated ground-truth labels. As a result, we run again the proposed algorithm on the corrected 4,999 video pairs. Figure 7 updates the ROC curve with an AUC of 0.9418 which is identical with the result on the initial list.

6   Conclusion

In this work, we propose a K frame selection algorithm and an identity similarity measure which employs simple correlations and no learning. It is verified on fast video-based face verification on YTF and achieves comparable performance with VGG-face. Particularly, the selection and pooling significantly reduce the computational expense of processing videos. The further verification of the proposed algorithm include the evaluation of video-based face expression recognition. As shown in Fig. 5 of [24], the assumption of group sparsity might not hold under imperfect alignment. The extended Cohna-Kanade dataset include mostly well-aligned frontal faces and thus is not suitable for our research purpose. Our further experiments are being conducted on the BU-4DFE database[5] which contains 101 subjects, each one displaying 6 acted facial expressions with moderate head pose variations. A generic problem underneath is variable disentanglement in real data and a take-home message is that employing geometric cues can improve the descriptiveness of deep features.

References

1. Abu-El-Haija, S., Kothari, N., Lee, J., Natsev, P., Toderici, G., Varadarajan, B., Vijayanarasimhan, S.: Youtube-8m: a large-scale video classification benchmark. arXiv: 1609.08675, September 2016
2. Boureau, Y.L., Bach, F., LeCun, Y., Ponce, J.: Learning mid-level features for recognition. In: Proceedings of the IEEE Conference on Computer Vision and Pattern Recognition (2010)
3. Boureau, Y.L., Ponce, J., LeCun, Y.: A theoretical analysis of feature pooling in visual recognition. In: Proceedings of the International Conference on Machine Learning (2010)
4. Crosswhite, N., Byrne, J., Parkhi, O.M., Stauffer, C., Cao, Q., Zisserman, A.: Template adaptation for face verification and identification. arxiv, April 2016. https://arxiv.org/abs/1603.03958
5. Donahue, J., Hendricks, L.A., Guadarrama, S., Rohrbach, M., Venugopalan, S., Saenko, K., Darrell, T.: Long-term recurrent convolutional networks for visual recognition and description. In: Proceedings of the IEEE Conference on Computer Vision and Pattern Recognition, pp. 2625–2634 (2015)
6. Fan, W., Yeung, D.-Y.: Face recognition with image sets using hierarchically extracted exemplars from appearance manifolds. In: 7th International Conference on Automatic Face and Gesture Recognition, pp. 177–182. IEEE (2006)
7. Hadid, A., Pietikainen, M.: Selecting models from videos for appearance-based face recognition. In: Proceedings of the 17th International Conference on Pattern Recognition, ICPR 2004, vol. 1, pp. 304–308. IEEE (2004)
8. Huang, Z., Shan, S., Wang, R., Zhang, H., Lao, S., Kuerban, A., Chen, X.: A benchmark and comparative study of video-based face recognition on COX face database, IEEE Trans. Image Process. **24**, 5967–5981 (2015)
9. Jia, Y., Shelhamer, E., Donahue, J., Karayev, S., Long, J., Girshick, R., Guadarrama, S., Darrell, T.: Caffe: convolutional architecture for fast feature embedding. arXiv:1408.5093 (2014)
10. Kemelmacher-Shlizerman, I., Seitz, S.M., Miller, D., Brossard, E.: The megaface benchmark: 1 million faces for recognition at scale. In: Proceedings of the IEEE Conference on Computer Vision and Pattern Recognition (2016)
11. Learned-Miller, E., Huang, G.B., RoyChowdhury, A., Li, H., Hua, G.: Labeled faces in the wild: a survey. Advances in Face Detection and Facial Image Analysis, pp. 189–248 (2016)

---

[5] http://www.cs.binghamton.edu/~lijun/Research/3DFE/3DFE_Analysis.html.

12. Mian, R.: Unsupervised learning from local features for video-based face recognition. In: 8th IEEE International Conference on Automatic Face & Gesture Recognition, FG 2008, pp. 1–6. IEEE (2008)
13. Parkhi, O.M., Vedaldi, A., Zisserman, A.: Deep face recognition. In: British Machine Vision Conference (2015)
14. Park, U. Jain, A. K., Ross, A.: Face recognition in video: Adaptive fusion of multiple matchers. In: IEEE Conference on Computer Vision and Pattern Recognition, CVPR 2007, pp. 1–8. IEEE (2007)
15. Pigou, L., van den Oord, A., Dieleman, S., Herreweghe, M.V., Dambre, J.: Beyond temporal pooling: recurrence and temporal convolutions for gesture recognition in video. arxiv, June 2015. https://arxiv.org/abs/1506.01911
16. Schroff, F., Kalenichenko, D., Philbin, J.: FaceNet: a unified embedding for face recognition and clustering. In: Proceedings of the IEEE International Conference on Computer Vision (2015)
17. Stallkamp, J., Ekenel, H.K., Stiefelhagen, R.: Video-based face recognition on real-world data. In: IEEE 11th International Conference on Computer Vision, ICCV 2007, pp. 1–8. IEEE (2007)
18. Sun, Y., Chen, Y., Wang, X., Tang, X.: Deep learning face representation by joint identification-verification. In: Advances in Neural Information Processing Systems (2014)
19. Taigman, Y., Yang, M., Ranzato, M., Wolf, L.: DeepFace: closing the gap to human-level performance in face verification. In: Proceedings of the IEEE International Conference on Computer Vision (2014)
20. Thomas, D., Bowyer, K.W., Flynn, P.J.: Multi-frame approaches to improve face recognition. In: IEEE Workshop on Motion and Video Computing, WMVC 2007, IEEE (2007)
21. Venugopalan, S., Xu, H., Donahue, J., Rohrbach, M., Mooney, R., Saenko, K.: Translating videos to natural language using deep recurrent neural networks. In: Proceedings of the Annual Conference of the North American Chapter of the Association for Computational Linguistics: Human Language Technologies (2014)
22. Wolf, L., Hassner, T., Maoz, I.: Face recognition in unconstrained videos with matched background similarity. In: Proceedings of the IEEE Conference on Computer Vision and Pattern Recognition (2011)
23. Xiang, X., Dao, M., Hager, G.D., Tran, T.D.: Hierarchical sparse and collaborative low-rank representation for emotion recognition. In: IEEE International Conference on Acoustics, Speech and Signal Processing (ICASSP), pp. 3811–3815. IEEE (2015)
24. Zhang, Y., Martinez, A.M.: A weighted probabilistic ap-proach to face recognition from multiple images and videosequences. Image Vis. Comput. **24**(6), 626–638 (2006)

Complementing SRCNN by Transformed Self-Exemplars

Andreas Aakerberg[✉], Christoffer B. Rasmussen[✉], Kamal Nasrollahi[✉], and Thomas B. Moeslund[✉]

Visual Analysis of People (VAP) Laboratory, Aalborg University, Aalborg, Denmark
{aaaker11,cbra12}@student.aau.dk, {kn,tbm}@create.aau.dk

Abstract. Super-resolution algorithms are used to improve the quality and resolution of low-resolution images. These algorithms can be divided into two classes of hallucination- and reconstruction-based ones. The improvement factors of these algorithms are limited, however, previous research [9,10] has shown that combining super-resolution algorithms from these two different groups can push the improvement factor further. We have shown in this paper that combining super-resolution algorithms of the same class can also push the improvement factor up. For this purpose, we have combined two hallucination based algorithms, namely the one found in Single Image Super-Resolution from Transformed Self-Exemplars [7] and the Super-Resolution Convolutional Neural Network from [4]. The combination of these two, through an alpha-blending, has resulted in a system that outperforms state-of-the-art super-resolution algorithms on public benchmark datasets.

Keywords: Super-Resolution · Convolutional Neural Network · Self-Exemplars

1 Introduction

Cameras have become an increasing part of everyday life, and they are used for anything between astronomy, microscopy and surveillance. In some occasions the quality of the images delivered from the respective camera is too low and an enhancement is needed. An example is the video feed from surveillance cameras, which can be used for different purposes, but are mainly of interest in the occasion of robbery, vandalism or other illegal acts. If the quality of the recorded material is high, it may assist the police in identifying criminals. However, the output quality of the video cameras is often compromised due to factors such as a wide field-of-view, limited resolution, compression artefacts and poor lighting conditions. Due to this, it can be difficult to recognise individual faces in the images captured by the cameras, which decreases the usability of the recorded footage. This is problematic, as the face is a key biometric when performing person authentication.

A way to solve this problem is to update the currently installed cameras with better hardware, install more of the present hardware or a combination of

© Springer International Publishing AG 2017
K. Nasrollahi et al. (Eds.): VAAM 2016/FFER 2016, LNCS 10165, pp. 127–136, 2017.
DOI: 10.1007/978-3-319-56687-0_11

both. However, these can be expensive methods compared to a software solution. Enhancing the quality and spatial resolution of the images from the already installed surveillance cameras using a SR method, may be sufficient to make identification of the faces possible. Besides increasing the image quality to assist the human perception a study also found that performing SR can be helpful in order to improve performance of a number of other computer vision tasks such as scene recognition and edge detection [3].

Work by [9,10] has shown that combining different SR algorithms can be beneficial. As there is a large selection of SR algorithms, whether it is single or multiple image methods, these vary in regards to how the SR image is created. Therefore by combining methods that vary significantly, positive aspects of both can be merged. Generally SR falls within two categories, using either a single or multiple LR images to create a HR image. Often known as hallucination and reconstruction methods respectively [11]. Current state-of-the-art SR methods are within the deep learning domain using CNN. The method of CNN originally dates back to 1979 [5] but until recently it has not been dormant due to long training times. However, through the possibilities brought forth by GPU computing, training a CNN has become much more efficient and the method is state-of-the-art across multiple domains within computer vision and image processing. Namely, the SRCNN algorithm of [4] showed that with the advances in training of CNN it is possible to learn the filters and biases through back-propagation to produce an end-to-end mapping between a LR and HR from an external set of images. This algorithm is one of the state-of-the-art SR algorithms. We show in this paper, that the performance of this algorithm can be improved if it is complemented with a dictionary based algorithm like the SelfEx which is a single hallucination based SR algorithm [7]. SelfEx creates an internal dictionary across a number of different scales from which a HR patch can be created. This aims to take advantage of the fractal nature of natural images where patterns reoccur at different scales.

In this work SR is performed using two different hallucination based SR algorithms of SRCNN in [4] and SelfEx in [7]. SR is only performed on the Y (luminance) component of the YCbCr space, and the quality of the alpha blended HR images is evaluated using quantitative methods on a number of testing sets. Including both publicly available test sets commonly used within SR research, and sets made for the face recognition scenario set out in this paper.

The rest of this paper is organized as follows: the related work in the literature is reviewed in the next section. Then, in Sect. 3, the proposed method for combining the two mentioned algorithms is explained. Section 4, reports the obtained experimental results. Finally, Sect. 5 concludes the paper.

2   Related Work

Much work has been done on SR algorithms since the early proposals in the seventies which was based on optimisations performed in the frequency domain [6]. Current research is mostly within hallucination based SR methods relying on deep-learning networks.

In [10] reconstruction and recognition-based SR algorithms is combined in order to improve face recognition. Here key-frames in video is selected based on face quality and enhanced with the hybrid SR. In [9] alpha-blending of a HR image created by a CNN based SR algorithm and a bicubic upscaled counterpart is performed to create HR video for better action recognition.

In [4] the SR algorithm aims to learn the relationship between a LR image and its HR counterpart using a CNN. The actual learning is done between LR and HR patches by solving the regression problem of finding a mapping that resembles the transition from a LR patch to the corresponding HR patch given by

$$X \approx F(Y), \tag{1}$$

where X is the ground truth image, Y is the LR input and $F(Y)$ is the LR to HR mapping function. The learned model can then be used to predict missing HR details of any LR image during testing. However, the actual process of achieving a higher spatial resolution is not performed directly in the CNN, but rather in a pre-processing step using bicubic interpolation.

The SRCNN consists of three layers where the first layer of the network convolves patches from the LR image with filters, such that the image becomes represented by activation maps. This layer is denoted as the patch extraction and representation layer and can be expressed as:

$$F_1(Y) = max(0, \ W_1 * Y + B_1), \tag{2}$$

where the $*$ symbol represents the convolution operation and $F_1(Y)$, W_1, B_1 are the activation maps, weights and biases for the first layer, respectively.

In the second layer another set of convolutional operations are applied to patches of the activation maps. By convolving the corresponding patches from all the activation maps with their respective filters and summing the results, a new set of activation maps are created. This layer performs a non-linear mapping given as:

$$F_2(Y) = max(0, W_2 * F_1(Y) + B_2). \tag{3}$$

In the last layer, the reconstruction layer, yet another convolutional operation is applied to the activation maps. The results are summed and averaged to find the respective pixels of each position in the resulting HR image, which, in the best case, should be similar to the ground truth. This operation can be expressed as:

$$F(Y) = W_3 * F_2(Y) + B_3. \tag{4}$$

Throughout the convolutional layers the features are continually built from the activation maps from low to high level features, i.e. the first layers contains generic features such as edges while deeper layers contains more complex features.

Another method for SR in the hallucination based category which creates HR images without the use of any extensive external LR-HR learning is the SelfEx [7]. Rather, for a given image, an internal dictionary is created that can be used to take advantage of the fractal properties often present in natural images.

With the use of this a number of different scales can be created for a given LR image from which a potential HR patch result can be found. The internal dictionary searches across the different scales for an optimal match for a given LR patch. This method of internal dictionary search is coined self-exemplars (SelfEx). Typically internal systems only search for matches by translating across images, however, this can be an issue in images due to issues such as change in shape, orientation, and potential perspective distortion. Therefore SelfEx takes this into account when searching for a HR match and calculates a transformation matrix accordingly for the extra degrees-of-freedom.

As described in [7] the general overview of creating a HR image with the SelfEx method for a given LR image I is as follows:

1. Blur and subsample I to create a downsampled image I_D.
2. For each patch P in I, find the homography that warps P to the best patch match Q in I_D.
3. From Q, find the patch Q_H from the LR image I. This is the HR patch from the original LR image.
4. With the inverse of the homography found in step 2, unwarp the patch Q_H to find the estimated HR patch P_H. Place P_H at corresponding position to P in the resulting HR image I_H.
5. Repeat steps 2–4 for all patches in I until the SR image is created.
6. Finally, run the iterative backprojection method such that I_H satisfies the reconstruction constraint for the given image I.

3   The Proposed Method

The purpose of this work is to investigate whether two different hallucination based SR algorithms can complement each other in order to increase general SR performance. We have intentionally chosen to blend algorithms which are known to have different super-resolution performance on certain types of images. The SRCNN is generally known to perform well on diverse images while the SelfEx has higher performance on images with repeating patterns, such as e.g. architectural images. This actual blending of the two algorithms is done by alpha-blending the super-resolved outputs from the two algorithms as seen in Eq. 5:

$$\beta = \alpha \cdot S_1 + ((1 - \alpha) \cdot S_2) \tag{5}$$

where α is the blend coefficient, S_1 and S_2 are the output images of the two SR algorithms and β is the alpha blended output image.

The optimal blend percentage for a given test set is found by iteratively changing the blend percentage of the two SR algorithms in steps of 1, from 0 to 100 while evaluating the change in PSNR. This evaluation is then averaged over a number of different test-sets in order to settle on a blend percentage which can be used more generally. The final blend percentage α_{final} is determined by taking the average value of the optimal blend percentages of all test-sets as seen in Eq. 6:

$$\alpha_{final} = \frac{1}{n} \cdot \sum_{i=1}^{n} \alpha_i \tag{6}$$

where α_i is the optimal blend percentage for dataset i.

4   Experimental Results and Discussion

4.1   Datasets

As no re-training is performed in this work, the following datasets is used both to find the optimal blend percentage and evaluate the results. These datasets are the Set5 [2], Set14 [14], BSD100 [8], URBAN100 [7], 50 images from both the AR Face Database [1] and the Siblings Face Database [12]. These datasets have been chosen as they contain a wide variety of images, and are all commonly used to evaluate state-of-the-art SR algorithms. The face specific datasets are included to evaluate the performance of the proposed SR on face images, to see if the algorithm can perform better or worse for class-specific objects.

4.2   The Obtained Results

The results will be assessed and compared to state-of-the-art SR algorithms using both the PSNR and Structural Similarity (SSIM) measures. Even though a high score in these measures does not necessarily correlate with the most visually pleasing result, they are used due to their near de-facto standard for comparison of SR algorithm performance. The PSNR is an objective full reference method which uses Mean Squared Error (MSE), but overcomes the intensity sensitivity problem of MSE, by scaling the MSE according to the dynamic range of the image. PSNR expresses the ratio between the LR image A and the HR image B in decibels and is defined as:

$$PSNR(A, B) = 10 \log_{10} \frac{MAX_B^2}{MSE(A, B)}, \tag{7}$$

where MAX_B is the maximum pixel value of the HR image.

The SSIM model is based on image degradation as perceived change in structural information, luminance and contrast which makes this method superior to MSE and PSNR according to [13]. The SSIM index is calculated as:

$$SSIM(A, B) = \frac{(2\mu_A\mu_B + c_1)(2\sigma_{AB} + c_2)}{(\mu_A^2 + \mu_B^2 + c_1)(\sigma_A^2 + \sigma_B^2 + c2)}, \tag{8}$$

where:

μ_A is the average of A, μ_B is the average of B, σ_A^2 is the variance of A, σ_B^2 is the variance of B, σ_{AB} is the covariance of A and B and c_1 and c_2 are stabilising variables utilising dynamic range of pixel values.

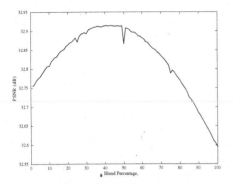 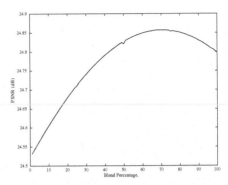

Fig. 1. Change in PSNR on Set5 ×3 for different values of α.

Fig. 2. Change in PSNR on URBAN100 ×4 for different values of α.

4.3   Blend Percentage

Figures 1 and 2 illustrates examples of how the PSNR changes as the two algorithms are blended. In all experiments a blend percentage of 0% indicates use of only the SRCNN HR image, while 100% denotes using only the SelfEx HR image. In specific cases where one algorithm is significantly better than the other, the blend percentage will be in either the high or low end, which is visible on Fig. 2. Here the blend percentage is rather high, to the favour of SelfEx, which is due to the SelfEx algorithms high performance on architectural images found in the URBAN100 dataset. However even though the SelfEx algorithm outperforms the SRCNN on this specific dataset (PSNR 24.80 vs. 24.52 on scale ×4) the optimal blend percentage for this dataset does not become higher than 72%, which indicates that the output from SRCNN can still contribute with valuable pixel information when blending. The slight drop in PNSR which can be seen in Figs. 1 and 2 at α=50 is also existent on the remaining datasets. The cause of this does however require further investigation, which has not been conducted in this work.

By evaluating the PSNR performance when blending from 0 – 100% on all the six test-sets in three different scaling factors and averaging the results, we found the best blend percentage to be 47% SelfEx and 53% SRCNN. This is of course a compromise as the optimal blend percentage varies from each dataset. The results, measured in PSNR and SSIM when using a blend percentage of 47%, and the individual optimal blend values for each test-set can be seen in the following section.

4.4   Comparison with State-of-the-Art

All super-resolved images are created with implementations of the SR algorithms provided by the respective authors. However, in order to be able to blend and compare the super-resolved images from the two algorithms, the images must be of the same dimension. As the SRCNN slightly crop the final HR image, due to the border problem associated with the convolutional operations, and the SelfEx does not, the images can not directly be blended or compared. We solve this issue by cropping the SelfEx HR images, such that these becomes of the same dimensionality as the SRCNN HR and ground truth image.

Table 1 shows the average results for three different up-scaling levels for a number of different test datasets. Note that the values in this table cannot be directly compared to the ones found in the work of [7], as they did not crop the HR images. Our methods improves the PSNR performance on all evaluated datasets when using the empirically found blend value of 47%.

Table 1. Average performance of our method compared to state-of-the-art methods. Red color indicates the best performance and blue color indicates the second best performance, excluding results produced with the optimal blend percentage.

Dataset	Scale	Bicubic PSNR/SSIM	A+ PSNR/SSIM	SelfEx PSNR/SSIM	SRCNN PSNR/SSIM	Our method using optimal blend percentage PSNR/SSIM/Blend %	Our method using fixed 47% blending PSNR/SSIM
Set5	×2	33.66/0.9299	36.54/0.9544	36.47/0.9533	36.66/0.9541	36.84/0.9548/47	36.84/0.9548
	×3	30.39/0.8677	32.59/0.9088	32.59/0.9077	32.75/0.9081	32.92/0.9106/43	32.91/0.9107
	×4	28.42/0.8099	30.28/0.8603	30.34/0.8606	30.48/0.8618	30.70/0.8669/43	30.69/0.8670
Set14	×2	30.23/0.8689	32.28/0.9056	32.22/0.9035	32.45/0.9066	32.57/0.9071/36	32.56/0.9069
	×3	27.54/0.7741	29.13/0.8188	29.15/0.8200	29.29/0.8217	29.40/0.8238/40	29.40/0.8238
	×4	26.00/0.7025	27.32/0.7491	27.38/0.7521	27.50/0.7518	27.63/0.7561/41	27.62/0.7564
BSD100	×2	29.32/0.8349	30.64/0.8782	30.98/0.8831	30.89/0.8795	31.18/0.8865/52	31.17/0.8863
	×3	27.15/0.7380	28.11/0.7817	28.28/0.7874	28.28/0.7842	28.41/0.7897/49	28.41/0.7896
	×4	25.92/0.6693	26.68/0.7084	26.84/0.7150	26.84/0.7108	26.96/0.7173/49	26.96/0.7171
URBAN100	×2	26.56/0.8382	29.20/0.8941	29.30/0.9026	29.13/0.8968	29.46/0.9033/60	29.45/0.9026
	×3	24.46/0.7354	26.03/0.7980	26.46/0.8095	26.24/0.7997	26.53/0.8099/66	26.50/0.8086
	×4	23.14/0.6583	24.32/0.7193	24.80/0.7386	24.52/0.7236	24.86/0.7392/72	24.82/0.7366
AR Face DB	×2	37.16/0.9680	40.02/0.9795	39.85/0.9789	39.90/0.9789	40.15/0.9795/48	40.15/0.9795
	×3	33.52/0.9292	35.67/0.9480	35.65/0.9492	35.83/0.9487	36.06/ 0.9511/44	36.06/0.9511
	×4	31.12/0.8850	32.88/0.9086	32.77/0.9098	32.95/0.9077	33.23/0.9133/43	33.23/0.9135
Siblings Face DB	×2	34.79/0.9087	36.29/0.9388	36.17/0.9276	36.28/0.9290	36.32/0.9290/33	36.32/0.9289
	×3	32.62/0.8614	33.77/0.8916	33.66/0.8793	33.70/0.8800	33.78/0.8808/48	33.78/0.8807
	×4	31.36/0.8317	32.36/0.8626	32.23/0.8487	32.26/0.8483	32.37/0.8503/48	32.36/0.8502

Figures 3, 4, 5, 6 and 7 show visual comparisons of different algorithms compared against the proposed method in this paper on different test images. The PSNR/SSIM values is included in the figure captions. As it can in these comparisons, the images produced by our method are slightly more visually pleasing. There is however still some images which does not benefit from blending, like it is the case with the Butterfly image from Set5 seen in butterfly.

4.5   Discussion

The results do not indicate that alpha-blending the two SR algorithms increase SR performance in certain domains more than others, such as face images or architectural images. It means the increase in performance is not class-specific. It is however interesting that regardless of the dataset used, the blended HR image results in the best PSNR score in all cases. This indicates that the SRCNN and SelfEx can complement each other in order to improve SR performance. Even though the SelfEx algorithm has better performance than the SRCNN on

Ground truth   Bicubic   **33.89/ 0.9043** SRCNN   **35.25/ 0.9249** SelfEx   **35.17/ 0.9240** Blended   **35.37/ 0.9261**

Fig. 3. Baby image from Set5 using ×3 upscaling.

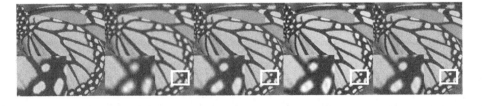

Ground truth   Bicubic   **24.01/ 0.8174** SRCNN   **27.95/ 0.9056** SelfEx   **26.85/ 0.9000** Blended   **27.70/ 0.9083**

Fig. 4. Butterfly image from Set5 using ×3 upscaling.

Ground truth   Bicubic   **23.71/ 0.8785** SRCNN   **27.04/ 0.9413** SelfEx   **27.06/ 0.9497** Blended   **27.29/ 0.9498**

Fig. 5. Poster image from Set14 using ×3 upscaling.

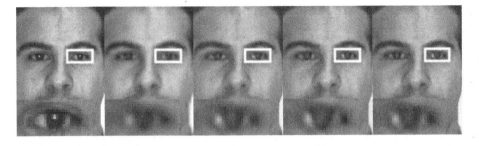

Ground truth   Bicubic   **32.46/ 0.9135** SRCNN   **35.27/ 0.9380** SelfEx   **34.61/ 0.9359** Blended   **35.16/ 0.9392**

Fig. 6. Example image from AR Face DB using ×3 upscaling.

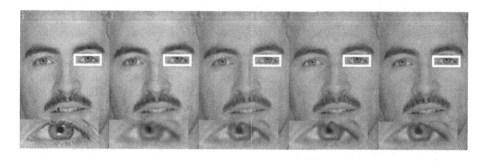

Ground truth   Bicubic   **29.88/ 0.7792**   SRCNN   **30.43/ 0.8053**   SelfEx   **30.41/ 0.8049**   Blended   **30.47/ 0.8063**

Fig. 7. Example image from AR Face DB using ×3 upscaling.

architectural images, the SR performance can still be improved by blending with the HR counterpart produced by the SRCNN.

As future work one could try other blending methods than alpha-blending and include experiments with blending other types of SR algorithms. Furthermore instead of blending at a fixed blend percentage, an adaptive blending method could possibly produce better results. This method could treat different areas of the image according to content, and then use the best suited SR algorithm in this area at varying blend percentages.

5   Conclusion

In contrast to previous work, where SR algorithms from different categories has been combined, we have show in this work that SR algorithms from the same category can also complement each other in order to improve SR performance. This has been done by alpha-blending the HR images produced by two hallucination based SR algorithms, namely the SRCNN and the SelfEx. We have observed improvement when using this method, on six different datasets, across different scaling levels. This indicates that both the used algorithms can benefit from each others HR output. This finding can possibly lead to further research in the area of combining different SR algorithms in order to improve SR performance.

References

1. Martinez, A.M., Benavente, R.: The AR face database. CVC Technical report 24. http://www2.ece.ohio-state.edu/~aleix/ARdatabase.html. Accessed 27 April 2016
2. Bevilacqua, M., Roumy, A., Guillemot, C., Alberi-Morel, M.: Low-complexity single-image super-resolution based on nonnegative neighbor embedding. In: British Machine Vision Conference, BMVC 2012, Surrey, UK, 3–7 September 2012, pp. 1–10 (2012). http://dx.doi.org/10.5244/C.26.135

3. Dai, D., Wang, Y., Chen, Y., Gool, L.J.V.: How useful is image super-resolution to other vision tasks? CoRR abs/1509.07009 (2015). http://arxiv.org/abs/1509.07009
4. Dong, C., Loy, C., He, K., Tang, X.: Image super-resolution using deep convolutional networks. IEEE Trans. Pattern Anal. Mach. Intell. **38**(2), 295–307 (2016)
5. Fukushima, K.: Neocognitron: a self-organizing neural network model for a mechanism of pattern recognition unaffected by shift in position. Biol. Cybern. **36**(4), 193–202 (1980). http://dx.doi.org/10.1007/BF00344251
6. Gerchberg, R.W.: Super-resolution through error energy reduction. J. Mod. Opt. **22**(8), 709–720 (1974)
7. Huang, J.B., Singh, A., Ahuja, N.: Single image super-resolution from transformed self-exemplars. In: IEEE Conference on Computer Vision and Pattern Recognition (2015)
8. Martin, D., Fowlkes, C., Tal, D., Malik, J.: A database of human segmented natural images and its application to evaluating segmentation algorithms and measuring ecological statistics. In: Proceedings of 8th International Conference Computer Vision, vol. 2, pp. 416–423, July 2001
9. Nasrollahi, K., Escalera, S., Rasti, P., Anbarjafari, G., Baro, X., Escalante, H.J., Moeslund, T.B.: Deep learning based super-resolution for improved action recognition. In: 2015 International Conference on Image Processing Theory, Tools and Applications (IPTA), pp. 67–72, November 2015
10. Nasrollahi, K., Moeslund, T.B.: Finding and improving the key-frames of long video sequences for face recognition. In: Fourth IEEE International Conference on Biometrics: Theory Applications and Systems (BTAS) 2010, pp. 1–6 (2010)
11. Nasrollahi, K., Moeslund, T.: Super-resolution: a comprehensive survey. Mach. Vis. Appl. **25**(6), 1423–1468 (2014)
12. Vieira, T.F., Bottino, A., Laurentini, A., De Simone, M.: Detecting siblings in image pairs. Vis. Comput. **30**(12), 1333–1345 (2014). http://dx.doi.org/10.1007/s00371-013-0884-3
13. Wang, Z., Bovik, A.C.: Mean squared error: love it or leave it? A new look at signal fidelity measures. IEEE Sig. Process. Mag. **26**(1), 98–117 (2009)
14. Zeyde, R., Elad, M., Protter, M.: On single image scale-up using sparse-representations. In: Proceedings of the 7th International Conference on Curves and Surfaces, pp. 711–730 (2012). http://dx.doi.org/10.1007/978-3-642-27413-8_47

Human Head Pose Estimation on SASE Database Using Random Hough Regression Forests

Iiris Lüsi[1(✉)], Sergio Escalera[2], and Gholamreza Anbarjafari[1]

[1] ICV Research Group, Institute of Technology, University of Tartu, Tartu, Estonia
{iirisl,shb}@icv.tuit.ut.ee
[2] Computer Vision Center, Universitat de Barcelona, Barcelona, Spain
sergio@maia.ub.es

Abstract. In recent years head pose estimation has become an important task in face analysis scenarios. Given the availability of high resolution 3D sensors, the design of a high resolution head pose database would be beneficial for the community. In this paper, Random Hough Forests are used to estimate 3D head pose and location on a new 3D head database, SASE, which represents the baseline performance on the new data for an upcoming international head pose estimation competition. The data in SASE is acquired with a Microsoft Kinect 2 camera, including the RGB and depth information of 50 subjects with a large sample of head poses, allowing us to test methods for real-life scenarios. We briefly review the database while showing baseline head pose estimation results based on Random Hough Forests.

1 Introduction

Many researchers have conducted research on modelling human movements in games and movies using different computer graphics techniques [1–4]. Such visualization has been used for improving human-computer interaction by means of emotion recognition, detection of people and human activity recognition [5–7]. Hence, in order to improve human-computer interaction it is necessary to develop algorithms that can interpret the behavioural movements made by humans and also mimic these actions in a natural way.

Over the years it has become quite common to use large databases to train and test active appearance models (AAM) that pinpoint and track the locations of landmark points in a human face [8–10]. Recently a hybrid method which adopted Lucas-Kanade optical flow and active appearance model that utilizes gradient descent was proposed [11]. As a different approach, the correlation between appearance and shape was used in [12]. This type of models detect and track face landmarks easily when the head orientation is near-frontal, with

---

The original version of this chapter was revised: The spelling of the second author's name was corrected. The erratum to this chapter is available at DOI: 10.1007/978-3-319-56687-0_14

© Springer International Publishing AG 2017
K. Nasrollahi et al. (Eds.): VAAM 2016/FFER 2016, LNCS 10165, pp. 137–150, 2017.
DOI: 10.1007/978-3-319-56687-0_12

only slight changes in angle, but tend to go awry when the proportions of the face change due to rotation. To prevent that, in [13] a method using auxiliary attributes was proposed.

Face standardization has been also addressed in order to solve the different point of view problem, which transforms skewed facial images to frontal ones. In [14] an automatic method for standardizing a face was presented. Key points, eye corners, were used to align and standardize the face for better future recognition. First AAM was used to extract feature points, and then an affine model was built, after which transformation was performed. Their method can fail in an uncontrolled environment as faces are not always symmetric (people can have different eye shapes, asymmetric features or facial expressions) and because occlusions may hinder eye detection. Moreover, in this work only roll angle was corrected, while yaw and pitch were disregarded.

Yang et al. [15] analysed more deeply the failures of conventional AAM models and proposed a method that first estimated the head pose directly from the image with the help of convolutional networks. On an average face-database, they were able to estimate the pose with about 4 degree accuracy. Unlike classic AAM models, the authors applied the rotated mean face shape to the image instead of a frontal one. This way they achieved a more accurate initial guess for facial landmarks, thus getting better results. There have been several techniques proposed for robust tracking by incorporating geometric constraints to correlate the position of facial landmarks [15,16]. Even though single step face alignment methods have been proposed [17,18], the most common and recent approach for face alignment is to model the relationship between texture and geometry with a cascade of regression functions [19,20]. Many methods used RGB-D cameras to conduct real-time depth-based facial tracking and tried to register a dynamic expression model with observed depth data [21–23].

However, most commented approaches for head pose estimation heavily rely on lighting conditions. In the same way, 3D head pose estimation from still images may be not accurate enough for some real-life applications. In order to have accurate head orientation recognition in real-life scenarios, the method would have to be trained with a large variety of poses in a all kinds of different lighting conditions. On the other hand, training with highly dispersed data could make the classification less reliable and produce false detection of angle or facial landmarks. To cross that gap, in [24] the depth-data and RGB data from Kinect were used. As a preliminary step the authors constructed a 3D head shape-model. After which they took three RGB images of the subject, from the left, the right and the front. These images were fitted onto the 3D AAM. Later the 3D AAM was aligned to the input 3D frame by benefiting from using the RGB data as constraining parameters.

Fanelli et al. [25] proposed a head pose estimation purely based on depth data. In their work, a high-definition depth-scanner was used to train a random Hough forest for classification and pose estimation. The trees in the forest were trained to classify for each depth patch whether they were part of the head or not. For each face patch, the location of the middle of the head was also estimated. This was necessary as it could be used as the nominal head location, thus providing sufficient information to move a 3D head model based on poses and location. With the help of several mean-shifts, the actual rotation and location could be estimated. Fanelli et al. [26] also based on Microsoft Kinect 1, but the sensor at that time gave fairly inaccurate results due to the low quality of available depth information. With this work, a depth database, BIWI, was also provided. However, adding different AAM type algorithms on top of Fanelli's framework has produced fairly accurate real-time facial landmark tracking applications [27,28]. Now that the Kinect 2 is available with much more accurate depth information and higher resolution RGB images, the results of depth-based head pose estimation algorithms could be improved upon and further analysed to achieve faster and smoother facial landmark detection and tracking [29,30].

One of the most important concepts to understand about the 3D sensors and the algorithms trained on the data acquired by them, is that the RGB-D data provided by a sensor is unique, as some outputs are denser, while others produce a lesser degree of error. Due to this fact, a method trained on a set of data from one sensor is incompatible with data from other sensors. The necessity for a head pose database for Microsoft Kinect 2 arises from the fact that nowadays this is one of the most accurate and easily available RGB-D sensors. Additionally, for further development of depth-based recognition methods, a variety of databases with heads in different poses is needed; thus, in this paper, we present the baseline results on SASE database, which is gathered with the Kinect 2 and can contribute to future research within the depth-related facial analysis field.

Gall et al. introduced Hough forests which are random forests adapted to perform a generalized Hough transform in an efficient way [31]. Hough forests can be regarded as task-adapted codebooks of local appearance that allow fast supervised training and fast matching at test time [32,33]. As the entries of such codebooks are optimized to cast Hough votes with small variance, and also their efficiency permits dense sampling of local image patches or video cuboids during detection, they achieve high detection accuracy. The flexibility of Hough forests permits extensions of the Hough transform to tasks such as object tracking, pose estimation and action recognition.

In [34] the problem using depth data that can be captured by the Kinect sensor [35] was addressed. In that work, in order to achieve robustness and speed, the pose estimation task within a regression and the Hough voting framework was formulated. Then random regression forests [36,37] were applied to predict joint locations from each pixel and accumulate these predictions with Hough voting, which were treated as likelihood distributions.

In this paper, we propose a 3D head pose estimation system using Hough forests, a special case of random classification and regression forests, on the SASE database. This database was presented in ECCV2016 and will be part of an international challenge, thus will not be publicly avalible at the moment. Even though works have been published with this method by Fanelli et al. [25,26,28], they were implemented using data from either a high definition laser scanner or from a low quality sensor Kinect 1. In this paper, we publish the baseline results for the SASE database, which was compiled using Kinect 2.

The rest of the paper is organized as follows: in Sect. 2 an overview of random Hough forests for 3D head poses is given. In Sect. 3 the details of the SASE database and the experimental results are given. Finally Sect. 4 concludes the paper.

2 Hough Forests 3D Head Pose Estimation

2.1 Kinect 2

The Microsoft Kinect 2 consists of 3 main components, namely, RGB camera, IR emitter and IR sensor. The RGB resolution of this sensor is 1080×1920 which is the resolution of a full HD image, in comparison to the Kinect 1's 480×640. The IR is used to employ time of flight technology to calculate the distance of each point. Which results in 1 mm depth accuracy at around 1 m distance. Even though this version also gives false information at very abrupt edges (70+ degrees), the failure angles are steeper than the ones with Kinect 1 [38].

These differences are the reason that makes it meaningful to try the head pose estimation method that worked adequately well on data from a sensor with a lower resolution on the SASE database to achieve baseline results, as random regression forests are a relatively simple method to implement and work well in real-time scenarios, thus not setting the bar impossibly high for the challenge.

2.2 3D Head Pose Estimation Problem

3D head pose and location estimation becomes important in the case of RGB-D camera-based applications that deal with the mimicking of human poses and facial expressions. Having an illumination invariant head detection and pose estimation could prove to be a great asset for gaming in the dark, video conferences etc. There exist many approaches to this issue; however researchers have not paid much attention to the Microsoft Kinect2 sensor. in that regard.

In order to calculate head poses, the initial pose of the person was taken as the reference pose. The initial pose has a frontal orientation, in which the subject is looking at the camera. Considering the noise of the sensor, 20 frames of this pose were used to average a good starting value for further calculations. After which markers were used to calculate the pairwise difference between an averaged initial pose and the current pose.

In this paper, the head pose is viewed in a 3D Cartesian coordinate system. The x-axis is defined horizontally and parallel to the sensor, the right side is positive, the y-axis is defined vertically, pointed upwards, the z-axis is defined perpendicular to both of these axes, so that they form a left-hand system. In this coordinate system, the head pose can be defined as a set of six parameters, angles for pitch, yaw and roll as seen in Fig. 1 part (b), and 3D location coordinates x, y, z. The central point of the head is considered to be the nose tip because this is easy to locate using depth information and fits the application of the database.

PITCH   YAW   ROLL

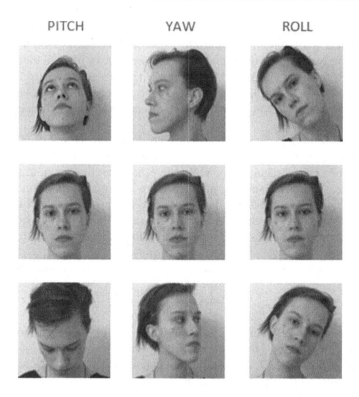

Fig. 1. Rotation angles yaw, pitch and roll, explained

The random regression forest is used to estimate a parameter vector $\theta = (x, y, z, \alpha, \beta, \gamma)$. The accuracy is calculated separately for the 3D-location and the rotation of the head as they cannot be measured by the same units.

2.3 Hough Random Regression Forests for 3D Head Pose and Location Estimation

Classification and regression trees (CRT) are a supervised learning method that provide a powerful tool which enables to cluster a complicated dataset into similar subsets such that very simple estimators can be used. In the non-leaf nodes of the tree are binary tests that are used to cluster the data, whereas in the leaf nodes the decision is made.

In case of classification and regression, there are two types of values stored in each leaf-node: the ratio of positive samples to all the samples that reached the leaf p_c. This can also be viewed as the probability of a sample that has reached the leaf node, being positive in nature.

Random forests are a collection of randomly generated CRT. Hough random regression forests are random forests adapted to perform generalised Hough transform in an efficient way. Hough forests are sets of decision trees trained on labelled data. Features from a video frame or image are mapped onto leaf nodes, where each leaf is attributed a probabilistic vote in the Hough space. The training process is partly governed by randomness that originates from random selection of samples from the training step. This part of the process is very similar to the boot-strapping method well-known in statistics. The training is also controlled by measures that make sure that the tree nodes are optimal for this classification problem.

There are two types of measures to be considered at each non-leaf node when choosing a test from a set of randomly generated tests. One of them is directly related to the classification error, while the other one aims to minimize within class variance and covariance to produce more accurate estimation results. In case of a large variance within a dataset, the confidence intervals of the estimation become too wide, resulting in low and statistically doubtful accuracy.

The measure for classification error can be formulated as:

$$E_C = \frac{|S_L| \cdot \sum_c p(c|S_L) \cdot \ln(p(c|S_L))|}{|S|} +$$
$$\frac{S_R| \cdot \sum_c p(c|S_R) \cdot \ln(p(c|S_R))}{|S|}, \tag{1}$$

where S stands for all samples, S_L, S_R signify samples that the test decided to send to the left and the right child, respectively. The $p(c|S_L)$ means the conditional probability of the sample having value $c \in 0, 1$ aka the ratio of positive samples in the data that will be sent to the left child. This is a common error measure for binary classification trees.

The measure that minimizes the within class variance, under the assumption that (x, y, z) and (α, β, γ) are independent from each other. This means only covariance between angles or between offset vectors is allowed.

$$E_V = \ln(|\Sigma^v| + |\Sigma^a|) - p(1|S_R) \cdot \ln(|\Sigma^v| + |\Sigma^a_R|) -$$
$$p(1|S_L) \cdot \ln(|\Sigma^v| + |\Sigma^a_L|). \tag{2}$$

Here Σ^a stands for the covariance matrix of angles; Σ^v is the same for offset vectors.

There are many ways to combine those two measures for clustering of the data; however in this paper tests are chosen by maximising the value of:

$$E_C + (1 - e^{-d/\lambda}) * E_V \tag{3}$$

Here d stands for the depth of the node and λ is a coefficient, set to be 5.

In that sense, the Hough forests can be thought of as an implicit codebook optimised for Hough-based detection. Since the trees consist of binary tests that are very fast, this results in a method that can utilise dense sampling, which leads to improved detection accuracy.

2.4   Construction of a Tree

Let the number of training samples be denoted by N. Then for building a random tree, N samples with repetition are randomly picked from the original set of patches, resulting in a set S_tree. This process of choosing samples is where the randomness of this method originates from.

At each non-leaf node of a tree, a binary test is generated. The test consists of parameters such as the size and location of two rectangles within the patch. One rectangle R_1 is described by $x1, y1, h1, w1$; the other one R_2 is represented similarly. One of the test parameters is also a threshold τ, which decides the outcome of the binary test.

$$|R_1|^{-1} \sum_{p \in R_1} I(p) - |R_2|^{-1} \sum_{p \in R_2} I(p) \geq \tau, \tag{4}$$

where I denotes the integral of the depth image and p a pixel within the depth patch. All patches that pass the test are sent to the right, and the ones that fail are sent to the left. This process is repeated until the maximum depth of tree, 8 in this paper, or the minimum number of samples per node, here 50, is reached. Each leaf will store the mean of offset vectors and rotation angles of all the patches that reached it, together with their covariance and the concentration of positive head-patches within all the patches that reached that leaf. The binary tests are chosen to find the best trade-off between discrimination by class and minimising the error of the offset vectors.

3   Experimental Results

3.1   SASE Database Details

The database used in this paper contains RGB-D information (424×512 16-bit depth frames and 1080×1920 RGB frames) obtained using the Microsoft Kinect 2 sensor of different head poses of 50 subjects, including 32 male and 18 female in the age range of 7–35 years old. The subjects were asked to move their heads slowly in front of the device to achieve different combinations of yaw, pitch and roll rotation. Altogether around 600+ frames of each subject were recorded. For those frames where the nose tip location was attainable, the ground truth of the 3D nose tip location and head orientation described by yaw, roll, pitch angles. The rest of the samples were retained, as more sophisticated methods like ICP can be used in the future to label them. The depth information (scaled for display purposes) and corresponding RGB data can be seen in part (a) in Fig. 2.

In this section, details of the setup and recording process are explained thoroughly. Overall the recording process elapsed about a month as the subjects were recorded during a number of sessions, which differed in the number of people captured.

The software used for the capture was a python script written using the Kinect 2 python library and OpenCV. The laptop used for the capturing process has an i5-4200u processor with an integrated graphics card and 8 GB of RAM. It also carried an SSD to speed up the frame rate. However, due to restrictions of the processor of the laptop, the frame rate was measured to be at 5 fps.

The head poses in the database are with values of yaw varying from −75 to 75, pitch and roll varying from −45 to 45. These constraints were chosen because they represent the maximum angles that can be achieved under normal conditions by a human sitting in front of a camera, and only moving the head while not changing their body position. The aforementioned restrictions were achieved experimentally and are not necessarily applied to all humans but rather seem to be an average trend.

The angle limitations are different for each subject. This is due to the fact that not all people can rotate their head the same exact amount. In order to avoid this problem, all the people were trained in advance, so that they did not rotate their heads too much during the capturing process. Also participants were free to perform different facial expressions in the different poses when capturing the data in order to have a more natural database. This resulted in a collection of mostly neutral faces with some happy expressions mixed in. It is important to note that this database is not focusing on representing various emotions and thus cannot be used for emotion recognition applications.

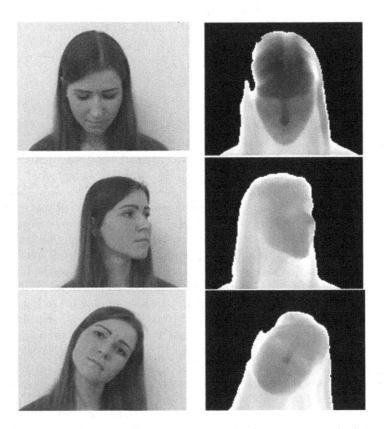

Fig. 2. (a) Cutouts from the database, for rows as (pitch, yaw, roll): (−32, 0, 3), (2, −49, 2) and (3, −1, −39), respectively.

3.2   Obtaining Samples

In this section, it is described how patches of size $m \times n$, in this case $m = n = 20$, are chosen from the depth data. First the depth is segmented, everything that is further than 1.2 m is set to zero. However since sometimes the wall is closer to the Kinect sensor a depth value is sampled from the wall to further segment out unwanted depth values. From around the head, positive patches, which will be used to train the trees in the forest, are extracted. Each patch is described by its location and 3D offset from the location of the head, aka the nose tip in this case. In case of training a tree for each subject a fixed number of frames is chosen at random from each subject. From each frame 10 positive locations are picked at random and all such possible patch locations are saved into a positive sample file. The negative samples are sampled from the rest of the frames' nonzero areas, again only 10 for each frame. These restrictions are set in order not to make the data for one tree too large. No offset from centre needs to be found for them, as they will not cast a vote for the head location nor the head orientation. This process is illustrated in Fig. 3.

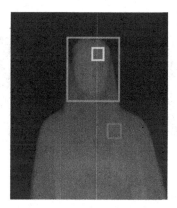

Fig. 3. Sampling process. Patches within the green rectangle, like the yellow one, are picked as positive samples. The ones outside, like the red one, are picked as negative. (Color figure online)

In testing of the algorithm 28 subject are picked as a test set. The trees are trained on this data and then tested on validation set consisting of 12 unused subjects. Another forest is trained on the previously used 40 samples and tested on the remaining 10. This is directly related to the challenge that this database will be used for.

Since the amount of data is huge and to achieve randomness for each frame 4 patches are chosen for training to for a large set of patches P. However the number of patches is still too large and time-consuming as many frames are similar to one another. So $N = 10000$ patches are sampled at random from the set P. Altogether, 10 trees were built. For Hough voting, only leaves with positive ratio of 1 are used. It is also important to note that leaves with lower variance are more trustworthy in this scenario. A lot of outliers are still produced, which can be removed with the help of statistics and shifting the mean towards denser areas. Some success cases are illustrated in figure sucess (Fig. 4). These angles had an approx error of 2–7 mm in location and 5 degrees in pose.

However, because of this methodology sometimes not enough patches are able to vote for the head location. This is one of the reasons for this method failing. It also has similar troubles in case of very large pitch angles as the detection of face area is largely based on marker locations. However in these cases the most visible part is the head and very little of face. This could be resolved by better sample set creation method and perhaps a more supervised clustering for the samples in the training process. This will not solve all of the failures though, as the density of such samples is too low to constitute a special case in the decision tree.

It also fails in cases where glasses hide important parts of the face, such as nose. This is mainly cause by the fact that Kinect 2 uses ToF methodology. However glasses are reflective and return erroneous depth values. This will leave us without the most important and distinctive patches being able to vote for the result. An example of this can be seen in Fig. 5.

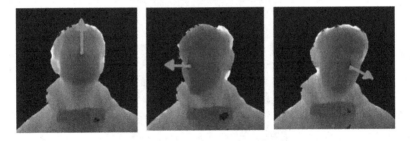

Fig. 4. Success cases from one subject, at (yaw, pitch, roll) being (0, 17, 2), (22, −5, 3) and (14, −10, −12), respectively

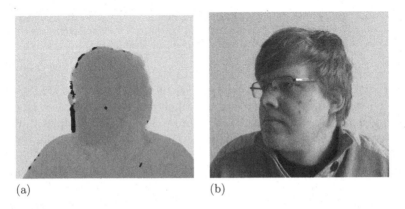

(a)   (b)

Fig. 5. (a) depth image occluded by glasses, (b) corresponding RGB

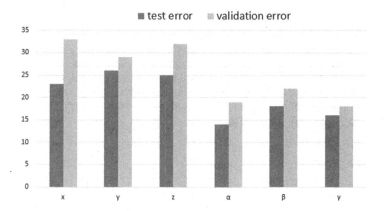

Fig. 6. The illustration of the error for the locations and angles of the estimated poses as reported in Table 1

Table 1. Estimation errors

Parameter	x	y	z	α	β	γ
Test error	23	26	25	14	18	16
Validation error	33	29	32	19	22	18

In this paper the a case is also considered a failure when there is no notable centre point or high density areas in the votes. If the voted location/angles are very sparse their mean can not be considered a good estimate for the head pose.

The errors are illustrated with the barplot in figure errors (Fig. 6). The estimation errors should be considered separately for the location vectors and the angles as they are from a different metric. However, and overall goodness measure can be considered to be the sum of mean errors of all the angle parameters. Let θ_i denote the parameter value at each frame and $\hat{\theta}_i$ the estimated parameter value. Then, the overall score can be defined as:

$$ErrorScore = \frac{1}{N} \sum_{i \in I} |\alpha_i - \hat{\alpha}_i| + |\beta_i - \hat{\beta}_i| + |\gamma_i - \hat{\gamma}_i|, \tag{5}$$

where I stands for indices of all testing set frames, where $|I| = N$ is the number of samples. The overall baseline score for development (training on train and testing on validation set) is 59 and the baseline score for testing stage (training with train plus validation data and testing on the test set) is 48.

4   Conclusion

In this paper a 3D head pose estimation algorithm using Hough forests was applied on a recently developed 3D head pose database, SASE, which was acquired using Kinect 2. This work was benefiting from the fact that SASE has higher quality depth information from an easily usable device. The 3D head pose estimation results reported in this paper represent the baseline score of an upcoming head pose international competition on the proposed SASE database.

Acknowledgement. This work has been partially supported by the Estonian Research Grant (PUT638), Spanish projects TIN2013-43478-P and TIN2016-74946-P, the European Commission Horizon 2020 granted project SEE.4C under call H2020-ICT-2015, and the Estonian Centre of Excellence in IT (EXCITE) funded by the European Regional Development Fund.

References

1. Palmas, G., Bachynskyi, M., Oulasvirta, A., Seidel, H.-P., Weinkauf, T.: MovExp: a versatile visualization tool for human-computer interaction studies with 3D performance and biomechanical data. IEEE Trans. Visual. Comput. Graphics **20**(12), 2359–2368 (2014)
2. Cao, C., Wu, H., Weng, Y., Shao, T., Zhou, K.: Real-time facial animation with image-based dynamic avatars. ACM Trans. Graphics **35**(4), 126 (2016)
3. Sollfrank, T., Hart, D., Goodsell, R., Foster, J., Tan, T.: 3D visualization of movements can amplify motor cortex activation during subsequent motor imagery. Frontiers Hum. Neurosci. **9** (2015)
4. Shuster, G.S., Shuster, B.M.: Avatar eye control in a multi-user animation environment, 7 December 2015. US Patent App. 14/961,744
5. Arellano, D., Varona, J., Perales, F.J.: Generation and visualization of emotional states in virtual characters. Comput. Animation Virtual Worlds **19**(3–4), 259–270 (2008)
6. Chen, H., Li, J., Zhang, F., Li, Y., Wang, H.: 3D model-based continuous emotion recognition. In: Proceedings of the IEEE Conference on Computer Vision and Pattern Recognition, pp. 1836–1845 (2015)
7. Aggarwal, J.K., Xia, L.: Human activity recognition from 3D data: a review. Pattern Recogn. Lett. **48**, 70–80 (2014)
8. Yan, S., Liu, C., Li, S.Z., Zhang, H., Shum, H.-Y., Cheng, Q.: Face alignment using texture-constrained active shape models. Image Vis. Comput. **21**(1), 69–75 (2003)
9. Liu, X.: Generic face alignment using boosted appearance model. In: IEEE Conference on Computer Vision and Pattern Recognition, pp. 1–8. IEEE (2007)
10. Koutras, P., Maragos, P.: Estimation of eye gaze direction angles based on active appearance models. In: IEEE International Conference on Image Processing, pp. 2424–2428. IEEE (2015)
11. Adeshina, S.A., Cootes, T.F.: Automatic model matching using part based model constrained active appearance models for skeletal maturity. In: 2015 Twelve International Conference on Electronics Computer and Computation, pp. 1–5. IEEE (2015)
12. Zhou, H., Lam, K.-M., He, X.: Shape-appearance-correlated active appearance model. Pattern Recogn. **56**, 88–99 (2016)
13. Zhang, Z., Luo, P., Loy, C.C., Tang, X.: Learning deep representation for face alignment with auxiliary attributes (2015)

14. Li, Q., Cheng, Z., Qi, S., Zhang, H., Liu, X., Deng, Y., Yi, M., Yuan, Q., Wang, T., Chen, S.: Automatic facial image standardization based on active appearance model. In: Information Technology: Proceedings of the 2014 International Symposium on Information Technology, p. 151. CRC Press (2015)
15. Yang, H., Mou, W., Zhang, Y., Patras, I., Gunes, H., Robinson, P.: Face alignment assisted by head pose estimation, arXiv preprint arXiv:1507.03148 (2015)
16. Vlasic, D., Brand, M., Pfister, H., Popović, J.: Face transfer with multilinear models. ACM Trans. Graphics **24**(3), 426–433 (2005)
17. Sun, Y., Wang, X., Tang, X.: Deep convolutional network cascade for facial point detection. In: IEEE Conference on Computer Vision and Pattern Recognition, pp. 3476–3483. IEEE (2013)
18. Zhang, J., Shan, S., Kan, M., Chen, X.: Coarse-to-fine auto-encoder networks (cfan) for real-time face alignment. In: Fleet, D., Pajdla, T., Schiele, B., Tuytelaars, T. (eds.) ECCV 2014. LNCS, vol. 8690, pp. 1–16. Springer, Cham (2014). doi:10.1007/978-3-319-10605-2_1
19. Cao, X., Wei, Y., Wen, F., Sun, J.: Face alignment by explicit shape regression. Int. J. Comput. Vision **107**(2), 177–190 (2014)
20. Xiong, X., De la Torre, F.: Supervised descent method and its applications to face alignment. In: IEEE Conference on Computer Vision and Pattern Recognition, pp. 532–539. IEEE (2013)
21. Weise, T., Bouaziz, S., Li, H., Pauly, M.: Realtime performance-based facial animation. ACM Trans. Graphics **30**(4), 77 (2011)
22. Kazemi, V., Sullivan, J.: One millisecond face alignment with an ensemble of regression trees. In: IEEE Conference on Computer Vision and Pattern Recognition, pp. 1867–1874. IEEE (2014)
23. Traumann, A., Daneshmand, M., Escalera, S., Anbarjafari, G.: Accurate 3D measurement using optical depth information. Electron. Lett. **51**(18), 1420–1422 (2015)
24. Wang, H.-H., Dopfer, A., Wang, C.-C.: 3D AAM based face alignment under wide angular variations using 2D and 3D data. In: IEEE International Conference on Robotics and Automation, pp. 4450–4455. IEEE (2012)
25. Fanelli, G., Gall, J., Van Gool, L.: Real time head pose estimation with random regression forests. In: IEEE Conference on Computer Vision and Pattern Recognition, pp. 617–624. IEEE (2011)
26. Fanelli, G., Weise, T., Gall, J., Gool, L.: Real time head pose estimation from consumer depth cameras. In: Mester, R., Felsberg, M. (eds.) DAGM 2011. LNCS, vol. 6835, pp. 101–110. Springer, Heidelberg (2011). doi:10.1007/978-3-642-23123-0_11
27. Yang, F., Huang, J., Yu, X., Cui, X., Metaxas, D.: Robust face tracking with a consumer depth camera. In: IEEE International Conference on Image Processing, pp. 561–564. IEEE (2012)
28. Fanelli, G., Dantone, M., Van Gool, L.: Real time 3D face alignment with random forests-based active appearance models. In: IEEE International Conference and Workshops on Automatic Face and Gesture Recognition, pp. 1–8. IEEE (2013)
29. Lüsi, I., Escarela, S., Anbarjafari, G.: SASE: RGB-depth database for human head pose estimation. In: Hua, G., Jégou, H. (eds.) ECCV 2016. LNCS, vol. 9915, pp. 325–336. Springer, Cham (2016). doi:10.1007/978-3-319-49409-8_26
30. Lüsi, I., Anbarjafari, G., Meister, E.: Real-time mimicking of Estonian speaker's mouth movements on a 3D avatar using Kinect 2. In: International Conference on Information and Communication Technology Convergence, pp. 141–143. IEEE (2015)

31. Gall, J., Yao, A., Razavi, N., Van Gool, L., Lempitsky, V.: Hough forests for object detection, tracking, and action recognition. IEEE Trans. Pattern Anal. Mach. Intell. **33**(11), 2188–2202 (2011)
32. Leibe, B., Schiele, B.: Interleaving object categorization and segmentation. In: Christensen, H.I., Nagel, H.-H. (eds.) Cognitive Vision Systems. LNCS, vol. 3948, pp. 145–161. Springer, Heidelberg (2006). doi:10.1007/11414353_10
33. Lehmann, A., Leibe, B., Van Gool, L.: Fast prism: branch and bound hough transform for object class detection. Int. J. Comput. Vis. **94**(2), 175–197 (2011)
34. Holt, B., Bowden, R.: Static pose estimation from depth images using random regression forests and hough voting. In: VISAp. 2012-Proceedings of the International Conference on Computer Vision Theory and Applications, vol. 1, pp. 557–564 (2012)
35. Moeslund, T.B., Hilton, A., Krüger, V.: A survey of advances in vision-based human motion capture and analysis. Comput. Vis. Image Underst. **104**(2), 90–126 (2006)
36. Lepetit, V., Fua, P.: Keypoint recognition using randomized trees. IEEE Trans. Pattern Anal. Mach. Intell. **28**(9), 1465–1479 (2006)
37. Shotton, J., Sharp, T., Kipman, A., Fitzgibbon, A., Finocchio, M., Blake, A., Cook, M., Moore, R.: Real-time human pose recognition in parts from single depth images. Commun. ACM **56**(1), 116–124 (2013)
38. Smisek, J., Jancosek, M., Pajdla, T.: 3D with kinect. In: Fossati, A., Gall, J., Grabner, H., Ren, X., Konolige, K. (eds.) Consumer Depth Cameras for Computer Vision, pp. 3–25. Springer, London (2013)

Spatio-temporal Pain Recognition in CNN-Based Super-Resolved Facial Images

Marco Bellantonio[1]([⊠]), Mohammad A. Haque[2], Pau Rodriguez[1],
Kamal Nasrollahi[2], Taisi Telve[3], Sergio Escalera[1], Jordi Gonzalez[1],
Thomas B. Moeslund[2], Pejman Rasti[3], and Gholamreza Anbarjafari[3]

[1] Computer Vision Center (UAB), University of Barcelona, Barcelona, Spain
marco.bellantonio@est.fib.upc.edu, {prodriguez,poal}@cvc.uab.es,
sergio@maia.ub.es
[2] Visual Analysis of People (VAP) Laboratory,
Aalborg University, Aalborg, Denmark
{mah,kn,tbm}@create.aau.dk
[3] iCV Research Group, Institute of Technology, University of Tartu, Tartu, Estonia
{tt,pejman,shb}@icv.tuit.ut.ee

Abstract. Automatic pain detection is a long expected solution to a prevalent medical problem of pain management. This is more relevant when the subject of pain is young children or patients with limited ability to communicate about their pain experience. Computer vision-based analysis of facial pain expression provides a way of efficient pain detection. When deep machine learning methods came into the scene, automatic pain detection exhibited even better performance. In this paper, we figured out three important factors to exploit in automatic pain detection: spatial information available regarding to pain in each of the facial video frames, temporal axis information regarding to pain expression pattern in a subject video sequence, and variation of face resolution. We employed a combination of convolutional neural network and recurrent neural network to setup a deep hybrid pain detection framework that is able to exploit both spatial and temporal pain information from facial video. In order to analyze the effect of different facial resolutions, we introduce a super-resolution algorithm to generate facial video frames with different resolution setups. We investigated the performance on the publicly available UNBC-McMaster Shoulder Pain database. As a contribution, the paper provides novel and important information regarding to the performance of a hybrid deep learning framework for pain detection in facial images of different resolution.

Keywords: Super-Resolution · Convolutional Neural Network (CNN) · Recurrent Neural Network (RNN) · Pain detection

---

The original version of this chapter was revised: The spelling of the sixth author's name was corrected. The erratum to this chapter is available at DOI: 10.1007/978-3-319-56687-0_14

© Springer International Publishing AG 2017
K. Nasrollahi et al, (Eds.): VAAM 2016/FFER 2016, LNCS 10165, pp. 151–162, 2017.
DOI: 10.1007/978-3-319-56687-0_13

1   Introduction

Pain is a prevalent medical problem that reveals as an unpleasant experience and needs to be managed effectively as a moral and professional responsibility [5]. Traditionally, pain is measured by 'self-report'. However, self-reported pain level assessment requires cognitive, linguistic and social competencies of the affected person. These aspects make self-report unfeasible to use for young children and patients with limited ability to communicate [37]. Thus, the notion of computer vision-based automatic pain level assessment was introduced [31,32].

Facial pain expression can be considered as a subset of facial expression and expresses emotion valley regarding to experiencing pain [2]. It can also provide information about the severity of pain that can be assessed by using the Facial Action Coding System (FACS) coding from [6,52]. For a long time the FACS has been used to measure facial expression appearance and intensity. Thus, vision-based approaches came into the scene to measure pain by using features from facial appearance change. Prkachin first reported the consistency of facial pain expressions for different pain modalities in [45] and then together with Solomon developed a pain metric called Prkachin and Solomon Pain Intensity (PSPI) scale based on FACS in [47].

The task of assessing the pain level from facial image or video is rather challenging. A substantial body of literature has been produced in the recent years to address the challenges [3,10,29,46,48]. A glimpse of the reason why pain level detection is difficult can be found in Fig. 1 [14]. From the facial images in the figure, we can see that the pain and non-pain frames may not present enough visual difference; however, the self-report tells a different story about having pain and non-pain status. The challenges also increase in the presence of external factors like 'smiling in pain' phenomenon and gender difference (male's vs female's way of experiencing) to pain [28,30,53]. This in turns result to a non-linearly wrapped facial emotion levels in a high dimensional space [51].

Recent advances in facial video analysis using deep learning frameworks such as Convolutional Neural Networks (CNN) or Deep Belief Networks (DBN) provide the notion of realizing non-linear high dimensional compositions [49]. Deep learning architectures have been widely used in face recognition [18,35,43,55], facial expression recognition [24,56], emotion detection [21,23,49]. Pain level estimation using a deep learning framework was also proposed [57]. Employing deep learning framework for pain level assessment from facial video entails two kinds of information processing from facial video sequences: (i) spatial information, (ii) temporal information. Spatial information provides pain related information in the facial expressions of a single video frame. On the other hand, temporal information exhibits the relationship between pain expressions revealed in consecutive video frames.

While exploring spatial and temporal information from facial images, face quality (e.g. low face resolution) can also play important role as studied in [11–13]. The first limitation of the image resolution is created by the imaging acquisition devices or the imaging sensors [41]. The spatial resolution of the image capture is determined by the sensor size or the number of sensor elements. So, for increasing

Fig. 1. Pain and non-pain facial expression is sometimes very difficult to distinguish visually. Examples from the UNBC-McMaster shoulder pain database [38]. The pain frames are at the left and the non-pain frames are at the right.

the spatial resolution of an imaging system, one of the easy ways is to increase the sensor density by reducing the sensor size. However, as the sensor size decreases, the amount of light incident on each sensor also decreases, causing the shot noise [41]. Also, the hardware cost of a sensor increases by making sensor density greater or corresponding image pixel density. Applying various signal processing tools is the other approach for enhancing the face resolution. One of the famous techniques is Super Resolution (SR). The basic idea behind SR methods is to obtain high resolution (HR) image from low resolution (LR) image or images [42,54]. Huang and Tsai [17] as pioneers of SR proposed a method in order to improve spatial resolution of satellite images of earth, where a large set of translated images of the same scene are available. They showed that the better restoration can be achieved rather than spline interpolation by using multiple offset images of the same scene and a proper registration. Since then, SR methods become common practice for many applications in different fields such as remote sensing [34], surveillance video [4,36], medical imaging such as ultrasound, magnetic resonance imaging (MRI), and computerized tomography (CT) scan [22,39,40,44].

The desire for HR stems from two principal application areas:

- Improvement of resolution for human interpretation: in these applications, human is ultimate goal for system. SR methods improve resolution and visual quality in captured image. For example, a doctor can diagnose or treat with image capture from outside and inside the patient's body.
- Helping representation for automatic machine perception: SR methods are used to improve the resolution and image quality, for facilitating the machine processing. SR methods are used in various problems such as optical character recognition (OCR) problem or machine face recognition [1,9,15,50].

In this paper, we investigate the plausibility of using a Recurrent Neural Network (RNN) [57] to exploit the temporal axis information from facial video using Long Short-Term Memory (LSTM) [8,16] to estimate pain level expression in the face. The RNN is fed with the features extracted by a CNN that explores spatial information. We employ a SR technique to generate super-resolved high-resolution images from low resolution faces and we employ the CNN+RNN based deep learning framework to observe the performance. We report our results through the publicly available challenging database called UNBC-McMaster Shoulder Pain database [38]. The major contribution of the paper are as follows:

- Analyzing the pain detection performance fluctuation due to facial image resolution.
- Determining the impact of employing SR techniques in pain expression detection.
- Employing a hybrid deep learning framework by combining CNN and RNN to exploit spatio-temporal information of pain in video sequences.

The rest of the paper is organized as follows. Section 2 describes the proposed methodology for pain level assessment. Section 3 presents the experimental environment and the obtained results. Section 4 contains the conclusions.

2   The Proposed Pain Detection Framework

In this section we first describe the facial pain-expression database to be used in our investigation. We then describe the procedure of generating facial images with different resolutions and, finally, the deep learning-based classification framework for the experiment.

2.1   The Database

We use the UNBC-McMaster Shoulder Pain database collected by the researchers at McMaster University and University of Northern British Columbia [38]. The database contains facial video sequences of participants who had been suffering from shoulder pain and were performing a series of active and passive range of motion tests to their affected and unaffected limbs on multiple occasions. The database also contains FACS information of the video frames, self-reported pain scores in sequence level and facial landmark points obtained by an appearance model. The database was originally created by capturing facial videos from 129 participants (63 males and 66 females). The participant had a wide variety of occupations and ages. During data capturing the participants underwent eight standard range-of-motion tests: abduction, flexion, and internal and external rotation of each arm separately. Participants' self-reported pain score along with offline independent observers rated pain intensity were recorded. At present, the UNBC-McMaster database contains 200 video sequences with 48398 FACS coded frames of 25 subjects.

2.2   Obtaining Pain-Expression Data with Varying Face Resolution

We created multiple datasets by obtaining the original images from the UNBC-McMaster database and then varying the resolutions by down-up sampling or SR algorithms. The down-up sampling was accomplished by simply down-sampling the original images and then up-sampling the down-sampled images to the same resolution of the original images by employing a cubic-interpolation.

In order to generate SR images, a state-of-the-art technique, namely example-based learning [26] is adopted. The work in [26] is an extension of [25] which uses kernel ridge regression in order to estimate the high-frequency details of the underlying HR image. Also a combination of gradient descent and kernel matching pursuit is considered and allows time-complexity to be kept to a moderate level. Actually the proposed method improves the SR method presented in [7]. In this algorithm, For a given set of training data points $(x_1, y_1), ..., (x_l, y_l) \subset \Re^M \times \Re^N$, the following regularized cost functional is minimized.

$$O\left(\{f^1, ..., f^N\}\right) = \sum_{i=1,...,N} \left(\frac{1}{2} \sum_{j=1,...,N} \left(f^i(x_j) - y_j^i\right)^2 + \frac{1}{2}\lambda \left\|f^i\right\|_H^2 \right) \quad (1)$$

where $y_j = \left[y_j^1, ..., y_j^N\right]$ and H is a reproducing kernel Hilbert space. Due to the reproducing property, the minimizer of Eq. 1 is expanded in kernel functions:

$$f^i(\cdot) = \sum_{j=1,...,l} a_j^i k(x_j, \cdot), \quad for \quad i = 1, ..., N \quad (2)$$

where k is the generating kernel for H which, is choosen as a Gaussian kernel $\left(k(x, y) = exp\left(-\left\|x - y\right\|^2 / \sigma_k\right)\right)$. Equation 1 is the sum of individual convex cost functionals for each scalar-valued regressor and can be minimized separately. The final estimation of pixel value for an image location (x, y) is then obtained as the convex combination of candidates given in the form of a softmax:

$$Y(x, y) = \sum_{i=1,..N} w_i(x, y) Z(x, y, i) \quad (3)$$

where $w_i(x,y) = exp\left(-\frac{|d_i(x,y)|}{\sigma_C}\right) / \left[\sum_{j=1,...,N} exp\left(-\frac{|d_j(x,y)|}{\sigma_C}\right)\right]$ and Z is the initial SR image that is generated by a bicubic interpolation.

We use the down-sampled images as input to the SR algorithm and obtain the super-resolved images.

2.3 Deep Hybrid Classification Framework

We use a combination of CNN and RNN based hybrid framework to exploit both spatial and temporal information of facial pain expressions for pain detection. The hybrid pain detection framework is depicted in Fig. 2. In order to extract discriminative facial features, we fine-tune VGG_Faces [43], a 16-layer pre-trained CNN with 2.6M facial images of 2.6K people. Concretely, we replace the last layer of the CNN by a randomly initialized fully-connected layer with the three pain levels to recognize, and set its learning rate as ten times the learning rate of the rest of the CNN.

Once, fine-tuned, we extract the features of the fc7 layer of the fine-tuned model and use them as input to a Long-Short Term Memory (LSTM) Recurrent Neural Network (RNN) [16]. LSTMs are particular implementations of RNN that make use of the forget (f), input (i), and output (o) gates so as to solve the vanishing or exploding gradient problems, making them suitable for learning long-term time dependencies. These gates control the flow of information through the model by using point-wise multiplications and sigmoid functions σ, which bound the information flow between zero and one:

$$i(t) = \sigma(W_{(x\to i)}x(t) + W_{(h\to i)}h(t-1) + b_{(1\to i)}) \tag{4}$$

$$f(t) = \sigma(W_{(x\to f)}x(t) + W(h \to f)h(t-1) + b_{(1\to f)}) \tag{5}$$

$$z(t) = tanh(W_{(x\to c)}x(t)) + W_{(h\to c)}h(t-1) + b_{(1\to c)}) \tag{6}$$

$$c(t) = f(t)c(t-1) + i(t)z(t), \tag{7}$$

$$o(t) = \sigma(W_{(x\to o)}x(t) + W_{(h\to o)}h(t-1) + b_{(1\to o)}) \tag{8}$$

$$h(t) = o(t)tanh(c(t)), \tag{9}$$

where $z(t)$ is the input to the cell at time t, c is the cell, and h is the output. $W_{(x\to y)}$ are the weights from x to y. More detail can be found in the original implementation [33].

Labels are predicted sequence-wise, $i.e.$ given a sequence of n frames $f_i \in \{f_1, ..., f_n\}$, the target prediction is the pain level of the f_n frame. Thus, training is set so that the information contained in the past frames is used in order to predict the current pain level. We optimize the LSTM with $Adam$ [27] with an initial learning rate of 0.001 so as to alleviate the hyper-parameter tuning problem.

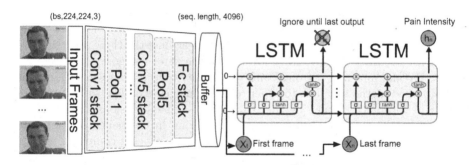

Fig. 2. The block diagram of the deep hybrid classification framework based on a combination of CNN and RNN

3 Experimental Results and Discussions

3.1 Experimental Environment

As stated in the previous section, we evaluated the performance of pain detection in varying face resolution by employing the hybrid deep learning framework on the UNBC-McMaster Shoulder Pain database [38]. The video frames of the database showed patients who were suffering from shoulder pain while they were performing a series of active and passive range-of-motion tests. The pain indexes were computed by following Prkachin and Solomon Pain Intensity (PSPI) scale from [47] and the pain levels vary in the interval 0–16 based on the FACS codes. Following [20], we classified each pain index into three categories of no pain (pain index lower than 1), weak pain (pain index between 2 and 6) and strong pain (pain index greater than 6). The three categories have been balanced by dropping consecutive no-pain frames at the beginning and at the end of each video, or by discarding entire video sequences which do not contain pain.

We applied the down-up sampling and SR algorithm described in Sect. 2.2 to generate three experimental datasets. The first dataset was created by using the original images from the UNBC-McMaster database (also used by [19]). The second and third datasets were denoted by 'SR1/4' and 'SR1/2', and were created by employing down-up sampling with the values 1/4 and 1/2, respectively, on the first dataset. The fourth dataset were denoted by 'SR2', and was created by employing the SR algorithm from Sect. 2.2 on the down-sampled images with factor 1/2. The LSTM network was configured with 3 hidden-layers of 64 hidden-units each and a temporal window of 16 consecutive video frames. For the purpose of comparison, the experimental setup of the LSTM was kept fixed for all the experiments against the three datasets. The performances was estimated with leave-one-subject-out cross-validation protocol.

3.2   The Obtained Results

Table 1 shows the results of the proposed system against the three sets. Here we report the accuracy in percentage for each of the three categories, namely "No pain", "Weak Pain" and "Strong Pain". From the experiments we can claim that the proposed method applied to super resolved images is crucial since it reaches better performance than using the plain down-sampled versions. The latter is denoted by the amount of improvement appearing in the pain detection rate using the super-resolved images as the subjects, while being compared against that of the LR ones. In other words, when recognizing the pains using the super-resolved images, a more powerful SR method leads to recognition rates closer to the case of considering the original ones. From the results we can see that pain detection is much better in super-resolved images compared to down-sampled ones by a large margin in case of strong pain, while for the other two levels, namely no-pain and weak pain, the performances are slightly better. This is due to the fact that stronger pain (compared to weak or no pain case) imposes more changes on the face and these changes are more pronounced on super-resolved images hence the detection accuracy improves by far in the strong pain class compared to the other classes. In order to see how temporal information affects the final results, we provide the SR2 accuracy when using a linear classifier on the plain CNN features against the LSTM predictions, which aggregates the temporal information in Table 2. Here the results are reported for each subject in the considered data set. As it can be seen, temporal information improves the predictions for a large margin, a 16% in average, meaning that spatial features are not enough for determining the pain level on facial images. Thus, the temporal variation of the frames allows for finding higher level facial features, like FACS, which are central for predicting the PSPI pain score [48].

Table 1. Pain detection results for the four experimental datasets created from the UNBC-McMaster [38] database

Semantic ground truth	Pain index	$SR^{1/4}$	$SR^{1/2}$	SR2
No pain	0, 1	55.3%	62.22%	55.78%
Weak pain	2, 3, 4, 5	73.1%	67.7%	75.94%
Strong pain	>6	18.36%	5.86%	39.45%
F1-score		0.67	0.66	0.69
Total	0–16	62.43%	62.64%	65.34%

From Table 2 we notice that in two cases, specifically subject number 7 and subject number 8, the LSTM failed to improve the accuracy of the CNN. After a detailed study of the dataset, we notice that sometimes, for both subjects, the pain index changes very rapidly among consecutive frames. The same pattern occurs (in a lighter form) also for subject 6, which improvement in the accuracy is not as good as for the other subjects. In addition, subject 7 is the only one

Table 2. Comparison between CNN and LSTM performances on SR2 dataset (in accuracy %). The CNN relies on the information of a single frame, while the LSTM takes into account variations on the images in the temporal axis. As it can be seen, the LSTM enhances the accuracy prediction for all subjects, reaching a 16% in average.

Subj.	1	2	3	4	5	6	7	8	9	10	11	12	13	14	AVG
CNN	40.9	50.3	52.0	50.7	50.3	42.5	**29.3**	**47.3**	50.4	44.0	50.0	51.3	51.9	30.2	45.8
LSTM	**58.0**	**61.5**	**63.0**	**65.6**	**82.5**	**48.0**	28.0	40.0	**81.0**	**65.4**	**82.0**	**66.0**	**65.5**	**60.5**	**61.9**

that contains only one video for the validation set, while subject 8 contains three videos, among which one very noisy with only 20 frames. We think that the aforementioned differences could be the key problems which leads to such a different performance for different subjects.

4 Conclusions

We investigated the performance of a recurrent deep learning framework trained against super-resolved high-resolution images for pain level classification. The system is a combination of CNN and a LSTM used to exploit both spatial and temporal information in videos. We evaluated our proposed method on UNBC_McMaster database by down sampling by different factors and by applying a super-resolution algorithm. From the experimental results of the pain detection performances we concluded that super-resolution and temporal information are key for obtaining good recognition results. Our experiments also showed that including deep temporal information within the model increases the generalization capabilities in discriminating among different levels of pain. Employing super-resolution techniques lead to an improvement of the performances in our pain detector. Down-sampling, on the other hand, worsen the system capabilities.

References

1. Capel, D., Zisserman, A.: Super-resolution enhancement of text image sequences. In: 2000 Proceedings of the 15th International Conference on Pattern Recognition, vol. 1, pp. 600–605. IEEE (2000)
2. Craig, K.D., Prkachin, K.M., Grunau, R.E.: The facial expression of pain. In: Handbook of Pain Assessment. Guilford Press (2011)
3. Craig, K.D., Hyde, S.A., Patrick, C.J.: Genuine, suppressed and faked facial behavior during exacerbation of chronic low back pain. Pain **46**(2), 161–171 (1991)
4. Cristani, M., Cheng, D.S., Murino, V., Pannullo, D.: Distilling information with super-resolution for video surveillance. In: Proceedings of the ACM 2nd International Workshop on Video Surveillance & Sensor Networks, pp. 2–11. ACM (2004)
5. Debono, D.J., Hoeksema, L.J., Hobbs, R.D.: Caring for patients with chronic pain: pearls and pitfalls. J. Am. Osteopath. Assoc. **113**(8), 620–627 (2013). doi:10.7556/jaoa.2013.023

6. Ekman, P., Friesen, W.: Facial Action Coding System: A Technique for the Measurement of Facial Movement. Consulting Psychologists Press, Palo Alto (1978)
7. Freeman, W.T., Jones, T.R., Pasztor, E.C.: Example-based super-resolution. IEEE Comput. Graphics Appl. **22**(2), 56–65 (2002)
8. Gers, F.A., Schmidhuber, J.A., Cummins, F.A.: Learning to forget: continual prediction with LSTM. Neural Comput. **12**(10), 2451–2471 (2000)
9. Gunturk, B.K., Batur, A.U., Altunbasak, Y., Hayes, M.H., Mersereau, R.M.: Eigenface-domain super-resolution for face recognition. IEEE Trans. Image Process. **12**(5), 597–606 (2003)
10. Hadjistavropoulos, T., LaChapelle, D.L., MacLeod, F.K., Snider, B., Craig, K.D.: Measuring movement-exacerbated pain in cognitively impaired frail elders. **16**, 54–63 (2000)
11. Haque, M.A., Nasrollahi, K., Moeslund, T.B.: Real-time acquisition of high quality face sequences from an active pan-tilt-zoom camera. In: 2013 10th IEEE International Conference on Advanced Video and Signal Based Surveillance, pp. 443–448, August 2013
12. Haque, M.A., Nasrollahi, K., Moeslund, T.B.: Constructing facial expression log from video sequences using face quality assessment. In: 2014 International Conference on Computer Vision Theory and Applications (VISAPP), vol. 2, pp. 517–525, January 2014
13. Haque, M.A., Nasrollahi, K., Moeslund, T.B.: Quality-aware estimation of facial landmarks in video sequences. In: 2015 IEEE Winter Conference on Applications of Computer Vision, pp. 678–685, January 2015
14. Haque, M.A., Nasrollahi, K., Moeslund, T.B.: Pain expression as a biometric: why patients' self-reported pain doesn't match with the objectively measured pain? In: 2017 IEEE International Conference on Identity, Security and Behavior Analysis (ISBA), February 2017 (submitted)
15. Hennings-Yeomans, P.H., Baker, S., Kumar, B.V.: Recognition of low-resolution faces using multiple still images and multiple cameras. In: 2008 2nd IEEE International Conference on Biometrics: Theory, Applications and Systems, BTAS 2008, pp. 1–6. IEEE (2008)
16. Hochreiter, S., Schmidhuber, J.: Long short-term memory. Neural Comput. **9**(8), 1735–1780 (1997)
17. Huang, T.S., Tsay, R.Y.: Multiple frame image restoration and registration. In: Advances in Computer Vision and Image Processing, pp. 317–339 (1984)
18. Huang, Z., Wang, R., Shan, S., Chen, X.: Face recognition on large-scale video in the wild with hybrid Euclidean-and-Riemannian metric learning. Pattern Recogn. **48**(10), 3113–3124 (2015)
19. Irani, R., Nasrollahi, K., Moeslund, T.B.: Pain recognition using spatiotemporal oriented energy of facial muscles. In: 2015 IEEE Conference on Computer Vision and Pattern Recognition Workshops (CVPRW), pp. 80–87, June 2015
20. Irani, R., Nasrollahi, K., Simon, M.O., Corneanu, C.A., Escalera, S., Bahnsen, C., Lundtoft, D.H., Moeslund, T.B., Pedersen, T.L., Klitgaard, M.L., Petrini, L.: Spatiotemporal analysis of RGB-D-T facial images for multimodal pain level recognition. In: The IEEE Conference on Computer Vision and Pattern Recognition (CVPR) Workshops, June 2015
21. Kahou, S.E., Bouthillier, X., Lamblin, P., Gulcehre, C., Michalski, V., Konda, K., Jean, S., Froumenty, P., Dauphin, Y., Boulanger-Lewandowski, N., Chandias Ferrari, R., Mirza, M., Warde-Farley, D., Courville, A., Vincent, P., Memisevic, R., Pal, C., Bengio, Y.: Emonets: multimodal deep learning approaches for emotion recognition in video. J. Multimodal User Interfaces **10**(2), 99–111 (2016)

22. Kennedy, J.A., Israel, O., Frenkel, A., Bar-Shalom, R., Azhari, H.: Super-resolution in pet imaging. IEEE Trans. Med. Imaging **25**(2), 137–147 (2006)
23. Khorrami, P., Paine, T.L., Brady, K., Dagli, C., Huang, T.S.: How deep neural networks can improve emotion recognition on video data. In: 2016 IEEE International Conference on Image Processing (ICIP), pp. 619–623, September 2016
24. Kim, B.K., Roh, J., Dong, S.Y., Lee, S.Y.: Hierarchical committee of deep convolutional neural networks for robust facial expression recognition. J. Multimodal User Interfaces **10**(2), 173–189 (2016)
25. Kim, K.I., Kim, D., Kim, J.H.: Example-based learning for image super-resolution (2004)
26. Kim, K.I., Kwon, Y.: Example-based learning for single-image super-resolution. In: Rigoll, G. (ed.) DAGM 2008. LNCS, vol. 5096, pp. 456–465. Springer, Heidelberg (2008). doi:10.1007/978-3-540-69321-5_46
27. Kingma, D., Ba, J.: Adam: a method for stochastic optimization. arXiv preprint arXiv:1412.6980 (2014)
28. Kunz, M., Gruber, A., Lautenbacher, S.: Sex differences in facial encoding of pain. J. Pain **7**(12), 915–928 (2006)
29. Kunz, M., Mylius, V., Schepelmann, K., Lautenbacher, S.: On the relationship between self-report and facial expression of pain. J. Pain **5**(7), 368–376 (2004)
30. Kunz, M., Prkachin, K., Lautenbacher, S.: Smiling in pain: explorations of its social motives. Pain Res. Treat. **2013**, e128093 (2013)
31. Kunz, M., Scharmann, S., Hemmeter, U., Schepelmann, K., Lautenbacher, S.: The facial expression of pain in patients with dementia. Pain **133**(1–3), 221–228 (2007)
32. Lautenbacher, S., Niewelt, B.G., Kunz, M.: Decoding pain from the facial display of patients with dementia: a comparison of professional and nonprofessional observers. Pain Med. **14**(4), 469–477 (2013). http://painmedicine.oxfordjournals.org/content/14/4/469
33. Léonard, N., Waghmare, S., Wang, Y.: Rnn: Recurrent library for torch. arXiv preprint arXiv:1511.07889 (2015)
34. Li, F., Jia, X., Fraser, D.: Universal HMT based super resolution for remote sensing images. In: 2008 15th IEEE International Conference on Image Processing, ICIP 2008, pp. 333–336. IEEE (2008)
35. Li, H., Hua, G.: Hierarchical-PEP model for real-world face recognition. In: Proceedings of the IEEE Conference on Computer Vision and Pattern Recognition, CVPR 2015, pp. 4055–4064 (2015)
36. Lin, F.C., Fookes, C.B., Chandran, V., Sridharan, S.: Investigation into optical flow super-resolution for surveillance applications (2005)
37. Lucey, P., Cohn, J.F., Matthews, I., Lucey, S., Sridharan, S., Howlett, J., Prkachin, K.M.: Automatically detecting pain in video through facial action units. IEEE Trans. Syst. Man Cybern. Part B (Cybern.) **41**(3), 664–674 (2011)
38. Lucey, P., Cohn, J.F., Prkachin, K.M., Solomon, P.E., Matthews, I.: Painful data: the UNBC-McMaster shoulder pain expression archive database. In: 2011 IEEE International Conference on Automatic Face Gesture Recognition and Workshops (FG 2011), pp. 57–64, March 2011
39. Maintz, J.A., Viergever, M.A.: A survey of medical image registration. Med. Image Anal. **2**(1), 1–36 (1998)
40. Malczewski, K., Stasinski, R.: Toeplitz-based iterative image fusion scheme for MRI. In: 2008 15th IEEE International Conference on Image Processing, ICIP 2008, pp. 341–344. IEEE (2008)
41. Milanfar, P.: Super-Resolution Imaging. CRC Press, Boca Raton (2010)

42. Nasrollahi, K., Moeslund, T.B.: Super-resolution: a comprehensive survey. Mach. Vis. Appl. **25**(6), 1423–1468 (2014)
43. Parkhi, O.M., Vedaldi, A., Zisserman, A.: Deep face recognition. In: British Machine Vision Conference, vol. 1, p. 6 (2015)
44. Peled, S., Yeshurun, Y.: Superresolution in MRI: application to human white matter fiber tract visualization by diffusion tensor imaging. Magn. Reson. Med. **45**(1), 29–35 (2001)
45. Prkachin, K.M.: The consistency of facial expressions of pain: a comparison across modalities. **51**, 297–306 (1992)
46. Prkachin, K.M., Berzins, S., Mercer, S.R.: Encoding and decoding of pain expressions: a judgement study. Pain **58**(2), 253–259 (1994)
47. Prkachin, K.M., Solomon, P.E.: The structure, reliability and validity of pain expression: Evidence from patients with shoulder pain. **139**, 267–274 (2008)
48. Prkachin, K., Schultz, I., Berkowitz, J., Hughes, E., Hunt, D.: Assessing pain behaviour of low-back pain patients in real time: concurrent validity and examiner sensitivity. Behav. Res. Ther. **40**(5), 595–607 (2002)
49. Ranganathan, H., Chakraborty, S., Panchanathan, S.: Multimodal Emotion Recognition Using Deep Learning Architectures. Institute of Electrical and Electronics Engineers Inc., United States (2016)
50. Sezer, O.G., Altunbasak, Y., Ercil, A.: Face recognition with independent component-based super-resolution. In: Electronic Imaging 2006, pp. 607705–607705. International Society for Optics and Photonics (2006)
51. Sikdar, A., Behera, S.K., Dogra, D.P.: Computer vision guided human pulse rate estimation a review. IEEE Rev. Biomed. Eng. **PP**(99), 1 (2016)
52. Sikka, K., Ahmed, A.A., Diaz, D., Goodwin, M.S., Craig, K.D., Bartlett, M.S., Huang, J.S.: Automated assessment of children's postoperative pain using computer vision. Pediatrics **136**(1), 124–131 (2015)
53. Vallerand, A.H., Polomano, R.C.: The relationship of gender to pain. Pain Manage. Nurs. **1**(3, Supplement 1), 8–15 (2000)
54. Yang, J., Huang, T.: Image super-resolution: historical overview and future challenges. In: Super-Resolution Imaging, pp. 20–34 (2010)
55. Yang, J., Ren, P., Chen, D., Wen, F., Li, H., Hua, G.: Neural aggregation network for video face recognition. arXiv preprint arXiv:1603.05474 (2016)
56. Yu, Z., Zhang, C.: Image based static facial expression recognition with multiple deep network learning. In: Proceedings of the 2015 ACM on International Conference on Multimodal Interaction, ICMI 2015, pp. 435–442. ACM, New York (2015)
57. Zhou, J., Hong, X., Su, F., Zhao, G.: Recurrent convolutional neural network regression for continuous pain intensity estimation in video. arXiv preprint arXiv:1605.00894 (2016)

Erratum to: Video Analytics

Kamal Nasrollahi[1]([⊠]), Cosimo Distante[2], Gang Hua[3],
Andrea Cavallaro[4], Thomas B. Moeslund[1],
Sebastiano Battiato[5], and Qiang Ji[6]

[1] Aalborg University, Aalborg, Denmark
kn@create.aau.dk
[2] Institute of Applied Sciences and Intelligent Systems, Lecce, Italy
[3] Stevens Institute of Technology, Hoboken, NJ, USA
[4] Queen Mary University of London, London, UK
[5] Università di Catania, Catania, Italy
[6] Rensselaer Polytechnic Institute, Troy, NY, USA

Erratum to:
K. Nasrollahi et al. (Eds.):
Video Analytics, LNCS,
DOI: 10.1007/978-3-319-56687-0

In the original version of the papers starting on p. 137 and p. 151, the spelling of Sergio Escalera's name was incorrect. The original chapters were corrected.

The updated original online version for these chapters can be found at
DOI: 10.1007/978-3-319-56687-0_12
DOI: 10.1007/978-3-319-56687-0_13

© Springer International Publishing AG 2017
K. Nasrollahi et al. (Eds.): VAAM 2016/FFER 2016, LNCS 10165, p. E1, 2017.
DOI: 10.1007/978-3-319-56687-0_14

Author Index

Printed in the United States
By Bookmasters